SUPERCOACH

SUPERCOACH

THE LIFE AND TIMES OF

JACK GIBSON

ANDREW WEBSTER

ALLEN&UNWIN

First published in 2011

Allen & Unwin
Sydney, Melbourne, Auckland, London

83 Alexander Street
Crows Nest NSW 2065
Australia
Phone: (61 2) 8425 0100
Fax: (61 2) 9906 2218
Email: info@allenandunwin.com
Web: www.allenandunwin.com

Cataloguing-in-Publication details are available
from the National Library of Australia
www.trove.nla.gov.au

ISBN 978 1 74237 809 1

Set in 12/16 pt Bembo by Midland Typesetters, Australia
Printed and bound in Australia by Griffin Press

10 9 8 7 6 5 4 3 2 1

For Judy and the Gibson family

The newspaper articles quoted in this book have been taken from Jack Gibson's personal scrapbooks, meaning that in most cases the date, page number and other details have been cut off. All newspaper articles are cited by author and name of publication throughout.

Unless otherwise stated, all quoted material comes from interviews conducted by the author or information offered by Jack's friends and family.

CONTENTS

PROLOGUE

BIG JACK WON'T let go.

Here, within the warm peach walls of the aged-care centre buried in bushland on the edge of the Sutherland Shire, he sits in a blue leather chair, in his flannelette pyjamas, as his wife Judy strokes his chest and kisses his forehead and gently runs her hand through his fuzzed and fading grey hair. 'I've got a visitor for you,' she says.

The supercoach smiles. He is content, comfortable, but this is a man whose life is in decline. His glazed, darkened eyes wander around the warm peach walls, searching for a way to conquer— if only for a second—the dementia that has gripped and torn him down. He made players into better players and even better men: some visit him, most cannot. They're embarrassed they can't bring themselves to do it but prefer to remember 'Coach' as he was.

Suddenly, the eyes sharpen and they lock on yours. In the dressing-room, that look alone made footballers fight through pain and fatigue and a lack of talent to do extraordinary things that would normally seem beyond them. Not this day. This is the look of a man who has beaten the demons in his mind, but knows they will soon return. Yet you just know, buried deep inside there somewhere, there's been a revelation. He's squaring you up and you're waiting for him to ask the question he's asked thousands before, always in his signature drawl: 'What's doin', kid?'

If only he could say it.

Sometimes the words come out but not today. So you shake his hand instead. For most of his life, those hands did the talking. He relied on them. Trusted them. Now they are one of the few things that work, and he grips your hand so tightly that you need to use your other hand to yank it free.

This was the first and only time I met Jack Gibson. It was the morning of 17 April 2008.

Later that evening, at the Royal Hall of Industries at Moore Park, the leathered bull-necks of his former teammates and players strained in crisp white shirts beneath black tuxedos. It is the Centenary Ball—a celebration of rugby league's hundred years of existence. As the evening rolled along, the Team of the Century was slowly revealed. Arthur Beetson, Noel Kelly, Graeme Langlands, Ron Coote are among them. All of them groundbreakers, in their own way. All of them touched by Jack Gibson in some way also. When he was revealed as the Coach of the Century at the end of the night, there was scant surprise, warm applause ... and then confusion.

Where was he? Because Jack's condition had been a source of mystery and speculation for so long, much of the room wondered why he wasn't there to accept.

Three weeks later, the Gibson family waited in a darkened room and the peach walls were no longer so warm. A chest infection that had overwhelmed Jack for weeks had degenerated into pneumonia. It was a Sunday evening when the wandering eyes stopped searching and closed for the last time as he slipped into unconsciousness. There was no respirator; there were no tubes. He wasn't in pain. All that was left was time and the inevitable.

For the next week, Judy and her children—Susan, Tracey, Joanne, Matt and John—slept on whatever they could find: wheelchairs, spare beds, inflatable mattresses. They had seen it coming. A few weeks earlier, Jack had grabbed Joanne's hand when it was just the two of them. 'I've had enough,' he told her.

But not yet. The longer the Gibsons held their vigil that week, the more it became apparent that Big Jack wasn't ready. 'He fought and fought and it was agonising to see the man fight,' says Matthew. 'The king of the castle did not want to let go.' By the time Friday evening came around, the Gibson family understood why.

●

The Sydney Cricket Ground is lit up like a supernova as the crowd swells for the Centenary Test between Australia and New Zealand on 9 May 2008. Those same leathered bull-necks from the Centenary Ball are straining again, this time beneath button-down shirts and ties tucked beneath specially crafted green and gold blazers as the game's greatest players wait to be paraded around the famous ground.

The SCG. The old girl. She is sparkling with a sense of occasion on this night. Jack left his imprint on her over the years as much as any other individual. Bradman will always have the keys to the joint—but Jack had a spare set.

In the 1950s and '60s, he galloped all over her as a fearless forward for Eastern Suburbs. That's when the hands did *all* of the talking. He'd captained Easts in the 1960 grand final against the might of St George. He played for Wests against them in 1963, when his connections with Sydney's underworld tipped him that referee Darcy Lawler had gambled heavily on the Dragons. 'We can't win,' he told Noel Kelly, who was sitting next to him in the dressing-room.

For all the blood he'd spilt on the SCG—some of it occasionally his—the Gibson legend was cemented years later when his hands held a cigarette and his understanding of footballers as much as football secured him the premierships he never won as a player. The first came with Easts in 1974 and 1975, when he would stand in the dimly lit rooms, a mischievous grin on his face, as he tipped the champagne bottle into the mouths of his players.

It was the same after the 1983 grand final when Parramatta had won their third successive premiership on his watch. He stood in the middle of the SCG, resplendent in his iconic kangaroo fur coat that weighed a ton, when a Parramatta trainer put the champagne bottle to his lips. Jack angrily waved it away. By the time they had found their way into the rooms, newly elected Prime Minister Bob Hawke edged his way into almost every photo. Not Jack, even if he was entitled to. It was never about him, even when it always was.

The SCG. The old girl. All the defining moments of his football career had played out here and those that defined his life weren't far away. Down the road, in the backstreets of Surry Hills near Central Station in the 1950s, he would stand on the door of Sydney's secret and heady world of Thommo's Two-up School. He wasn't just the hands. He was the muscle.

Rise up and pan north, coming down in the city at the New South Wales Leagues Club. In 1954, he spotted Judy from across the room and even though she was with another man he knew there and then there was no other woman for him.

Rise up again and sweep east, coming down to the neon delights of Kings Cross. In the '60s, he would come here to play away his last cent on the card tables at the casinos. In the '70s, when he was considered one of the city's biggest SP bookmakers, he was here settling up with those who had punted with him. In the late '80s, he was walking the same streets, slipping into the grubby nightclubs and interrogating their dark characters in search of the drug dealer who had sold the lethal dose of heroin that claimed the life of his son Luke at the age of 25.

Now rise up and return to the SCG and the night of the Centenary Test.

Ian Heads, the respected journalist and author who helped Jack pen four books, is in the dining room of the Trustee's Reserve beneath the MA Noble Stand attending a function where some of the game's leading players are being inducted as life members. Earlier in the week, Judy had told him that Jack was close to letting go, so they had carefully crafted a media statement to be released at the relevant time.

With the speeches over, Heads turns on his mobile phone. A message. He walks out of the function and listens. Judy's voice is typically calm and stoic. She delivers the news they had been expecting.

Heads pulls SCG Trust chairman Rodney Cavalier aside and tells him the news. The chairman hushes the room. 'Ladies and gentlemen, I regret to inform you that Jack Gibson has passed away.' A collective sigh. Disbelief and grief hang in the air. James McCarthy, a trainee priest, delivers a prayer. Jack, a devout Catholic, would have approved. From that point on, the news shoots around the SCG like a pinball. This match, this occasion, has taken on new meaning.

Peter Sterling is high up in the Brewongle Stand in the Channel Nine commentary box. Jack coached him at Parramatta and in 1981 had told the little blond halfback to kick to the seagulls as advice to fix his ailing kicking game. Sterling had not a single clue what that meant—until he was standing at one end of the SCG that Sunday afternoon, the leather in his hands as he looked up and down field to where the seagulls were picking at the sacred turf. Now Sterling is on-air and doing his piece to camera with co-commentator Matthew Johns before the Test match. His earpiece crackles. The news comes down the line from a producer: the man who had taught him almost everything he knew about life, and a little bit about football, was gone. 'I can't remember what I said,' Sterling recalls. 'I just wanted to get to a commercial break.'

By now, the players who had been named in the Team of the Century started to make their way down to the Members' Stand in preparation for a lap of honour. Graeme Langlands and Bob Fulton are standing in front of the Australian dressing-room when they hear. Wally Lewis is stepping out onto the turf when someone tells him. 'Suddenly the whole night changed,' Lewis remembers. 'You could *feel* him.' Noel Kelly is in the middle of the ground when the word finds its way to him. 'That's Jack,' he says to no one in particular. Before the team had left the field, Jack's death is announced to the crowd. Midway through a minute's silence, a Kiwi supporter in the Brewongle Stand screams out. He is frog-marched from the stadium before a fight could start. He misses Australia's easy 28–12 win over New Zealand.

As far as Matt Gibson was concerned, the best way to honour his father was to leave his family and get his arse to the SCG even though the match was over. He'd bought tickets but only realised he'd forgotten them when he reached the old entrance to the cricket ground on Driver Avenue. He sought out the most senior gate attendant. On match day, Jack always made a habit of exchanging a few words with the man on the door. 'I knew your father well,' the veteran attendant says. 'How is your father, anyway?'

He let Matt in. His scruffy, unshaven appearance rouses the interest of some in the Members' Reserve, but when they learn he is Jack Gibson's son they pump his hand. 'I felt the need to go, but I don't know what drove me there,' he says. 'They were just the people I wanted to be with.'

Call it coincidence. Call it serendipity. But Judy Gibson knows Jack determined the precise moment of his exit. 'It seems very strange that he could hang there for a week and then go at that time. He controlled the moment.'

At 6.32 p.m., with the focus of the game he loved on the SCG, with the family he loved surrounding him, within the warm peach walls, Big Jack decided he was ready to let go.

1   THE BOSS

THEY WERE ALWAYS Craven As back then, pinched between middle finger and thumb so tightly that he had to really suck it back, right down to the cork-tip filter, to inhale the last breath of its nutty goodness. In the early hours of this morning in July 1950, he'd have another in his mouth before the one he'd just flicked away, arcing through the cool winter air, had landed on the York Street pavement.

Jack had been there for hours, leaning against his black Pontiac, chaining the Cravens as he waited for one of the well-marinated patrons to emerge from the din of the Celebrity Club. He was 'hot-plating'—working as an illegal taxi service as such—one of the inventive ways Jack would subsidise the things that filled his world then: drinking, gambling, chasing skirt.

He held his own at all three but it was the punt—the turn of the card or the bob of the racehorse's head—that determined whether he would be shuffling into the pawnbrokers that week.

His tiny weekly wage of a few pounds working as a clerk at an engineering company in the Sutherland Shire was never enough. In their spare time, he and good mates Bobby Dodd and Alan David did some SP bookmaking on the side, running their rookie operation out of a small shed on a vacant block in the Shire. 'If our clients knew what our bank was between us,' Dodd said years later, 'they'd never have bet with us.'

Not that Jack would ever complain about misfortune. He knew how it rolled. Years later, when he coached, he would growl whenever someone suggested that luck prejudiced the outcome of a match, let alone life. He drew on many lines of inspiration but one of his favourites was this: 'Luck is where preparation meets opportunity.'

Surely, though, he reflected differently on the early hours of this morning in 1950. Joe Taylor emerged from the Celebrity Club and, through his black horn-rimmed glasses, eyed the muscular 21-year-old leaning against the Pontiac. Jack flicked away his cigarette and Taylor slid into the back seat. Taylor was done for the night and was making a beeline to his residence on Village High Road in Vaucluse.

This was the chance meeting where the legend of Jack Gibson started—and probably some of the myth, too. Either way, this much is clear: meeting Joe Taylor changed everything.

Taylor wasn't drunk on this morning like many of his clientele— or any morning for that matter. He was a teetotaller and prided himself on the fact. Legend has it the only drop of grog that passed his lips was when a prankster replaced his ginger ale with flat beer. Nobody tried the gag twice. Joe Taylor was no fool and less likely to tolerate one. He was also on the rise. He owned the Celebrity Club—that was legal. Down the road, in the darkened backstreets of Surry Hills, he operated the legendary Thommo's

Two-up School—that was not. As the years rolled on, he would open illegal casinos and sly grog joints, a necessary evil in those days because of 6 p.m. closing times. He managed footballers and boxers. He was an impresario and restaurateur but also one of Sydney's most fearsome punters with almost no regard for money. As David Hickie wrote in *The Prince and the Premier*, which details the rise of organised crime in Australia: 'Joe "The Boss" Taylor was, for nearly 40 years, one of the biggest powers behind the scenes of Sydney's illegal gambling rackets.' Jack had a more succinct way of putting it: 'He's as powerful as two governments.'

Joe was Jack's style of man: self-made and independently wealthy. He mixed as easily with politicians and high-ranking members of the police force as with the punter needing to lend a few quid to get home. He had a soft, almost solemn touch but had a short fuse when provoked. When Taylor was in his 70s and a young buck pushed his luck too far, The Boss required only a few sweetly timed punches to end the matter. 'He'd fight Jesus Christ,' said one witness of that incident. What appealed to Jack was that Taylor smacked of underworld cool. Taylor often wore a black suit, black tie and crisp white button-down shirt. Whenever possible, he wore a tinge of red somewhere, usually a handkerchief, for good luck. It was Joe's favourite colour. Like most serious gamblers, he was stubbornly superstitious.

Jack was Joe's style of man, too. It only required a few more trips over time between the Celebrity Club and Vaucluse for Taylor to take a shine to the quiet yet imposing young footballer, who had earlier that year played a handful of third-grade matches for St George. Taylor had been toying with the notion of sponsoring a team in next season's thriving Eastern Suburbs A-grade rugby league competition. A player like Jack could be useful, Taylor thought. So could the muscle.

The muscle on the door at Thommo's for some time had been 38-year-old William John 'Bobby' Lee. Like most of the bouncers in town, he was a former boxer. At 3.30 a.m. in May of 1951, Bobby Lee was shot five times while drinking at the low-rent Ziegfeld nightclub in King Street. Notorious gunman John 'Chow' Hayes had pulled the trigger, apparently as payback after Hayes' nephew had been shot a month earlier.

Lee didn't survive. Jack got his job.

●

Those hands. They were imposing, thick-fingered claws, even back then, and he knew how to use them. Jack and Bob Dodd were drinking at a pub in Cronulla when a mug came up wanting to pick a fight with the biggest bloke in the bar. For some men, alcohol prompts them to do this.

'Piss off,' Jack said out of the corner of his mouth. 'I'm having a drink with a mate.' The mug left but soon returned. 'Piss off,' Jack warned again. 'I'm having a drink with a mate.' When the mug tried his luck a third time, a word hadn't passed his lips before Jack's right hand had sat him on the floor.

Another time and another mug. This one king-hit Bobby as he was chatting to a girl at Oyster Bills, a nightclub in Sylvania. Jack cleaned him up, too. When the three of them were sitting in the holding cell at the nearest police station hours later, Jack eyeballed the guy and told him ever-so-slowly: 'When we get out of here, I'll give you a headstart. You'll need it.' They never sighted him again.

That's how Jack talked, even then: slow, deliberate, like he meant it. He was regularly mistaken for having a brooding, sour demeanour. Those close to him knew better, but it was a handy way to be considered when you worked at an illegal two-up ring. Thommo's Two-up School was as much an institution as it was illegal: to those who won and lost fortunes there, those who couldn't get in, and the police who turned a blind eye to—or profited from—its very existence. It had been in clandestine operation since 1910, when former boxer George Guest founded it. He'd called it Thommo's after his ring name of Joe Thomas. When he died in 1954, he left all of it to Joe Taylor in his will, although the truth of it was that Taylor had been a hidden principal and running it for years.

The Game floated around the inner-city backstreets like a ghost, always one step ahead of the police. Spotters—'cockatoos' as they were known—would keep watch, usually lighting a cigarette as a signal that the law was near. On the very rare occasions when the police *did* catch the ghost, Taylor would pay them off.

The Game had various locations, mostly around Paddy's Market near Central Station. There was a big room off Elizabeth Street and another off Dixon Street around the corner. By the time Jack started working there, it was operating out of an old barn off Reservoir Street where punters would step off the busy streets and walk through a maze of dark alleys, weaving through the buildings surrounding the ring before being guided there by a doorman holding a torch.

Jack entered the scene precisely around the time when Thommo's was becoming fashionable for Sydney's well-to-do set yet still a haven for men—no women, sorry—from all walks of life. Pimps. Doctors. Wharfies. Politicians. Criminals. Bookmakers and butchers. An eclectic tangle that would jam the arc of the ring, every one of them staring up into the swinging light bulbs that illuminated the green baize mats below, a smog of cigarette smoke hanging above them, as the two King George VI pennies—the King's head shined on one side, the Kangaroo and its long tail blackened on the other—came down and bounced off the floor and fortunes (or weekly wages) were won or lost. They'd do this from the moment the doors swung open at 6 p.m. and were still going at three o'clock the next morning.

And they *were* fortunes; hundreds and often thousands of pounds determined on the run of the coins. Cashed-up American sailors would flood the ring post–World War II, but by the early 1950s, when Jack was making his way, the money came from everywhere: from Supreme Court judges to prominent horseracing trainers. On one famous night, radio personality Jack Davey lost £2000 on a spin, shrugged his shoulders and walked out, and then held a champagne party for two days.

This was money and a world far removed from what Jack had ever known. And here he was, suddenly standing right in the middle of it, playing rugby league for the Celebrity Club on the weekends, but from Monday to Friday keeping a watchful eye on what went down at Thommo's—with Joe Taylor keeping a watchful eye on him.

Jack needed a father figure like The Boss in his life, because there was every chance his father was at the Caringbah Hotel, or a nearby wine bar, getting his fill before riding his pushbike home to their house in Telopea Avenue, where Jack lived with his mum, Florence, and sisters and brother. His father would doze away in the shed down the back, and while Jack loved him it was clear the grog had got him. His best years were over. Jack's were all ahead of him.

●

It hadn't been an easy life for John Cooper Gibson, who was of Scottish descent, had fought in the Second Boer War at the age of twenty around the turn of the century and then later during World War I in 1915. During his time in South Africa after the Boer conflict, he met up with his brother Frank, who had gone there in search of diamonds and then to America in search of gold. After that, Frank was never sighted again. For as long as anyone can remember, the Gibsons were always looking for something more.

Upon his return to Australia, John married Florence Thompson and they lived, for a time, in southeast Queensland where John worked as a bush policeman. One night, John rushed to a sheep station at Goodooga on the New South Wales border to break up a knife-fight between Aborigines and shearers. He was struck from behind, losing the sight in one eye; the family then moved to Kiama, south of Sydney. When Jack was born on 27 February 1929, John was 51 and the world was on the precipice of the Great Depression. He was the couple's fourth and last child—after Frank, Rose and Norene—and while he was born John Arthur Gibson he was known, almost instantly, as Jack.

Living in uncertain times, John Gibson moved his family from Kiama to Sydney in search of a better life. Small businesses, from trash-and-treasure stalls to fish shops, started up as quickly as they closed. When Jack was seven, an uncle gave him five two-shilling pieces. 'I never knew there was that much money in the world,' Jack reckoned years later.

By the time Jack was eight, the family was living at Gladesville, but for his schooling he had been dispatched to St Gregory's at Campbelltown—an agricultural boarding college in the scrubland outside of Sydney and decades off becoming the crucible of international rugby league players it is today. He was the youngest of the 40 boarders and his daily letters to his parents hinted at homesickness. Midway through the following year, he left to attend Marist Brothers Eastwood, but by then he had developed a rebellious streak. He had no truck with the conformity of school.

By his own count, Jack figured he attended 'nine or ten schools' in Sydney—most of them Catholic—and was asked to leave many of them. He attended De La Salle Cronulla but was re-enrolled at St Gregory's on 20 April 1942, and remained there for another two years. 'He used to joke how he'd been expelled from ten schools,' says Brother Comans, one of Gibson's former classmates at St Greg's. His teachers regularly bawled him out for his untidy uniform. 'He didn't care,' says another, Brother Luke. 'The teachers were constantly on his back but he always had that amiable nature. He never took anything seriously, which annoyed them. But they couldn't feel animosity towards him for too long. Nobody could.'

He thrived on boarding-school life, though, and the camaraderie that accompanied it. He dabbled in some SP bookmaking with his peers, and his frequent losses prevented him from taking the train home when it was permitted. During his early teens, he started to fill out. He didn't get his large frame from his father, who was a slightly built man, but from Flo. She was imposing. Fair horserider, too, and fearless. When St Greg's played one-off rugby league matches against visiting Catholic schools from Parramatta or Kogarah or Bondi, Jack stood tall in the second row and used his growing physique to assert his authority. 'You could always depend on Jack to biff a few blokes,' says Brother Comans. 'We didn't always win, but they never got through the forwards because of Jack.'

While he excelled at sport, he never had much interest in academia. School records for his Intermediate exam at the end of third year in 1944 highlight that he failed English and both

Mathematics classes, although he excelled at woodwork and metalwork. 'I was probably the kid most likely to fail,' Jack once said of his school days.

By now, his family had moved to the end of Telopea Avenue in Caringbah on a large block that extended down to Yowie Bay. During summer, he delighted in taking his father's boat out and fishing for yellowtail, or galloping about on one of his mother's horses. It was idyllic but the family struggled in this time of war. Jack and Florence remained prolific letter writers during his time at St Greg's and on one occasion she wrote:

> My Dear Jack
> I am going to send you some fruit by today's train so you should get the parcel on Friday. I am sorry to tell you that I sold your football boots. I got 7/- when I sold them. I did not know if you would have sold them.
> Love from all
> Mum
> PS. I will put the 7/- I got for the boots in the bank for you.

The regular correspondence with his parents suggested Jack grew up in a home in which he was loved—and he loved back. But by the time he walked out of St Greg's at the age of fifteen, he was ready to leave everything behind. There was more to be learnt in the real world and when he and close mate John Toohey saved enough money they were heading north, tucked underneath the canvas covers of a freight train bound for Queensland and so much more; they were living in the moment. They were also trying to avoid the moment when they'd feel the thwack of the baseball bat the railway staff used at stations along the way to find unwanted stowaways.

The pair started off cutting cane, and money was tight. One afternoon after a hard day's work, Jack spied a ten-quid note on the floor of the crowded bar. He discreetly made his way towards it, stomped down his foot and didn't move for an hour as he waited for the right moment to pick it up. He probably could've held his own if it had degenerated into a fight. When some older cane-cutters twigged that the teenagers were from the Big Smoke, they asked: 'Can you blokes fight?' Jack's deadpan reply: 'Do you want to find out?' In the ensuing scuffle, the legend goes that Jack knocked three out, stepped into John's fight and belted him, too. Then he broke his right hand and was forced to return to Sydney.

By February 1946, Jack was mustering cattle and sheep on the remote Big Creek Station, stuck in the middle of rural Queensland near Cheepie, which is now a ghost town. He constantly wrote to his parents and relied on them for supplies:

Big Creek Stn
Cheepie via
Charleville, Qland
Sun. 31st March 46

Dear Mum & Dad & Norene

I was very pleased to hear from you again, also to know that you are well. I was very grateful to receive the parcel you sent me Dad. The bullets and battery were just the things I wanted most, also the tobacco and papers. Shot a big roo the other day with the rifle and will send the skin home when it dries out as they make very good mats.

The firm I am working for is called Webb and Gregg. It is a big Melbourne firm. They own about 10 sheep and cattle stations all together. I have been getting only £1/2/– each week but my boss said he would try to get me a £1 rise. I seem to get on with him extra well. The job is 10 times better than the last one at 'Kialla'.

Much Love

Jack xxx

By late 1949, Jack had seen enough of sheep and cattle and he returned to Sydney for good. But what to do? He loved sport and played A-grade footy for Cronulla, but for all his ability with his fists, Jack never had designs on being a boxer. He attended the New South Wales amateur titles at the old Police Boys Club in Woolloomooloo as an onlooker, but when the defending heavyweight had no opponent he stepped in. He humbled the champion for the first two rounds, but was so tired he couldn't lift his arms in the third and lost. It was his first and last time in a ring. Besides, he did his best work out of it. 'He was always trying to prove something,' says Peter Toohey, John's young brother. 'That he was macho. But there was always two sides to him.'

A hard man was forming on the outside, but the softness and compassion remained within. When John Toohey died from a leaking valve in his heart, Jack could not stop the tears for days.

2 GRENFELL

THE FIRST SCRAPBOOK he ever kept was a dark green Collins Graphic Analysis Book. He would methodically cut out each newspaper and magazine report that mentioned his name and glue it inside, in loose chronological order. On the opening page, a small two-paragraph story from *The Rugby League News* has been affixed and has yellowed with time. Playing third grade for St George against Manly, Jack broke the defensive line and galloped 35 metres to score the match-winning try. 'Gibson was the most conspicuous forward on the field,' said the last line of the report.

If only they knew, although Norm Provan had a suspicion about his toughness from those early beginnings when he packed down in the second row alongside Jack in the early months of 1950. 'All muscle and bone,' is how Provan remembers him. 'There wasn't anything skilful about him. He wouldn't fool you with dummies. But he would hit and hit hard.'

Alas, Jack's time in the Red V was short-lived. He left mid-season after playing just a handful of matches. After skipping training one evening, and then walking off after being replaced in a game, he was suspended for two matches by the club and never returned. Some former players believed he grew discontented with the lowly match fee. The following season, Provan was elevated to first grade; the course was set for him to become the Dragons' most successful captain. As Ernie Christensen suggested to the readers of *The Sun* years later: 'Many local fans tipped Gibson to do as well as Norm in the long run.'

It's easy to suspect Jack's budding career under Joe Taylor could explain the stagnation of his nascent football career. The young bloke was on the rise. He'd progressed from giving The Boss a lift home to working occasionally on the door at the Celebrity Club, usually dressed in a tuxedo. Taylor had already lined him up to play for the A-grade team of the same name the following season. Jack had also started putting in some hours at Thommo's—although not yet as the replacement for Lee, who was still happily breathing in late 1950. Beneath the swinging light bulbs, Jack met Taylor's son, Ron, who was a fast-emerging centre. By the time the Celebrity Club lined up for its debut match of the 1951 season, they were firm friends.

Almost instantly, the Celebrity Club became as outrageously fashionable and successful as the nightclub that bore the same name. It played most of its matches at suburban Waverley Oval on Bondi Road or at the Sydney Sportsground at Moore Park and the crowds regularly swelled above 10 000 fans. Of course, Taylor was among them. He'd usually be sitting next to the immaculately dressed and deeply sun-tanned Perce Galea, whose reputation was as big as Taylor's. In time, he became the 'uncrowned king of illegal casinos in Sydney'.

What Taylor and Galea had in common was that they liked to bet—and bet *big*. Sydney's senior competition was largely played on Saturdays—especially the match of the day—while A-grade football was a purely Sunday affair. Because there was no horseracing on the Sabbath, the options to bet were limited. Taylor's new team provided a new avenue for punting. As always, the wagers were thrown around like confetti.

Indeed, Taylor seemed to have a complete disregard for the value of money. As David Hickie wrote: 'When he was gambling, money was nothing more than betting ammunition. He gambled at cards, the horses and the greyhounds, and once said if he ever found himself with $500,000 he would love to bet it on a horse.' Bill Waterhouse—at one time regarded as the biggest bookmaker in the world—has said of Taylor: 'I don't really fear any punter, but if I could fear one, it would be Joe Taylor. The trouble with Joe is he is one of the few men in the world who completely doesn't give a damn about money.'

Taylor's often repeated philosophy was simple: 'Money wasn't worth having if you couldn't get the pleasure of giving it.' And he seemed not to care who he gave it to. It was a position of wealth Jack admired. Deeply. He wasn't that flush … but he was working on it.

Joe's philosophy was to back a favourite, and the shorter the price the more he would invest. He stacked the deck with his football team accordingly. He'd sought out and successfully signed hardened front-rower Jack 'Duck' Walsh from Western Suburbs and another ex-first-grader, Owen Bevan, brother of the legendary UK-based winger Brian. Then came the exceptional signing from St George of Jack Lindwall, a centre who had smashed point-scoring records while wearing the Red V of the famous club and whose older brother Ray was the fearsome Test fast bowler.

The Celebrity Club's players, young and old, were demonstrably aware they were playing for more than competition points. They felt The Boss's money on their shoulders, and knew they held it in their hands. Under coach Frank O'Connor, a former international who had played with South Sydney, they adopted a flowing style of footy. No surprise there: Taylor had promised the team a pound for every winning point scored by the end of the season. Whenever a break was made, and there was a scent of a try, there were three or four players lining up in support.

Watching from the back of the Waverley Oval grandstand, Taylor wasn't merely running an eye over his side. He was watching the young second-rower who was more than holding his own against grizzled forwards from the wharves and factories that made up the rest of the A-grade competition. Jack stood 6 foot 3 inches and weighed next to 100 kilograms. Hardly impressive stats these days—adequate for a damaging outside back—but in 1951 he was an imposing figure.

His physical attributes were only part of the deal. He was fearless and relished the tough stuff. Duck Walsh, who had played every position for Western Suburbs except fullback, halfback and hooker and captained them to the first-grade title five years earlier, took an instant shine to the young bull.

For all his effrontery, it remained to be seen if Jack was the man to replace Bobby Lee on the door at Thommo's. In these post–World War II years, the city had been infused with American sailors wanting to fight or make love—usually the former if they could not find the latter. Hard men were required out the front of every establishment. Lee was a tough bugger. When Chow Hayes threatened to shoot him at the Ziegfeld club in May that year, Lee tried to call his bluff. 'You wouldn't do it here, with all the lights shining and all the people around,' he reportedly said. Turns out

Chow would. He did. When Lee later died in hospital, Taylor felt comfortable that Jack was tough enough to replace him.

Jack was one of about 30 to 40 men who worked at Thommo's. Not as many as in the institution's heyday, the previous decade, but enough to ensure trouble was readily snuffed out. It was a dry house and while Taylor demanded every bouncer who worked for him turn away a drunken man, many punters got their fill before they walked in. The drunks weren't necessarily the ones they had to keep an eye on. It was the desperate man who had haemorrhaged his weekly pay in an hour. That man caused trouble, trying to snip a winner for a loan. Or worse, think about following him as he left the premises so he could roll him in one of the darkened streets of Surry Hills.

Joe Taylor needed employees whose mere presence kept such desperates in check. Jack's presence said as much. So did that of Alf O'Connor, who worked the main ring and was better known as Big Itchy. A legendary story about Big Itchy: one night, a punter tried to slip a counterfeit £5 note into the ring. He was taken outside, reportedly at gunpoint. Itchy then 'scrubbed' his face along the bitumen as a reminder not to do it again. Owen Moase was such a man, too. He was a former middleweight boxer and played in the forwards with Jack for the Celebrity Club side. He was missing some fingers on one hand. It didn't bother nor hinder him. Standing in the middle of it all was ringkeeper Nixy the Flea, who weighed 45 kilograms, perpetually wore a coloured handkerchief around his neck and puffed on a long cigar beneath the swinging light bulbs.

Thommo's was full of these Runyonesque characters: Step-aside Joe, who would move to the left whenever he tossed the pennies; Lemon Drops, who was known to throw eight or more heads in a row; Bondi Jack; Billy the Greek; Snowy the Lair.

In those early months, Jack's primary job was to ensure the winners got home safely by calling them a taxi or driving them home himself if the win was large enough. If they'd won thousands—which regularly happened if the King George pennies were running their way—he'd ensure nobody left the ring for twenty minutes while the winner had enough time to clear out before a losing punter had time to bite him.

When they weren't working at Thommo's, Ron Taylor and Jack were at the Trocadero dance hall in George Street where thousands of the city's twenty-somethings would converge on the weekends. Ron couldn't dance, so you'd find him in the corner reading the Sunday newspapers after the first editions hit the street at eight o'clock that night. Not Jack. His proficiency at the waltz and foxtrot was often enough to entice two girls back to the lounge where Ron had been thumbing the papers.

If they weren't there, they would be drinking at the Celebrity Club. And if they weren't there, Jack would be drinking with Bob Dodd at Oyster Bill's down south. And if he and Bob weren't there, they were somewhere punting on horses. And more often than not they would be losing. Jack was on a first-name basis with the pawnbrokers. One time, he pawned Dodd's new set of golf clubs that he'd received as a birthday present from this father. 'I never got them back,' Dodd remembers. 'But we got another set. Jack liked to gamble. On horses. We once went to Melbourne and he had that much money on him he had to put it in the hotel safe. I knew it when he had dough—and when he didn't.'

If Jack wasn't working into the early hours or drinking or punting he was playing footy. The Celebrity Club galloped to the A-grade premiership in 1951. The following season, they got better, their popularity soared ... and the betting interest intensified. So much so, there were suspicions that some teams were 'running dead' and backing against themselves. Taylor increasingly had disputes with coach Frank O'Connor about selections.

Eastern Suburbs—the district's senior club, a New South Wales Rugby Football League foundation club in 1908—was also starting to gnash its teeth over the Celebrity Club's growing popularity. On a 'free' weekend, a combined first- and second-grade team played Taylor's side and was defeated. By the time the Celebrity Club won their second A-grade premiership, Easts had seen just about enough. They pulled rank as they were entitled to do and called the cream of the A-grade competition's young players into grade. Jack, Ron Taylor, Barry Blundell and Maurie Kermond from the Celebrity Club were among them. Some initially baulked and refused to go before receiving letters from Easts that they would be banned for life if they didn't comply.

Players like Blundell were thrust into first-grade before the season was finished. It didn't help Easts as they struggled to eighth position and crowds struggled to reach more than 3000 each weekend. As for Jack, he was ignored. It was the same for the first match of the season in 1953 when Blundell, Taylor, Maurie Kermond and Dick Rowe stepped out onto Cumberland Oval against Parramatta.

Instead, Jack was ingloriously named on the bench for third grade. *Third grade.* Who would've envisioned that the young forward warming the pine of the reserves bench that day would, in time, leave an indelible mark on the club, the club he was playing against and the game itself? Not a soul—and that included Jack Gibson himself. Football was a pastime, as it was for most of those who played then. He had no grand designs. 'Once football becomes hard work, it is no good to me,' he would say. 'I only play for fun.'

●

Jack also played because he was good at it. After his debut in third grade, he was immediately elevated to reserves the following week for the match against Balmain at the Sydney Sportsground. Come Anzac Day, he was deemed ready for first grade after regular prop Ken Hunter had strained knee ligaments against Newtown the previous weekend and was ruled out. Easts lost 19–17 at Pratten Park, but Jack acquitted himself well enough on debut to ensure he was selected the following week.

That encounter against Manly lingers in the memory of those who witnessed it, because this was the scene in the middle of Brookvale Oval that day, with the match firmly in the balance in the second half: Jack Gibson, he of one-and-a-half first-grade appearances, head snapping out of the scrum and throwing wild punches at Manly counterpart Roy Bull, who was captain-coach and a respected international. Referee Bert Crowley sent them from the field and Jack's colours were nailed to the mast for the rest of his career. 'Jack and I worked off one principle: get in first,' says his former teammate Ferris Ashton. 'If you have to think about it, it was too late.'

Jack thought for about a nanosecond. But while he was instantly tagged as a wildman, he glued enough newspaper clippings in the dark green Collins Graphic Analysis Book to suggest his skills extended beyond that of a thug. So said the report in *The Sun* in June after Easts had lost 20–18: 'Canterbury half Carl Keogh was the best on the ground ... Not far behind was tall, rangy Eastern forward Jack Gibson, who absolutely revelled in the tough stuff and whose final try for Easts was the result of a smart gather off a dropped pass.'

And this in *The Sydney Morning Herald* after Easts' 26–18 win over Parramatta later that month: 'If anyone is to be singled out for special mention, it is Jack Gibson. This youngster is going places.

Yesterday he ran himself to a standstill with a glorious display.'
He received the *Herald's* £10 prize as their Man of the Match
and remained a contender for their best and fairest award as the
season progressed. State selectors were looking, too, and they had
no hesitation in naming him in the New South Wales side to
play against a touring American All-Stars side. While it was described as a 'benevolent' state team because the US team was so
inexperienced, it recognised his dramatic ascension from third-
grade reserve at the start of the season to valued forward by the
end of it. In the first week of September, Easts lost the minor semi-
final to St George, but the emergence of Gibson, Blundell and
Taylor as the next generation gave them hope for better days.

Instead, Easts unravelled in 1954. Captain-coach Col Donohoe
had been forced back to South Sydney because of the residential
rule enforced by the New South Wales Rugby League. Donohoe
had been particularly liked by his teammates, not least because
he had convinced local publicans to let his players drink beer
after training behind closed doors when hotels shut down at
6 p.m. Such things were important then. Ferris Ashton, the World
War II veteran who had shown Jack the ropes in the back row
the previous season, was the replacement and it did not rest easily
with some players. They had wanted the job to go to Frank
O'Connor, the coach from the Celebrity Club.

Jack continued to evolve as a player despite the coaching
upheaval. As Ashton recalls of the player and the man that season:
'He was nothing flash but gee he was a hard man. He made a
big difference to our scrum. Even back then Jack was taciturn
and droll, a great man with a one-liner. He was very, very dry
… and a very reliable forward.'

So reliable that midway through the season he was selected for
the Sydney second team. Shortly afterwards, he was clipping out

the newspaper report that named him in the New South Wales side to play Queensland in the interstate match at the Sydney Cricket Ground. Another newspaper report compared his form to that of a 'Hydrogen bomb'. It had been an expeditious rise, but it was about to come to a sudden halt, like one of the opposition forwards who ran into that stiffened right arm he would often thrust out when he ran into the teeth of the defence.

Two days after representing New South Wales, he and Ron Taylor were climbing into the Pontiac, pointing its big black beak due west and driving into the sunset. The police had zeroed in on Thommo's. The Game was up and The Boss had told them to get out of town.

●

That year, in 1954, New South Wales Police Commissioner Colin Delaney had created a ripple of laughter across the city when he publicly declared that Thommo's did not exist. In truth, it had enjoyed police protection for years thanks to healthy bribes for the lower ranks of the force.

The ripple became a tidal wave of trouble for Joe Taylor and others, including Jack. Thommo's was raided in May, but it was revealed in the press to be nothing more than a publicity stunt. Taylor knew the score: he closed The Game down and told his son and Jack to leave town. 'Things had become too hot,' says Ron Taylor. 'The coppers were onto us so we closed down for six months. Dad said we might as well go up bush and play a bit of football.'

The big black beak of the Pontiac came to a halt just over 350 kilometres west of Sydney in the small town of Grenfell, out on the western plains and surrounded by cattle and sheep farms. They had followed Blundell and old Celebrity Club brethren

Maurie Kermond and Dick Rowe, all of whom had been playing local footy out there since the start of the season and for reasons completely innocent compared to that of Jack and Ron, who had booked into the local pub, the Railway Hotel, on Main Street.

Of a weekend, they played for the local side, the Grenfell Goannas. The cold, hardened grounds were far removed from those in the city. If the side won, the boys from the city rarely had to buy a drink back at the Railway, which was usually rum poured by the publican. The next day, the local grocer would spy them and throw them a bag of apples for nothing. 'But if we'd lost,' says Ron, 'they'd be abusing us and telling us we couldn't play.'

It was a life far removed from the swinging light bulbs. In their spare time, the Eastern Suburbs boys would venture into the bushland and shoot at things. Anything. Usually trees. Sometimes a cow, by accident. During the week, Taylor worked in a wheat silo. As for Jack, he cut railway sleepers. He worked just six hours on his first day, and then noticed a few more were required on the second. By the end of the week he was clocking on at dawn and finishing at dusk. 'These country blokes are too smart for me,' Jack told Ron. They were both eventually sacked.

Thankfully, after just over two months, the heat around Thommo's subsided and Jack and Ron returned to Sydney in the September of 1954. Decades later, they returned for a Goannas reunion and were warmly embraced by the town. The line-up of fans, mainly women of various ages, stretched around the corner as they waited for Jack's autograph in his slow, sloping hand.

The problem back home was that their departure had torn the Tricolours asunder. This once-proud club had won just three matches and closed out the season with eleven consecutive losses.

Ferris Ashton was broken. 'I still don't know why it happened,' he says today of the exodus of players to the bush. 'What I do know is how much it hurt the club.'

3 FLOWERS

ALL THAT BRUTALITY on the field tended to mask one widely held belief: that Jack Gibson was a fine-looking man. His were classic, masculine features. The thick crop of dark brown hair, perfectly swept back matinee idol–style. The square jaw. The dark eyes and a cool, emotionless expression. There was nothing delicate about him and the girls dug it. If they spotted him at a dance or nightclub, they'd angle for an introduction through one of his friends. His cousin, Lila, was continually asked by her nurse friends about making his acquaintance.

The year before they had fled to Grenfell, he and Ron Taylor were lunching at the fashionable Italian restaurant Romano's in York Street as guests of a wealthy Easts sponsor. If an overseas celebrity was in town, this is where they dined. As the young footballers sat there feeling slightly out of place, a stunning brunette flounced past. She gave the room whiplash. It was the Hollywood actress Ava Gardner. 'She went straight over to the head waiter and wanted to know who Jack was,' Taylor recalls. Nothing came of it, but a point worth noting: at the time, Ava Gardner was married to Frank Sinatra.

Ava Gardner was the temptress who drove Sinatra to the verge of madness. It was never that dramatic when Jack Gibson glanced at Judy Worrad across a crowded room at the New South Wales Leagues Club in Phillip Street one Saturday night in late September in 1954. Nevertheless, the attraction was strong. It mightn't have been love at first sight but from all reports it followed soon after.

Judy Worrad was twenty years old and would've given Ava Gardner a run for her money. Two years earlier, she had stormed into the finals of the Miss Pacific beauty contest held at Bondi Beach. Then she won it, which was really no surprise to anyone. She never thought of herself as anything more than the girl who worked as a statistical analyst in the city, who lived in Warner's Avenue, whose parents were decent, hard-working souls. She didn't think she was better or worse than anyone else. Bondi was merely the name of the suburb she lived in, not a better way of life.

On this Saturday night, Judy was enjoying a cabaret show with a male friend. They were 'just casual', as she remembers it. Suddenly, Maurie Kermond appeared before her. Maurie had played with Jack at the Celebrity Club, then Easts, and then Grenfell that year. He knew Judy and told her that the bloke making eyes at her on the other side of the room wanted to meet her. She slipped a glance at Jack. She knew nothing of him, because she knew nothing of football. 'Bring him over,' she said.

They moved out on the floor and shared a dance. After a while, Jack got straight to the point. 'Can I take you home?' he asked. 'No, I'm here with someone,' Judy laughed back, equally amused and surprised by his front. She played it cool and passed on her phone number, but, on reflection more than 50 years later, she had known her life had changed forever. 'From the first time that I met him that night, he was always in my life.'

●

Other impressions? 'He must've been good looking—I wouldn't have backed up, otherwise,' she says. 'And he was actually shy. Quite shy.' That coyness didn't stop Jack from phoning her the next morning. He wanted to see her. That night.

On Sunday evenings, Judy and her girlfriends would head to the Bronte Surf Club for the weekly dance. Jack had said he would be keen on taking her, but when he didn't arrive on her front step by 7 p.m. she shrugged her shoulders and Miss Pacific slipped into the night alone. 'Where's he coming from?' her mother, Ellen, asked as she left. 'Caringbah,' her daughter replied. 'Where's that?' her mother's friend from next door chimed in. 'Cronulla,' she said. 'Forget it!' they laughed in unison. 'You won't see him again.' In the 1950s, Cronulla may as well have been another city.

But she did see him again. The next day, Jack eased the Pontiac up to the curb in front of the picture theatre in Bondi Junction where Judy worked part-time as an usherette. When she walked out to meet him, he didn't offer an apology or reason for not materialising the previous night, but as Judy moved closer his no-show became secondary. The car was full to the windows with flowers. Jack Gibson: fearless rugby league forward, muscleman on the door at Thommo's Two-up School, and apparently a romantic.

They started dating and soon Jack introduced her to his heady world of nightclubs and floorshows, as well as its illegal casinos.

On Sunday evenings, it was the Carlisle Club at No. 2 Kellett Street in Kings Cross, which Joe Taylor had opened the year before. After having a meal, Judy would play rummy at £1 a game in one room while Jack played solo, a form of euchre, in another.

Jack never concealed his connection to Joe Taylor and the dark world he operated in. 'He didn't look like a crim,' Judy thought. Jack was known around the eastern suburbs for his football as much as anything else. Late on Saturday evenings, when they stepped into the Celebrity Club, people knew him. In late November, they walked in and found their table near the stage. Judy immediately spied the orchid corsage on the table. It had been two months since Jack had filled his Pontiac with flowers for her and here he was presenting one more. 'Put it on,' he smiled. When she opened the box, an engagement ring twinkled back at her.

Jack had predictably hocked many of his possessions to buy it. 'It was a fair bit for him to get together,' remembers Bob Dodd. 'It was a fair amount for those days and it took a long time to save up for it. He really wanted to get engaged and really wanted that ring so he could propose. After he met Judy that was it. There was no one else. That was the end of his chasing.'

Judy knew the question was coming. 'I think we ought to get married,' he had casually suggested months earlier. 'It'll be good.' She hadn't given him an answer, although she hadn't entirely dismissed the idea. This time she nodded and then Jack proceeded to tell her about the nerve-racking events earlier in the day. 'Your mother grilled me,' Jack said—and she had. 'I hope you can look after her,' Ellen Worrad told him. 'I'll do my best,' was Jack's reply.

They were married on 21 May 1955 at St Anne's Catholic Church at Bondi with about a hundred guests in attendance.

Bob Dodd was Jack's best man, Ron Taylor a groomsman and Norm Erskine, the most popular nightclub performer of the day, crooned away at the reception in Bondi. They spent their honeymoon on the beach at Surfers Paradise, which hadn't yet been consumed by monstrous high-rise buildings. They would drink at the only pub on the strip and giggled at the fact that you were allowed to smoke cigarettes in the picture theatre. When they returned to Sydney, they rented a two-bedroom flat on Elouera Road in Cronulla but soon moved into a cheaper one-bedroom unit nearby.

Jack was still working for Taylor throughout the week at Thommo's, and was now earning more money because he had replaced Big Itchy O'Connor in the ring. On occasions, Taylor would ask him to slip into a dinner suit and bow tie and stand on the door of his after-hours nightclub, the Corinthian Room, down the end of George Street in Haymarket. Jack hated the tuxedo but not the extra cash. After patrons made their way past Jack, they were greeted by an elaborately presented glass case in the foyer that contained the bounced cheques of former clientele. It was a subtle reminder that the house never forgot a bad debt. By the time the last of the crowd had staggered out, dawn was threatening to break.

Those nocturnal hours hurt his football. That season had been a forgettable one. He'd played most of it in the lower grades, and had been called into the firsts on just four occasions. He was sent off in one match against Souths for punching. Jack relished the game, and respected his club, but he had new priorities. He was never going to meander along in life. Nobody made a self-made man but the man himself. Joe Taylor had taught him that. By the end of the year, Judy was pregnant and Jack was focused on building a house for his growing family. He borrowed heavily from the bank and bought a block of land at 137 Nicholson Parade near Gunnamatta Bay. Every penny was invested into building their home. Whenever he found a few spare hours, he'd clear the scrubland off the block. When that was done, he started digging the foundations. By September 1956, Judy had given birth to their first child, Suzanne.

To suggest his form wavered during those few seasons because his mind was elsewhere surely would have angered him. Of course he still cared. He hadn't rediscovered the form that led to his rapid rise from third-grader to representative player in his debut season—but he still had a sense of on-field authority. The legend was growing. He'd been sent off in 1955 for punching yet escaped with a caution at the judiciary hearing. He wasn't so lucky in early 1956. He started throwing punches against North Sydney and was sent off. He was suspended for two matches.

Don't dismiss it as pure thuggery. While there was, undeniably, wildman in his style, his aggression really stemmed from his competitiveness. He hated to lose. At anything. So it hurt to see Easts struggle through the 1950s as the great underachievers of the premiership. For the 1957 season, the Tricolours enticed brilliant Randwick rugby union players Tony Paskins and Rupert Mudge to the club after they had been playing league for Workington Town in England. Terry Fearnley, a prodigiously talented forward, had returned to the club after leaving for a season following a contract dispute with president Ray Stehr.

He and Jack were starting to relish their combination in the front row. What the pair lacked, and had done for seasons, was a top-class hooker. Ian Walsh had signed but departed before playing a match because he required a career-threatening kidney operation. Despite a spirited run at the end of the season in which

Easts strung together six wins from seven matches—including a shock victory over defending premiers St George—they finished eighth and out of the reckoning.

The following season, in 1958, they tanked again and finished seventh. That was the year Jack got his groove back. In late May, he was selected to represent Sydney against the touring Great Britain side after a rousing display for Easts against Manly at the Sportsground. The thought of pushing Manly rival Rex Mossop to the reserves bench no doubt pleased him. The fearless attitude that had served him well so far was respected by selectors and teammates alike. The press, too. In late July, he almost single-handedly ensured Easts beat North Sydney 13–9 at North Sydney Oval. 'The Great Gibbo, as his teammates call him, was punishing in all he did, whether running with the ball dwarfed in his ham-like claws or tackling Norths forwards,' oozed Jack Pollard in *The Daily Telegraph*. Truth was, Jack loathed the nickname 'Gibbo'. 'Who's Gibbo?' he'd say whenever someone used it.

In 1959, Dave Brown was appointed coach of Easts. He was the goal-kicking, record-breaking, premiership-winning icon who had been dubbed 'The Bradman of League' during the 1930s and '40s. But reputation made no difference as Easts again failed to reach the finals.

Stuff this, Jack thought. Before a match against Western Suburbs that season, he dragged Terry Fearnley aside in the dressing-rooms at Pratten Park. Neville Charlton, the ball-playing Magpies forward otherwise known as 'Boxhead', was in his sights. 'I'll make sure he's carried off today,' Jack promised. 'He's got a glass jaw.' As a scrum packed down in the twentieth minute, Jack kept his word: his two right-handed punches knocked Charlton out. Boxhead left the field on a stretcher. Easts still lost 38–10.

His frustration, even then, was the lack of preparation. What use was there in turning up to training twice a week, having a short discussion with the coach about tactics and then running through some basic drills? There was no forethought for success. 'It bores me,' he told Judy before trudging off to training one night.

At no stage did Jack covet the position of first-grade football coach, even if he silently thought he could do a better job.

4 THE BIG KICK

SO HERE HE is, Jack Gibson. Big Jack by now. The legend was stirring.

He was widely known as the immovable Eastern Suburbs forward and one of Joe Taylor's men: hard but as honest as the day was long—and some of the early morning, too. If he'd worked a rare Saturday night and pulled an all-nighter working at one of Joe's nightclubs, he'd stop his car—a La Salle, from the Cadillac stable, by now—outside a Catholic Church and attend mass. On a Sunday night, he and Judy would stop in at St Patrick's in The Rocks before heading to Kellett Street in the Cross, where they hit the illegal casinos.

As the 1960 rugby league season loomed, Big Jack—now 31—was also doting father to three daughters: Sue, Tracey and Joanne. Tracey was born in June 1958 and on Christmas Eve of that year the family hastily moved into their newly built house in Nicholson Parade. There were no curtains on the windows but Jack and Judy's expanding family could wait no more. Joanne was born in late March of 1960. Four days later, Manly beat Easts by a point at the Sportsground on the opening weekend of the season, which had started where the past dozen or so had ended for the Tricolours: miserably.

By now, Big Jack had other matters to attend to. The legend was stirring but what remained very discreet was his growing side interest as an SP bookmaker. The punt had been part of his realm since he and Bob Dodd and Alan David had run their own book as teenagers. He had seen for years the lure of the green turf and green baize. He had seen the intoxicating charm of the King George VI pennies tossed into the light of the swinging light bulbs. But this was different. This was risk on a grander—and dangerous—scale.

Since the 1930s, the SP bookmaker had been an intrinsic part of Australian life and a necessity because of the nation's passion for having a bet. You would find the SP in the corner of the local pub or club, the milkbar or the workplace. The SP would offer the odds on races and other sporting events at the fixed starting price, thus the term 'SP bookie' or, as more affluent customers preferred, 'turf accountants'. It was only legal for such bookmakers to operate at a racetrack and they had to be licensed. Those who operated elsewhere—or via the telephone—were operating illegally, although the police often turned a blind eye. As revealed at the 1962 Kinsella Royal Commisison into off-course betting, one in four Australians regularly punted with the local SP, of which there were an estimated 6000 nationwide. The Commission concluded that ten times more money was gambled off the track than on it. Bookies from the time reckon it was more.

Shortly after moving into the house at Nicholson Parade, Jack started to take his slice of the pie. It started through the trotting bookie Harry Mulray and two of Harry's biggest punters, Bob and

Jack Ingham, in the late 1950s. The Ingham boys had taken over the family poultry supply business from their late father, Walter, in 1951, and were starting to reap the rewards. The chicken kings also loved to bet. And big. By the late 1950s, they were said to be turning over £150 000 a week with Mulray. The bets were getting too much for the bookie, so Mulray introduced them to Jack so he could become a commission agent, whose job was to farm the bet around to other bookmakers.

'Jack got into the SP through Harry Mulray,' says a man familiar with the gambling scene then. 'He used to put all of the Inghams' bets on. Harry Mulray was a good trotting judge and sweet with the Inghams. Harry was getting in too much, so he gave the turnover to Jack. That's what gave Jack the big kick.' The 'big kick' was a shilling earned for every pound invested, and given how fearless the Inghams were when it came to the punt that was very good coin. The danger was if Jack decided to take the bet himself and not farm it around. The return often outweighed the risk, and soon enough Jack was fielding bets from other punters.

Meanwhile, the talk was that Taylor wasn't pleased about Jack branching off on his own, although it didn't sour their relationship. Jack kept working for The Boss, but he had also sparked a close friendship with two of the heaviest hitters in the city. The Ingham brothers were no fools. They were clever businessmen and didn't carelessly hand out their trust, especially when it came to the punt. Their betting arrangement showed how much trust they had in Big Jack.

●

While his bookmaking activities were unspoken, the press was tantalised by the fact that Jack juggled his football career with the late finishes of the nightclub business. 'Late nights, normally taboo with athletes, seem the right prescription for Eastern Suburbs rugby league forward Jack Gibson,' Ernie Christensen wrote in *The Sun*. 'He never gets to bed before 4am yet he is the best conditioned player in Easts' teams ... Gibson says that he always sleeps well and is keen to train when he rises.' In the same article, Jack said: 'If I had to rely on football for my living, I think I'd scout around for something easier.'

What never received a syllable of coverage was Jack's involvement in one of Australian publishing's most infamous episodes. It was the first time Rupert Murdoch was pitted against the Packer family and the incident sparked a newspaper war that reverberated through Australian publishing for decades. Years later, Jack and billionaire businessman Kerry Packer became close allies. But on this occasion, he sat on Murdoch's side of the fence.

He had already met Murdoch, who had become managing director of News Limited in 1953 at the age of 22 after his father, Keith, had died. In the late 1950s, as Murdoch started to lay the foundation blocks of his media empire, he'd attended Thommo's, which was only a few streets away from News Limited's Holt Street offices in Surry Hills. *Daily Mirror* reporter and playboy punter Bill Mordey organised a covert operation to ensure Murdoch and two friends from the United States found their way to the Game. After being driven down darkened alleys and swapping cars, they suddenly found themselves beneath the swinging light bulbs. Mordey reported afterwards that Murdoch and Jack got on well. Others recall Jack laying Murdoch's bets for him, although Murdoch rejects this. 'I am pretty sure that if I put any bets on I would have done it myself,' he says.

On the morning of 8 June 1960, their paths crossed again. When Murdoch bought Mirror Newspapers from John Fairfax and Sons, it meant Sir Frank Packer's Consolidated Press no longer had a place to print its regional newspapers. Sir Frank's pugnacious son Clyde honed in on the Anglican Press. It had been placed in the hands of a receiver-manager and Clyde spied an opportunity to solve his father's dilemma. Francis James, the hard-nosed founding editor of the weekly religious publication *The Anglican*, was having no truck with that. He approached Murdoch, who promised to keep his publication independent and out of the clutches of the Packers.

The situation reached boiling point on the night of 7 June when Clyde, his younger brother Kerry and a group of muscle-men broke in and took possession of the Anglican Press building in Queen Street, Chippendale. James phoned Murdoch, who hastily arranged his own muscle. That muscle was organised just after midnight by Frank Browne, the *Sunday Mirror's* larger-than-life sports columnist, who immediately went to Thommo's and offered some of the doormen some extra work. One of those men was Jack Gibson, and around 2.30 a.m. he and the rest of Browne's heavies stormed the Anglican Press and regained control for Francis James. In the process, Kerry Packer—the country's future billionaire and richest man—was badly bashed. The images were splashed all over the front page of that day's *Daily Mirror*.

Murdoch does not recall Gibson's involvement, because the media mogul wasn't present. 'But I do remember the lead-up to the fight and the actual night when the editor of the *Mirror*, the late Ian Smith, rang me several times with excited blow-by-blow stories,' Murdoch says. 'It is true that Kerry Packer was thumped by somebody as we talked about it together many years later.' But the late journalist Tom Prior reckoned Jack Gibson was involved. In his 1993 book *The Sinner's Club*, he recounts seeing a series of photos taken by *Mirror* photographer Don Sheahan. He wrote:

I recognised some familiar faces from Thommo's two-up game in Don's pictures, including Jack Gibson, who later won increasing fame as a rugby league coach and memorable rugby league commentator. 'Young Packer's the goer,' said Don. 'He really copped a thumping. Browne's mob weren't mucking around. They were earning their pay'.

Frank Browne was no doubt aware of Jack's form when he dragged him into the Murdoch–Packer brawl. A month after the Anglican Press showdown, with Easts looming as a serious threat to St George's domination of the premiership, he was set to reach the milestone of his hundredth first-grade game. South Sydney was the opponent and their home ground of Redfern Oval was the venue. Before the match, Jack walked to the centre of the field to a hero's reception as club president Bob Stuart grabbed the microphone and spoke glowingly of his long service to the club. 'And what's more,' Stuart said, tongue planted firmly in cheek, 'he's never incurred the wrath of a referee.'

After 35 minutes of play, referee Cliff Brown pointed to the sheds and Jack solemnly walked from the field. He was sent off five times during his playing career but this would always be the stand-out: dismissed for kicking Souths forward Russell Addison in the head during an altercation. When Addison regained his feet, he was also sent off for provoking the incident in the first place. Easts won the match and Jack was suspended for a month.

It was an unfortunate time to be sidelined because he was undoubtedly playing the best football of his career. So much so, he was seriously being touted as a prospect for the Australian squad to play in the World Cup in Britain and France at season's end. The reason, as far as Jack was concerned, was new coach Dick Dunn, who had been given the job that year but had the side humming along in second position on the ladder for the second half of the season. 'Dick Dunn gave me a specific job to do and showed confidence in me,' Jack said of the coach. 'I needed someone to show confidence in me. When it happened, that motivated me. Dick was the only coach who showed personal confidence in me even after I'd had poor games. He made me a better player. He was the best coach I had. He seldom used criticism; he preferred the good and positive things about a player.'

The belief that Easts could achieve something special was seeded the round before Jack's send-off against Souths when they had triumphed 7–4 over St George at the Sportsground. For the past five seasons, the men in the Red V had been unstoppable. Captain Ken 'Killer' Kearney ran a tight operation. Centre Reg Gasnier was lethal. Johnny Raper was so influential throughout this season he was already considered one of history's greatest lock-forwards. And then there was Norm Provan, Jack's old second-row teammate from the thirds in 1950 who was not only a central part of the Dragons machine but being groomed to take over from Kearney. Meanwhile, Easts were gnawing away at the Saints' dominance with young talent. John 'Straw' Andrews, in particular, was a crowd-pleasing fullback who thrived on running the ball. But it was the front row that had given them some backbone. In Ken Ashcroft, Jack and Terry Fearnley had finally found a competitive hooker to bookend. When Fearnley was ruled out for the rest of the season with a knee injury, Jack was given the captaincy. He thrived on the added responsibility.

By the finals series in early August, St George had finished three wins ahead as minor premiers, with Wests, Easts, Balmain and Canterbury log-jammed on equal points. Easts won the preliminary play-off against Canterbury 20–11 on a Tuesday night to ensure their progression, but lost to Wests 18–7 at the SCG the following

Saturday. In the minor semi-final, they met Canterbury again and what ensued was a hundred-minute epic that Easts eventually won—but it should never have been so hard. Jack had stirred his forwards in the first half with some inspirational runs. Easts led 9–0 at half-time, but the match was pushed into twenty minutes of extra play when referee Darcy Lawler inexplicably awarded a try to Canterbury winger Ken Rowlands with seven minutes remaining of normal time. The Easts players were dumbfounded. So was the crowd. Hadn't Lawler seen Rowlands fumble the ball further downfield as he attempted an intercept and regained it on the bounce? Evidently not. The explanation afterwards was that Lawler's vision had been obscured.

The gaffe didn't influence the final result. A try to winger Boyce Beeton two minutes into extra time and two goals to the other winger, Bob Landers, ensured a 16–9 win. 'It renews hope of East regaining its old-time glamour,' wrote George Crawford in *The Daily Telegraph*. Yet the prevailing sentiment heading into the final was that the golden run was about to come to an end. Easts were to meet Wests, the side that had humbled them at the SCG a fortnight earlier. Sure, the Magpies back line featured stars like centre Harry Wells and the legendary halfback Keith Holman, who had dismantled Easts previously, darting from the scrum base and with short grubber kicks. But the confrontation that would determine the result would be between Jack and his old sparring partner Neville Charlton. 'I understand Easts' general strategy will be a "battle of the giants" in the early stages,' Jim Mathers ominously predicted in the *Mirror*. There were no tougher giants than Gibson and Charlton.

In the end, there was none of the brutality many had expected. Jack had led the way in the forwards, although he had dropped the ball in some tackles, but his most telling play came late in the first half when he set up his side's second try. As Mathers colourfully reported: 'This sustained assault began with a man-sized effort by the slogging forward Jack Gibson, who skirted the sideline, and transferring his otherwise bellicose physique into the shape of a thoroughbred, he passed inside to winger Beeton who scored the try.' When Doug Ricketson scored a cracking try shortly after, to give them a 15–5 lead, the cry of 'Easts! Easts! Easts!' on the Paddington Hill echoed around the cricket ground. A Holman try late in the match silenced them briefly but Easts held on to win 20–15. Easts were in the grand final.

It was the first time since 1945 that they had reached the season-decider. In that 1945 match, Dick Dunn had been a lock-forward and had scored three tries in the win against Balmain. Now as coach, he was deliciously close to victory again. As the Easts players left the field, the 29 000 fans around the SCG rose to their feet and applauded. Then something extraordinary happened, underlining the significance of the result. Wests' vanquished players, bruised and broken, took the unprecedented step of forming a guard of honour before the gate of the Members' Stand. Jack Gibson led his boys through and into the rooms. The next day, George Crawford wrote in *The Telegraph*:

> The match restored to league touches of the colourful glamour that surrounded the great East teams of the past. It also brought a new outlook for the public, which had wearied after watching for five years Balmain, Wests and Manly in turn making unsuccessful attempts to dethrone St George.

Crawford then tipped St George to win the grand final. Indeed, as the match neared it was clear that Easts and their supporters were revelling in the fact that they had simply made it. They had 'risen from the ashes', as more than one rugby league roundsman described in their preview stories. Street processions were organised, special functions arranged. 'Easts can carry their flag on to the ground,' St George's po-faced secretary Frank Facer remarked. 'But St George will carry the JJ Giltinan Shield off the field as winners of the 1960 premiership for the fifth successive year.'

For about 28 minutes of the grand final, having held the Dragons machine to a 5–2 lead, Jack Gibson and his side held their own. Then the class of Dragons Reg Gasnier and winger Johnny King shone through just after half-time and the match burst open. St George won 31–6. Despite his disappointment, Jack wasn't complaining too loudly in the aftermath. He had noted the refereeing of Darcy Lawler with interest. Easts had won the penalty count 17–6. The front row of Gibson, Ashcroft and Bob McDonagh had dominated the feared Dragons front row of Bill Wilson, Ken Kearney and Kevin Ryan in the scrums. Lawler had given Easts every chance.

As for Jack's performance that season, there was no dispute that he was at the peak of his powers. He was overlooked for Australian selection, which astounded those who had watched him stand tall for Easts that season. 'For several years he has been Sydney's most underrated footballer,' George Crawford wrote as he named Jack one of *The Sunday Telegraph*'s players of the year:

> Gibson this year proved his qualities beyond doubt. As the only mature player for Eastern Suburbs, he did a remarkable job piloting a team of youngsters through to the premiership grand final. He did it with gutsy football, which could not fail to inspire the 12 youngsters around him.

Jack would have liked that.

5   ANY NEWS?

HE WOULD OPEN the bowling and come in off a medium length with a Keith Miller-style run. He would thunder in, clunk his left foot down and unleash the ball with the same fury he displayed on the football field. Sometimes, he got surprising lift and his bouncer snared him many wickets. But when the ball beat the batsman and thudded into his pads, or faintly kissed the edge of the willow, the rest of the Waverley boys would appeal to the heavens. The keeper. The slips. The ring of fieldsmen in close. All of them.

Hooowzzzzzzzaaaaaat?!!!!!!!!

Not Jack. Theatrics weren't his go. He preferred to turn around slowly, place his hands on his hips and stare down the umpire. His eyes would narrow and only then would he make his inquiry without expression … 'Any news?'

From 1957 to 1961, playing with the famed Waverley club, Jack was one of those rare sportsmen who picked up their first-grade cricket season just after their first-grade football season had finished. Having returned to the game of bat and ball at the age of 27, he took 92 wickets in five seasons of Sydney grade cricket, most of them in first grade. 'We all loved him,' says his fellow opening bowler, Dr John Morrison. 'He was a strong man physically and mentally and he could bowl all day.' He was as revered at Waverley as he was at Easts. One day at Manly Oval, he told officials that he had to leave early to play in a trial match for football. Could he play further up the order? Waverley was a strict club and such requests would normally be dismissed. But this was Jack. He came in at No. 3, blazed a quick-fire 30, and then was off.

The Waverley boys were shocked at how quiet he was: the man with the formidable reputation who brought his young daughters to home matches at Waverley Oval and rarely said a word. Two incidents, though, cemented the legend. Both involved the Bankstown club. 'We don't like them, and they don't like us,' says Morrison. After a match at Bankstown Oval one Saturday afternoon, a handful of Waverley players could not get to the nearest pub quick enough because of the oppressive heat. As they slowly sipped their ales, some of the Bankstown players on the other side of the room started heckling them. Jack endured it for so long. 'Won't be long, fellas,' he told his teammates, plonking down his glass. He walked over, whacked three of them, returned to his seat and calmly sipped his beer. 'We looked on him as our knight on horseback,' says Morrison. 'Our minder. We all felt quite safe when Jack was around.'

While the Waverley boys knew of Jack's reputation, the word hadn't filtered throughout Bankstown just yet. On another occasion, after another cricket match against Bankstown, he found himself at another local pub with just one other player. Some of the patrons became rowdy and knocked the schooner glass in his hand. Jack gave them a menacing look and that was enough for five of them to set upon him, schooner still in hand. They kicked him as he tried to cover himself on the ground. The following Saturday, Jack convinced his Easts teammate Terry Fearnley and two well-known professional boxers to front the same pub as he went in search of retribution. They entered the bar from different doors and the packed room fell silent. 'You could have heard a pin drop,' says Fearnley. 'They must have found out who he was.' As had been the case his entire life, Jack didn't use those big hands for the sake of it—only when necessary.

Cricket was just another way of testing himself. He'd often front at the nets at the SCG and bowl at the New South Wales side's best batsmen during training sessions. For hours on end, he'd bowl at legendary figures like Neil Harvey and Alan Davidson. He'd buy a brand-new two-piece ball because he knew it would swing more than a four-piece model. 'He was a cunning bugger,' says Bob Simpson, the former New South Wales and Test batsman who became the Australian team's most influential coach. 'He was ahead of the game, even then.'

It was Jack's reborn love of cricket that almost forced him to prematurely retire from his first love of rugby league as the 1961 season approached. He slipped a disc in his back while bowling in the nets at the SCG one afternoon that summer and had struggled with the incessant pain. The warmer the weather, the louder he grumbled. In late February, a week before his 32nd birthday, he told reporters it had healed but was uncertain about playing on. 'Unless I can do it easily in the trials, I think I'll give it away,' he said. He made it past the pre-season but when he was ruled out for the round-three match against St George it was clear he needed surgery. After the three-hour operation, in which the slipped disc was manipulated back into position, rumours floated around the game that doctors had ordered him to quit. 'I have not been told to give up rugby league,' he snapped. 'I will give up rugby league when I don't get any more enjoyment from playing.'

For Easts, too, the pressure was there to repeat the feats of the previous season. Coach Dick Dunn had slipped into the background and Terry Fearnley had been appointed captain-coach for the season. When it became clear after a few months that Fearnley was struggling with form and fitness after having a knee reconstruction, he asked for Dunn to be rushed back in as coach. While Jack's on-field presence was hampered by his back injury, he was finding his voice in a weekly column in *The Sun*. He had a theory about why Easts were continuing to hum along despite having none of the big-name stars of their rival clubs:

> People talk about the money in sport, but all I'm interested in is having a good game. By a good game, I mean winning games. I don't see the slightest fun in playing 80 minutes and ending up as loser. On the money angle, over at Easts we all get the same cut per game. No fancy fees for temperamental stars or fellows who will miss a few beats because it won't cost them anything. The system probably will change once Easts gets some money, but the change may not be for the best. We reached the grand final last season, and if we get there this year we will stretch our opposition to the limit.

Easts didn't make the grand final. They didn't even reach the play-offs. They had been in the top four all season and with three minutes remaining of their final-round match against Canterbury at the Sportsground appeared certain to stay there until the Berries conjured up a try. Ironically, George Crawford reckoned in *The Telegraph* that Canterbury's incentive-based pay system, in which players were awarded £20 for a win, had been the reason.

Jack Gibson would have scoffed at such a claim, but his column from mid-season proved to be prophetic. Money changes everything, he reckoned, and later that year it did. In mid-September, the Eastern Suburbs Leagues Club was opened and the neon sign on the front 'Easts to Win' started blinking for the first time. The club was built on Oxford Street, Bondi Junction, in a three-storey building that used to be the infamous Royal Surrey Hotel, where shady underworld figures once drank. Its rebirth as Easts Leagues netted the club a £50 000 surplus less than four months after its opening.

In the early weeks of 1962, Easts Leagues donated £1000 to the football club and cashed-up officials immediately started eyeing new talent. When they signed Neville Charlton from Wests, Jack was floored. Neither man had been particularly fond of the other. Rival prop forwards rarely were—and Charlton was probably still stinging from the two right-hand punches Jack had concussed him with in their memorable encounter during the 1959 season. So as far as Jack was concerned, Charlton's signing amounted to betrayal from his own club.

Then reports emerged about what they had paid for Charlton. Jack heard it was 600 quid. The newspapers reported Easts paid an £800 transfer fee to Wests and then signed Charlton to a two-year deal worth £800. Another version of the story said that the leagues club had given the football club a whopping grant of £3000, with £2000 of it covering the transfer fee and £800 going to Charlton. 'Easts' offer was just too good to refuse,' Charlton said.

Jack was livid. So much for playing from the heart. Easts president Bob Stuart said Jack would be moved to the second row to accommodate their new prized signing. Good luck. Big Jack wasn't having a bar of it. He wanted an immediate release.

The move surprised club officials. When they heard that Terry Fearnley also wanted out, amid wild speculation that Charlton would be given the captaincy, they were mystified. As for Jack, he was incensed the club would place a £500 transfer on his head. 'I will not play again with Easts,' he said as the issue started to boil in the press. 'I will approach the club for a reduction in the price placed on me. I feel they owe me this, at least. The club should look after the players who have stuck with it, before buying new players. They have paid more for Charlton than I have received in my nine seasons with the club.' In those nine seasons, he'd been paid a total £1500. Now Easts were trying to reap a third of that in letting him play elsewhere. 'If it's not reduced, I probably will not play at all,' he said. President Bob Stuart was stunned at how ugly the situation had become. 'We don't want to lose him,' he said. 'He has been a wonderful clubman and is held in high regard at Easts.'

The following night, Gibson and Fearnley fronted the Easts committee after Charlton had completed his first training session for his new club that afternoon. Fearnely was told he would not be going anywhere. As for Jack, they slashed the transfer fee in half to £250. The following night, Newtown secretary Jack Carey paid the fee and then Jack signed on to play the 1962 season for £500.

For years, Jack insisted that he never played for money, only the pure enjoyment of the game, but it had been a factor in his decision to leave. It opened him up to accusations of hypocrisy— and not for the first time. He was also angry with Fearnley for not following him out of the club. Fearnley had the right to appeal to the New South Wales Rugby League, but didn't proceed. Easts needed their man. He had been captain-coach the previous season, after all. After three weeks of stalemate with the club, Fearnley relented and signed on for another year for £400. 'I just weakened and stayed,' Fearnley recalls. 'I don't think Jack was that angry about leaving the club. I think he was dirty with me for not sticking with it and us going together.' Fearnley's hands were tied, but Jack wasn't prepared to accept that immediately. For him, matters of loyalty were easily defined even if, in reality, they were not.

After Jack officially signed with Newtown, he and Judy walked across the road to the Newtown Leagues Club on Stanmore Road but were told visitors weren't allowed in until after 8 p.m. on Saturday evenings, but welcome to the club anyway. They went to Kings Cross for a Chinese meal before Jack then headed to the Forbes Club, owned and operated by Perce Galea. 'I bit the house for 500 … and did the lot on baccarat,' he recalled years later. 'Actually, I had 60 or 70 quid in my kick so I did a bit more than 500. That was my pay for the year with Newtown. Gone. The only good thing to come out of the experience was that I learned from it. This was a one-off; I came away from the experience bruised but a little wiser. I didn't chase the lost 500 and I never let the punt beat me again.'

•

'It cracked like a Tom Thumb firecracker.' Jack was not referring to the usual sound of flesh and bone and cartilage colliding with each other. It was his left collarbone, and he cracked it early in the second half of the pre-season match between Newtown and Easts at Henson Park—the first showdown with Neville Charlton.

Newtown officials had shocked many when they appointed Jack as captain for their first match of the season against Manly. Five-eighth Tony Brown, who had been skipper for several seasons, was made vice-captain. If the appointment left some stalwarts privately aggrieved, they were soon mollified when Jack faced his former club for the first time.

Leading 9–2 early into the second half, Newtown had dominated in the forwards right up until the moment Jack and those around him heard the sickening sound in a tackle. He rushed to the sideline and was instructed by doctors not to take the field again. He returned anyway but looked like a seagull trying to fly with a broken wing, his face contorting each time he figured in the play. Easts second-rower Merv Cross, a medical student at the time who later became Australia's leading orthopaedic surgeon, said afterwards the show of bravery was lunacy. Newtown fell apart after Jack's injury but he'd earned the team's eternal respect by returning to the field. The following day, X-rays confirmed the break. 'I'll be back in two weeks,' Jack promised.

As the season played out, Jack's new teammates had a familiar feel to the Easts side of 1960. They had no constellation of superstars and were loaded with youngsters, but their unity and belief allowed them to be more than competitive. From the first round through to the last, Newtown were embedded in the top four. The previous season, they had finished second last. This time, they finished second behind St George and met them in the major semi-final at the SCG in the first week of the finals. If taking on the side that had won the last six premierships was something to fear for Newtown's young players, Jack wasn't letting on and he told them so before the match:

It is time someone started giving Newtown players a bit of credit for their ability—because they have plenty of it. You would think we were a team of mugs, who had just drifted into the competition. I've played a fair while—I'm not one of the new boys around the place—and for my money this team has as much talent as any other and can win the premiership. Out at Henson Park nobody has given a thought to the possibility of a defeat by Saints tomorrow. Most of the boys expect to win by a furlong and the St George legend that works so potently against Wests every time they meet won't be worrying the Blue colts. Saints are not going to get any respect from our fellows on what they have done in the past. The 'big bad wolf' stuff won't cut any ice with us.

Kaboom! The words were dynamite. They were the words you would expect from the captain, perhaps the coach. Yet they weren't delivered during an impassioned oratory after training at Henson Park on Thursday night. They weren't mouthed in the dressing-rooms at the SCG that Saturday afternoon. They appeared in his weekly column for *The Sun*, read by thousands. David could not have thrown a larger stone at Goliath. Come full-time, St George had won 30–9. Centre Reg Gasnier unfurled one of the virtuoso displays of his career and scored three tries. In the final minutes, Jack could hardly move. He'd tackled himself to a standstill. The following Saturday, Newtown faced Western Suburbs at the SCG again and it was a similar result. They were defeated 25–13. The gains achieved in their season had evaporated too quickly.

For Jack, there was always something outside football to distract him from the disappointment it usually brought him late in the year. He was spending less time working at Thommo's. His SP business was expanding well beyond the Inghams. Word had got around, and more bets from other punters were being taken. He slowly broke away from Joe Taylor, who wasn't entirely pleased with the situation. 'Joe liked having everyone around him,' says a punter from those times. 'There was no bad blood, but Jack wanted to make it on his own.'

And he had. He had a loving wife. He had three young daughters. On 4 December that year, when Luke was born, he had his first son. He had built a home for them all to live in. He was providing for them but answerable to no one but himself. He is unlikely to have thought about it, but Jack had reached what he'd been climbing towards since Joe Taylor had slid into the back of his Pontiac outside the Celebrity Club in the early morning of July 1950. He'd become his own man.

6 'WE CAN'T WIN'

TRADE A PLAYER a year too early rather than a year too late. This was the principle Jack Gibson followed as a coach. As the 1963 season approached, it was the ruthless decision Newtown made about him as a player.

For the Bluebags, it was a straightforward call: Jack was playing busted. He had struggled with an injured thigh muscle the previous season, but it was that temperamental disc in his back causing the most grief. His contribution in the pre-season matches had been pedestrian at best and when he was dropped for the trial match against Parramatta at Lidcombe Oval in early March he sensed retirement was near. 'The selectors might have made my mind up for me,' admitted Jack, who had just turned 34.

He was no fool. He sniffed the breeze and it reeked of an ugly standoff. Just as he had done when leaving Easts, he made the first move. He wanted Newtown to place him on the open transfer market—and without a fee. The club's retention committee agreed to his request because of his 'loyal service to rugby league', but the Newtown players were unhappy at their officials for not showing their captain the same loyalty he'd showed them.

As it turned out, Jack's decision to walk was a gamble. It had been hinted that North Sydney was interested, but nothing came of it. It had been rumoured that Jack had spoken to Easts about playing for them for no fee, but they didn't want him either. Just before Anzac Day, with three rounds of the premiership already complete, Western Suburbs snapped him up. Secretary Bill Beaver declared Gibson would be 'invaluable help' to the club. Jack just wanted a start. 'I've never earned much out of football and I'm not looking for anything now,' he said. 'I love the game and just want the chance to play.'

After three matches in reserve grade, he was elevated to first grade for the match against Balmain at Leichhardt Oval. Selectors wanted to strengthen their pack. It sounded like a job Jack could handle. And from that point on, he became a crucial figure in the front row, alongside hulking prop Denis Meaney and the Australian hooker Noel 'Ned' Kelly. His arrival at Wests was timely. The Magpies had lost the last two grand finals against all-conquering St George, as well as the 1958 decider. Yet there was every indication that this was the season when Goliath might finally be toppled. Wests had beaten Saints on Anzac Day at the SCG, although the Dragons players were furious about the performance of referee Darcy Lawler. There were no such complaints, though, in late June when Wests beat them again. Jack had been instrumental in that 12–5 win, having sent bruising centre Peter Dimond over for a try. It was only the second time the Dragons had been beaten that season—both at the hands of Wests.

The serendipity was becoming impossible to ignore. Jack had started this season with his playing career ostensibly finished, yet he could see the premiership he'd failed to grasp in 1960 with Easts. He liked his Wests teammates, too. These working–class types from the fibro suburbs were his style of people. Jack's penchant for frequenting flashy illegal casinos and driving expensive cars seemed glamorous but he was nothing of the sort.

One Sunday afternoon, Jack invited the players and their wives and children to lunch at Nicholson Parade. 'We're all standing there looking at each other wondering if we had the right place,' Peter Dimond said years later.

> Then a butler opens the door, brings us in and takes the ladies' coats and hangs them up. We spend the rest of the night being served good food and drink by waiters. We knew he wasn't on that much as a player so we just left it at that ... I'm not breaking any new ground when I say Jack was mystery man. No one made any inquiries.

Few saw it as a chance to grandstand, and most accepted it as a gesture typical of the man.

Captain Arthur Summons had noted in those first few months how economical Jack was with his words. It had been the same at other clubs, and while playing cricket for Waverley. He was no mug, and certainly no mug lair. He wasn't sheepish by any means. He was renowned for simply asking 'What's doin'?' whenever he walked into the room, and Noel Kelly is convinced he discovered the greeting. The fact is, it just took some time to get to know Jack Gibson. 'And when you did, you realised what an intelligent and humorous fellow he was,' says Summons.

Jack clicked instantly with Noel Kelly, though. It was 'Ned' to everyone else but 'Snoz' to Jack, who delighted in how often Kelly's nose would bleed during a match. They often spear-fished together in Gunnamatta Bay, and Kelly would be petrified that Jack was 6 foot 3 inches of moving shark bait because he kept shoving every fish caught deep into his wetsuit. They had the same synergy on the field. If the opposition had scored, and they sensed Wests were beginning to wane, they'd try a set move. 'Sideswipe,' Jack would say to Snoz out of the corner of his mouth. From a short kick-off, with the ball hanging in the air, the two props would come flying in from opposite sides and crunch into the opposing player just as he caught it. 'It was like being hit by two buses,' is how Kelly remembers the move—and fondly.

After the last victory over St George, Wests were humming. If not for losses to Balmain and Easts in the last month of the 1963 home-and-away season, they might've edged the Dragons out of the minor premiership. As it turned out, they finished second and it set up a major semi-final blockbuster between the two teams at the SCG. There had been suggestions in the press in the days before the game that Jack would only play if it were a heavy ground, the conditions in which he had prevailed for his entire career. It was a furphy—and Noel Kelly wouldn't have accepted it, anyway. 'Hooker Noel Kelly is keen to have the experienced Gibson in the pack if only to assist in winning the ball,' Ernie Christensen wrote in *The Sun*.

Wests were the bull in the Dragons' china shop. They had done it earlier in the season by out-muscling and -bustling the premiers into error. Jack was crucial to it as much as anyone. In the semi-final, the same strategy had worked, but down the stretch, with two minutes left to play, St George still hung on grimly to an 8–7 lead. Wests fullback Don Parish almost levelled the scores with a penalty attempt from near the sideline, but it shaved the upright. But then a reprieve. Dragons fullback Graeme Langlands placed a foot behind the dead-ball line while fielding the kick. From the drop-out, the Maggies would have one last shot at it. Robert Gray captured the excitement of it in *The Sunday Mirror* the next day:

> Langlands kicked far down field where the ball reached the eager hands of Jack Gibson, the tough prop. Gibson crashed through and transferred to Kelly who, in a grinding, bumping run, bullocked his way through three desperate tackles. Scarcely a spectator among the 42,065 present kept his seat as Kelly flicked out a neat pass to young Rob McGuiness. Off McGuiness galloped, running diagonally across field with the St George cover defence steaming after him. An inspired dummy had all except lock Johnny Raper wrong footed as McGuiness sensed Smyth come inside him. Down McGuiness went with Raper around his ankles but the job was done and Smyth, running strongly, dived across. Thus those Western Suburbs Davids slew the St George Goliaths.

●

As the grand final neared, the gambling grapevine began to grow, twisting and turning about some suspicious betting activity. Days before the game, it found its way to Jack.

He was told that referee Darcy Lawler had backed St George, which had qualified for the decider having beaten Parramatta in the preliminary final thanks to typical Reg Gasnier brilliance. 'You've got no chance,' Jack was reportedly informed. It was said that Lawler had placed a bet of £600 on the Dragons. Jack had good reason to believe the whisper. Lawler had form. Regardless of his standing as the game's premier whistleblower, his performances had long attracted heavy suspicion. The British touring sides of 1958 and 1962 believed Lawler was, without question, a 'cheat'. There were also suspicions that Lawler had backed St George in the major semi-final a fortnight previously, but that miracle try had denied him.

In 1961 Jack had been a mere spectator at the Sportsground for the semi-final between Manly and Balmain. Manly led 5–2 at half-time and their confidence was high as they left the field, knowing they would have the wind at their backs for the second half. As coach Ken Arthurson made his way to the dressing-room, Jack pulled him aside. 'Ken, there's some disquieting news,' he told Arthurson, the future chairman of the league. 'The betting says you're "off".' In other words, Lawler had backed Balmain. Arthurson rejected the claim, but Jack was adamant: 'I'm just telling you what's going on.' Manly lost 10–5 as Lawler's whistle constantly sounded throughout in the second half, always in Balmain's favour.

Now here was Jack, two years later, facing the identical prospect of a Lawler rort. Yet this time it was a grand final. Jack had played in one against St George with Easts, had lost it, and now this opportunity in the autumn of his career was about to be snuffed out by a referee wanting to fatten his wallet.

Jack and his Wests teammates arrived at the SCG for the grand final on Saturday, 16 September 1963, to find the ground looking like a swamp. Rain the day before, then storms overnight and that morning, and then the playing of lower-grade deciders, had turned the sanctified turf of the SCG into sanctified, caking mud. Before the match, Jack spotted his long-time friend Bob Dodd in the Members' Stand and made his way over. 'We can't win today,' Jack said, explaining the predicament.

An hour before the match, Jack plonked down next to Noel Kelly on the bench in the change rooms. They were rummaging through their kitbags, pulling out their gear, when Jack repeated the remark: 'We can't win today. Fuckin' Lawler has backed them.'

Kelly didn't believe it. 'Turn it up, Jack,' he replied. 'It's the grand final.' 'I'm telling you we can't win,' Jack insisted. Kelly suggested they tell Wests secretary Bill Beaver, and he didn't believe it either. Other accounts over the years have suggested Beaver and Kelly knew of the alleged bet days before grand final day. 'Every other story you hear is just hearsay,' says Kelly. 'Any other story you hear but mine is bullshit. There was Jack, Bill and I that knew. We weren't going to tell anyone.' But captain Arthur Summons knew. 'Here we were, we had their measure all season, to have a referee affect the outcome of the game … I still get the shits about it,' Summons says. 'We were stunned. Dumbfounded. All I could think was that if we were the better side we could overcome all of it.'

As the 1963 grand final played out before the record crowd of 69 860, it became clear that they could not. The mud was the third enemy, as ambulance men were rushed onto the field to wash it from the players' eyes in the early exchanges. But as far as the players in the black-and-white jumpers were concerned, the first enemy was Lawler.

Just before half-time, with Wests trailing 5–0, Summons grubber-kicked the ball into the right-hand corner. Peter Dimond said later he had grounded it, but Lawler was adamant when quizzed afterwards that he never touched it. Summons detonated and was told to be quiet or he'd be sent off. It was just the first of many incidents that enraged the Wests players. Kelly always figured he had the measure of his opposite hooker, Ian Walsh, whenever they played but was constantly penalised by Lawler on this day for his deeds in the scrum. 'Walsh has never moved me in his life,' Kelly insists, still. In the end, the 18–7 penalty count hurt Wests as much as it bewildered them.

Yet the decision that forever haunts the Magpies players came with fifteen minutes remaining as the Dragons hung grimly to a 5–3 lead. St George fullback Graeme Langlands passed to winger Johnny King, who danced above the mud and down the wing. He shrugged off the tackle of his opposite, John Mowbray, but was knocked down by Wests fullback Don Parish, who had come across in cover. The old Wests players still insist they heard Lawler call the tackle. Back-rower John 'Chow' Hayes says he heard Lawler say, 'he's tackled' or 'you're tackled'. Others recall the referee instructing King to 'play it'. Instead, King jumped to his feet, dashed down the sideline and scored the match-winning try. Lawler awarded it.

That's when the blood of the Wests players boiled. As the wail of the full-time siren neared, Lawler reprimanded Jack for throwing punches in frustration. 'Send me off and I'll give you up,' he was overheard saying. Jack finished the game, and Wests finished it defeated. 'It was the biggest rort in grand final history,' Summons says angrily, still seething after all these years.

Some of the Wests players weren't aware of Jack's claims until they were back at the leagues club sipping their first beers. The following day, there was only a ripple of disquiet in the press. The squad for the Kangaroo tour of Great Britain and France had been named after the grand final and it had become the story of the day as much as St George's escalating supremacy. Arthur Summons received some consolation in being appointed captain–coach of the touring side.

Lawler died in 1994 at the age of 75 and never commented publicly on the allegations. But to this day, the Wests players believe Jack was right. Noel Kelly *knows* Jack was right. Three days after the grand final, Jack introduced him to the man who told them he had placed the bet for Lawler. 'We went for a waterski on the Tuesday, and he introduced me to the bloke who put his [Lawler's] money on,' Kelly says.

Years later, there was twenty or so of us former Magpies players on a bus on our way out to a match at Campbelltown, and we stopped into Warwick Farm at the races. We had a bet, and I was standing in the enclosure where the bookies are. A bloke came up to me and said, 'Do you remember me?' I said, 'No.' He said, 'I put Darcy's money on.' I never had the brains to ask him his name.

History records that in the minutes after the full-time siren in the 1963 grand final, *The Sun-Herald* photographer John O'Gready captured the image of a lifetime: St George's towering captain Norm Provan embracing the diminutive Summons, whose head barely reached the shoulders of his rival skipper. Both were coated in mud, and years later the image became the inspiration for the trophy that teams have played for on grand final day since 1982. 'The Gladiators', as O'Gready's award-winning photo was called, captured the mutual respect of those who played an unforgiving code.

What history forgets is how the Wests players thought the match stank like the sanctified mud they had battled and bled on. How those players still alive believe as much today. And how from that moment onwards, whether as a player, coach or man at the back of the grandstand, Jack Gibson never trusted a referee again.

●

For most of his adult life, Jack carried two items with him wherever he went. One item was a deck of cards. His desire to play whenever possible was almost obsessive. The other was The Wad. There was never a wallet. Never. It was The Wad. The Wad was a thick, indeterminable chunk of cash that was folded directly in half—*never* in a roll—and kept secure with two thick rubber bands. Whenever The Wad came out of Jack's pocket, it immediately caught the eye of those standing nearby.

Noel Kelly remembers seeing The Wad. Out of nowhere, Jack would sometimes tell him they were heading to Kings Cross, where they'd venture into the dark corners of various establishments, settling up on bets Jack had won and lost through his bookmaking enterprise. All Kelly wanted to do was leave, but Jack knew everyone. 'Jack was the King,' Kelly says.

Kelly also noticed the times when The Wad was nowhere to be seen. Sometimes, he would drop off the windfall to Jack's clients. Late one Saturday afternoon, Jack phoned him and asked if he could come around to the house. He handed Kelly a large bag of money as big as a banana box. Kelly couldn't estimate how much was in it but it was enough to make him nervous. A local doctor had backed jockey George Moore's rides all afternoon and was flying. Moore was the premier rider of the day and whenever he mounted a horse that season—especially if Tommy Smith trained it—he seemed to win. Kelly knocked on the doctor's front door and handed him his winnings. The doctor glanced inside the bag. 'Mate, take it back to him,' the doctor said. 'I'm not in any hurry and I reckon Jack's had a bad day today.'

Shortly afterwards, Kelly suggested to Jack that he give the bookmaking caper away. He had already seen Jack go close to selling Judy's car to cover gambling debts. Who knew where it would lead? 'I knew for a fact Jack was broke at the time,' Kelly says. 'I'd say to him: "Why don't you give it away?" Jack would reply: "What would I do?" ' Joe Taylor always knew the money would eventually come back, and Jack had the same philosophy. It was a matter of holding on. 'And there were times when he would sell my car,' says Judy.

A few weeks after George Moore had ripped the heart out of Jack's kitty, the money had come back. Jack and his daughter Sue, who was ten by then, were walking along a street in Cronulla. Jack discreetly took out The Wad, which was now an inch thick. He peeled off 200 quid and told his daughter to give the money to a frail elderly couple sitting at a table. Yet he didn't want them to know who the money had come from.

The fluctuations of his SP business did not prevent him thinking about the future. Throughout the 1964 season, as Wests struggled to find momentum after the miserable end to the previous year, Jack was already preparing himself for his life in football beyond playing. Over some quiet beers at a Cronulla pub one afternoon, he asked Arthur Summons: 'What do you think about coaching? In Sydney?'

Summons had led the Kangaroos to their first Ashes series win on English soil earlier that year. The Wests board had approached him about taking over as coach for the following season, but Summons had rejected it because they would only appoint him for one year and not three. 'I believe you need to coach for three years, and no longer than that,' he told Jack. 'After that, players get sick of you, you get sick of them, and you need new ideas.' Jack continued to press Summons on the art of coaching, even though Summons had never held such a position at club level. 'He never mentioned that there was an offer,' Summons says. 'I don't know if he was dabbling with the thought of getting into it. But he wanted to talk about it.'

Later that season, Jack retired. It didn't receive blazing headlines in the press, and the only clipping in his dark green Collins Graphic Analysis Book was a small twelve-paragraph story in *The Telegraph* headlined: 'Tough guy quits R.L.' With Wests out of the finals race, the cruel irony was that his last match was against St George at Kogarah Oval on 22 August. Wests were thrashed 37–10.

Later in life, Gibson spoke of his twelve seasons of playing first-grade rugby league with indifference. 'I loved the game as much as anybody. But I never had the intensity. To me it was just something I did on Sunday.' Of course, it went deeper than that. 'The only thing I regretted when I played is that I did have a tendency to look back over my shoulder and think: "You could have been a better player". I regretted that I never gave it the time that I should have.'

7 CINDERELLA

IT STARTED UP there on the low-sloping hill of the Sydney Sportsground with Jack following the play through his horn-rimmed spectacles, holding up one hand to block the sinking afternoon sun. The view that season of 1965 wasn't pretty. It hurt to watch Easts play so miserably. Yes, he'd stormed out of the club five years ago and vowed never to play for them again. Signing Nev Charlton was as good as treason in Jack's mind. But just as he could never get rugby league out of his system after retirement, so it was with the red, white and blue.

Call it morbid curiosity. Easts weren't in the mire but they had one foot in it. Terry Fearnley had retired the previous season and he reckoned the motivation had been sucked right out of the joint. They had a zippy halfback called Kevin Junee, who had earned New South Wales selection; another playmaker in John Peard, who was cocking the eyebrows of those who turned up early enough to watch the lower grades; and another kid called

Barry Reilly, better known as 'Bunny'. He was a lock-forward who would tackle a blade of grass if required. Jack's style of player.

The issue, it seemed, was the coach. Bert Holcroft was an Englishman who was articulate and could talk about the intricacies of rugby league for hours. During the day, he worked at the Mick Simmons Sports Store as a salesman. Whatever he was selling to his players, they weren't buying it. By the end of the season, Easts had won three of eighteen games. Jack put in for the job, barely mentioning the fact to a soul. When the committee vote was taken, Holcroft narrowly won. The after-vote words of JJ Brown, the elegantly spoken president, are rusted on to the Gibson legend: 'There's no use putting square pegs into round holes.' Jack's response: 'I don't know if I was the square peg or the round hole.' The translation was that the Easts committee knew how headstrong their former captain was. It wasn't prepared to hand him the keys to first grade quite yet.

So Jack returned to the Sportsground hill the following year and through his horn-rimmed spectacles watched Easts sink with the afternoon sun. It was mid-July when they dipped below the horizon. Holcroft conducted training sessions with a whistle and the players had tired of its shrill. At the Thursday night session before the game against Manly, he issued a warning. 'Listen, you've got to win this week,' he said in his thick English accent, which started to sound like fingernails on a blackboard to the players. 'Otherwise, it'll be a lap of the oval for every point you lose by.'

Was he *serious*? Did he believe they weren't *trying*? Did he think he was coaching the *juniors*? Manly smoked them 53–nil at the Sportsground, and true to his word Holcroft ordered 53 laps at the next training session. The side completed as many as they could before stopping and just staring at the coach. He'd lost them. They didn't win another game.

In the annual report at the end of the year, club secretary Jimmy Hunt wrote: 'It is painful to record. Your first-grade team did not win a single match. This has never before happened in your club's illustrious history and it must never happen again. Surely the club is due for a turn of fortune at the beginning of the 1967 season.'

At no stage throughout the carnage had Jack indicated he wanted to apply for the position again. Words were never his go, and only those who knew him well could interpret his subtle body language. If he was angry, for instance, he'd push the horn-rimmed specs back onto the bridge of his nose with his index finger ... and then say nothing. When Jack said he intended to apply for the Easts coaching job again, close friend Ron Massey roared with laughter. 'You're kidding?' Massey said. Index finger, specs pushed back. 'He got very dirty,' Massey recalls, smiling.

Applications were to be taken in November and the interest in saving Easts ran high. Club stalwart Ferris Ashton, former Canterbury coach Jack Hampstead and former Easts halfback Doug Doney all applied. So did Holcroft, much to the astonishment of the players. Holcroft wanted to stay if the club was 'getting new blood'. There was speculation the legendary Kangaroos and Souths fullback Clive Churchill wanted in, too. He denied it but left the door open: 'If I am approached by any club I would be interested.' Jack wasn't waiting for such a call and promptly applied. 'I would get plenty of enjoyment, physically and mentally, out of coaching the team,' he told *The Sun*.

This time, the square peg fitted the round hole: Jack narrowly won the vote. There was no reason submitted publicly but it had been an easy sell. Forty years after the appointment, Jack wrote about why he thought it had come to be. 'When I put in for the job again, there weren't many applicants. That made my task of getting appointed a lot easier.' It was self-effacement late in life. What he had promised the committee was an elimination of the schoolboy errors he'd been witnessing from the Sportsground hill for two years. 'Make sure they didn't kick the ball out on the full from the kick-offs,' he told them. 'Make sure they did kick the ball out when they got a free kick. Sort out the defence. Then we can win some football games.'

After his appointment, a young reporter from the *Mirror*, Peter Frilingos, phoned Jack for comment. 'We can't win them all next year but I'm sure we can win quite a few. I know I have the full support of the committee and I think our first duty is to make the players we have happy. This is essential if a team is to win.' They *were* happy despite the tortures of the past two seasons. They were young. They liked each other. They just needed direction. While Jack knew the value of treating his players with respect, he knew of the revolution that was coming for the game. He knew Easts needed discipline if they were to survive, let alone win some games.

He'd already cast a shadow upon the players. During the later months of the 1966 season, some noticed a mysterious black limousine regularly parked near the Sportsground, adjacent to Moore Park, where they trained. The windows were blackened, but they figured it was Jack running an eye over proceedings. The story sounds apocryphal—he was far too busy to hide in parked cars.

Besides, Jack was driving a brand-new Chevrolet by then.

•

The revolution Jack could foresee started as a murmur in November, became a flirtation for the code's powerbrokers for the pre-season series in March and was then thrust upon the Sydney premiership for the start of the season on April Fool's Day, 1967. Since the game's formation in Australia in 1908, the team in possession of the ball retained possession until they lost it. But in the 1960s, the winds of change from England blew all the way to Sydney and the law of unlimited tackles was about to be incinerated forever.

While controversial, the four-tackle rule was generally viewed in England as a favourable development. It had prompted teams to use the ball, to trust their skills, and it made the game immeasurably more entertaining to watch because the time with the pigskin was limited. Traditionalists took a different view. It meant more kicks down field, more scrums if it went into touch, more monotonous scrum penalties.

And what of Jack? No panic. He saw it coming and instead of arguing its merits thought about what was needed. For someone who had never coached before, who had lacked discipline on the field as a player, who had been sent off five times, who had been a square peg, he certainly seemed to have the foresight that others never expected of him. He had already identified defence as the fundamental deficiency in his team, but to triumph in this new era they had to be tackling automatons. And to be tackling automatons, they had to be fit. Super-fit. Jack knew the right man to prepare them for it.

George Daldry had known Jack for years. He had worked for Joe Taylor briefly after he returned to Australia having fought in the Army in World War II. He was there in the early hours of that July morning outside the Celebrity Club when the worlds of Big Jack and The Boss collided. During the war, Daldry had been captured by the Japanese in Malaysia and dispatched to the notorious Changi Prison. During his three years in those rancid cells, standing shoulder to shoulder with his fellow prisoners of war, Daldry made a personal vow: if he ever crawled out of the hellhole and back to Australia, he would spend the rest of his days searching for 'the fountain of life' to make up for stolen time. By the time Jack called upon him to train his team, Daldry was a personal trainer to the stars. He was always immaculately attired in black boxing boots, tiny shorts and a crisp white T-shirt, and the common remark about Daldry was how his supreme fitness belied his age (he was in his mid-40s). As an instructor at the gym in the City Tattersalls Club in Pitt Street, the man was an institution.

It took just one session with Jack's men to learn he'd taken on a significant task. Daldry decided to take them on a long road run: from the Sportsground, down to Elizabeth Street near Central Station, back along Cleveland Street and then a full lap of Centennial Park. That was the plan, anyway. They started off and Daldry set the pace, although it was a trot by his standards. When he hit Cleveland, he turned around to check the status of the players. They were hundreds of metres behind.

Eventually, though, he improved their endurance. They trained two and sometimes three times a week, usually at Centennial Park. Those who wanted to do extra work could train with Daldry at City Tatts and many did, lifting weights. The trainer was shocked at how small the forwards were compared to others he had worked with. What impressed him, what convinced him that they would win at least a few games, was their attitude. The players were continually encouraging and cajoling each other at training. They'd found a reason to believe. 'They had all bought in on Jack making a difference,' says Daldry.

Meanwhile, Jack was giving away nothing. At his first session, he had to be told who his first-grade side had been the previous season. Nobody considered it ignorant: just a sign that reputations meant little to him. And what of his own reputation? 'None of Big Jack's "man-about-town" way of living is likely to be passed on to Easts,' declared reporter Geoff Prenter in *The Sun*. 'Once he steps out of the spanking new Chevrolet and changes into the sea-blue tracksuit, the unconventional life Jack leads is forgotten.'

Jack predicted his players would be '10 points' better than the previous year. 'I can promise Easts fans greater success this season,' he said. Asked why he had taken on such a mountainous task, he replied: 'I think I can do something for them. And I think they can do something for me.'

The Easts committee had already done something for him. They'd opened the chequebook, ever so slightly, and spent on new stock. There was the sharp-shooting goal-kicker Allan McKean from St George and the charismatic winger from Souths, Bruce 'Larpa' Stewart. Yet the headline signing was the monstrous globe-trotting South African lock-forward Louis Neumann, who had played for Leeds in England. While the acquisitions were seen as favourable, the reality was that Easts were still far behind other cashed-up Sydney clubs. His side had cost about $4100 on transfer fees. Canterbury had paid only $100 less to St George to buy Kevin Ryan.

When it came to the captaincy, appointing Kevin Junee seemed a formality. Easts had used no less than six skippers during the disaster of the previous season. Junee had been sacked after one match but publicly declared his desire for the position again. 'I like the idea of being captain and was a bit disappointed when I got only one opportunity last year,' he said. The belief of many was that Junee was the team's best player. He was a natural choice as leader.

Jack had a different view on the matter, as he often did. For captain, he preferred a player on the wing in second grade.

Jim Matthews had been a rugby union junior at Sutherland, played a season for Leeton in the Riverina, and then been five-eighth for two years at Canterbury. Unwanted for the 1963 season, he successfully transferred to Easts and toiled away in the halves as the club struggled for success. By the end of 1966, he had been dumped to reserves.

His appointment hardly created a ripple in the press, but it certainly did within the confines of the club. 'Jimmy had qualities,' said Jack when he elaborated on the subject two years later. 'I knew he was tough enough. What I did was give Jim Matthews an opportunity.' This was going to be Matthews' seventh season of grade football, and that kind of experience in a young side appealed. He also had an ability to talk to players—anyone—and give it to them straight. With Peard sidelined for the season with glandular fever, he could also play five-eighth.

During the pre-season, Terry Fearnley had helped Jack train the side. He'd run with them, too, and was contemplating a comeback at the age of 33, so healthy was the vibe his old front-row partner had created. Discipline was the cornerstone of Jack's philosophy: if any player wasn't ready to train on the stroke of 6 p.m., they'd be dropped to reserves. 'If it's good enough for me and the others to be here on time, so it is for you,' he told them.

Nowhere did that Spartan mindset matter more than on the field. Defence would be king. So was the chase after the kick. So was possession. Yet the golden rule that had to be obeyed more than any other was that there would be no fighting. No cheap shots. No punches. No retaliation. Not even back-chat to the referee. Otherwise you'd be hooked from the field. 'One thousand Philistines were slain by the jawbone of an ass,' he would tell his men. 'And two thousand football games had been lost by the use of the same weapon.'

Meanwhile, those who knew of the Jack Gibson legend—throwing upper-cuts in scrums, kicking players in his hundredth first-grade match, frightening mugs on the cusp of two-up rings with a solitary glance—figured the world had officially gone mad.

As that season unfurled, though, it was the rookie coach who knew he'd provided the right blueprint for success—even if it didn't come early. Easts won two matches in the pre-season, but come the last day of April they had just one competition point from a scrappy 9-all draw with Newtown. But then the breakthrough: a 17–11 win at the Sportsground over North Sydney, who were captained by the great Test winger Ken Irvine. At half-time of that match, Jack did not address his players as a group. He was never one for grand dressing-room oratory. Instead, he quietly worked his way around the room, individually approaching each of his men and bringing it in so tight his nose was almost touching theirs, so close they could probably smell the scotch he often sipped at half-time. 'Do you think you can improve for me in the second half?' he whispered to them. 'Yes, Jack.'

That moment busted down the door. Having won their first match since late 1965, Easts then won six of their next seven matches, and suddenly the side that was the standing joke of the premiership the season before was now its 'Cinderella story', a cliché every newspaper roundsman chose to use in most stories about them. The real test, though, would be Canterbury, the competition leaders who were being inspired by new captain-coach Kevin Ryan. They were set down to meet for the coveted Match of the Day at the SCG—Easts' first appearance in the Saturday fixture in three seasons—a bog after heavy rain had lashed Sydney all week.

If redoubtable defence was ever needed, this was it. The Easts pack was small compared to most of their rivals. But they were agile. Jack wanted them to tackle and tackle low. 'The boys would ankle tackle a herd of charging elephants if Jack Gibson told us it was necessary,' Allan McKean said. By half-time, Easts led 13–nil, but it was the second half, with the Berries winning the scrums two-to-one, stalking the Easts tryline, that stirred something within the coach as he watched from the Members' Stand. Not only did his boys win 18–2 but their line was never crossed. In thirteen matches, they had given up just fifteen tries.

At full-time, all hell broke loose. Kevin Ryan whacked his big paw into Jack's big paw and shook it intently. 'If it's possible to enjoy losing a game, we enjoyed losing that,' he told him. 'You boys were much too good for us.' The rest of Canterbury's men were effusive in their praise. 'Boy, do they tackle,' said second-rower Kevin Goldspink. 'There seemed to be 26 of them on that field.' Their president, Eddie Burns, said he wanted to see Easts in the grand final before adding with a grin: 'Against us, of course.'

After Easts players had stood before the Paddo Hill and acknowledged their giddy fans, they turned towards the Members' Stand and were stunned to see the Canterbury players had formed a guard of honour, as a show of respect and acknowledgement of what they had just done.

Jack didn't speak to the press that afternoon. No need. The coach stood in a corner of the jubilant dressing-room, scanning the scene; one look at the tears welling in the big fella's eyes explained what the result had meant to him.

•

Of course, Jack's boys lost to Newtown the following week, but that's footy. The dream has to end some time, unless you are

St George. If you are St George, who have won the last eleven premierships and even though some experts believe some early season losses means your aura of invincibility is waning, by the time you are playing Easts you are still leading the comp.

Jack had rumbled with the Dragons for years and—notwithstanding the occasional victory—they had usually been the source of misery, not least in two grand finals. That had been as a player, not in his reincarnation as coach, and the fuse had been lit with the triumph over Canterbury.

Bob and Jack Ingham sensed it. They were still gambling heavily with Jack, and punting types from those days put the value of their bets at *hundreds* of thousands of dollars. But their friendship had also grown stronger. When the wealthy brothers sponsored the club's player of the year award, the humble rooster became the club's unofficial mascot. Now and then, a rooster would make its way into the dressing-room after a victory.

When Easts met the Dragons in mid-July, more than 18 000 fans pushed through the creaky turnstiles at the Sportsground to see if they could do it again. Snuffing out Canterbury was one thing, but silencing the Saints back line—sparkling with Test stars like Graeme Langlands, Billy Smith and, of course, Reg Gasnier—was another task altogether.

When the two sides left the muddy field that Sunday afternoon, with Easts having beaten the premier team of the past decade 15–9, there could be no dispute about Jack Gibson's side having the defence to win the competition. Gasnier, not one for hyperbole, called it 'inspired'. Captain-coach Ian Walsh could not recall defence being that intense, with two or three Easts players regularly pouncing on the player with the ball. None had been busier than Bunny Reilly, who was turning into the revelation of the season.

Afterwards, the Easts players posed for a team photograph—holding a cut-out rooster—and cheered like they had won the title. Jack was reaching for comparisons. 'You can call on champion horses for an extra effort and they give it,' he told the pressmen. 'That's how it was with our players.' Then they all headed to Easts Leagues Club where Dragons players bought the first drinks.

Daldry deserved the credit for the players' stamina, but it was the first-year coach who had brought harmony and discipline to the club. The mood at training was electric. 'What would you rate your performance out of ten at the weekend?' he'd ask one of the players. 'About a nine, Jack,' the player might reply. 'I'll say five,' he snapped back, tongue in cheek. They had all bought in, even to the strict edict of no fighting.

After the Roosters' win against Balmain at the SCG, leading referee Col Pearce burst into the rooms to declare: 'I've never seen cleaner football.' It was the first and only time Pearce ever did such a thing. Of all the changes Jack had brought to Easts, this was the one that caused bewilderment among the league cognoscenti aware of the coach's immediate past. 'Punching is a waste of time in football because it does nothing but get the offender and his team into trouble,' he said. 'A punch won't hurt most first-grade players, especially forwards.' He insisted there was no hard rule that insisted one punch meant the player should be dropped. 'Such a breach would be answerable to his teammates,' Jack said. And what of those who thought it a contradiction that a former player known for brawling had banned such behaviour as a coach? 'Coaches coach what they couldn't do. I couldn't play the game clean—but my teams have to.'

As the semi-finals drew nearer, it wasn't the way Easts were finishing the season so much as the way they had started it that might decide their premiership chances. Those early losses meant they could barely afford a single loss if they were to sneak in to the top four. When they fell to long-time rivals South Sydney at the SCG, it presented them with a clear equation for the final-round match against Parramatta: win.

Deep into that match at the Sportsground, Parramatta hung grimly to a 14–13 lead. As it had been all season, the Easts forward pack seemed to be dwarfed by the opposition. Hooker Ken Owens lost the first eleven scrums against Parra's veteran Billy Rayner. Yet, as it had also been all season, they somehow bucked against it. The lead changed four times, but this would be the one that mattered: Easts second-rower, Kevin Ashley, knocking over a field goal with twelve minutes remaining to take the lead 15–14. As the time slowly dissolved, as his men blindly tackled anything in front of them, as the Easts faithful rode every play, Jack's hands were working overtime.

The Craven As were going in and out of his mouth quicker than they ever had. For the past two years, he had sat on that hill in silence and thought he could do better, and here he was on the sideline, looking through horn-rimmed glasses again, only seconds away from taking a side that had not won a match the previous season into the play-offs.

When they did it, there were no tears as there had been after the win against Canterbury. He didn't reach for metaphors as he had done after the victory against St George. What it meant to him showed in those big hands that wouldn't stop shaking an hour after full-time. 'They said we couldn't do it,' he said. 'Well, look at these little fellows. What a mighty team they are.'

They were also a damaged one. Bodies were strewn across the dressing-room floor and there was a prevailing feeling afterwards that Easts had no chance in their semi against Canterbury at the SCG the following Saturday. 'Roosters today, feather dusters tomorrow,' an unnamed Canterbury player was quoted as saying in *The Sun*. Despite Easts' brave victory over them earlier in the season, the 9-stone (57-kilogram) weight difference in the pack would be too much. Bring it on, Jack thought. 'They had big forwards then—have they got any smaller?' he asked. 'The more confident Canterbury are, the better for us. We've been the underdogs all season and look where it's got us ... Although I'm not having a bet, I know we will finish on top.'

For one of the few times that season, Jack made the wrong call. The bruises and breaks from the previous win, the raw emotion of what they had achieved so far—all that meant nothing as Canterbury rolled over the top of them. Between them, Allan McKean and Jim Matthews landed just one penalty goal from ten attempts. But afterwards Jack was blaming nobody. 'Time ran out,' he said.

It surprised nobody that Easts finished that season with the best defensive record in the competition—less than 10 points per game. He had promised the committee some wins, but had brought them much more. 'At the start they didn't know I was going to win some football games, and neither did I,' was his later account of that debut season.

Yet success for Jack—as he would learn—was never measured in games won or points not scored. It was the happiness of his players that counted. On the last page of the green Collins Graphic Analysis Book, there is a newspaper clipping of the Easts dressing-room after their semi-final loss to Canterbury. The battered players are sitting around, with captain Jim Matthews holding a flapping rooster above his head.

Everybody, except the rooster, is laughing.

8   THE SAUSAGE-ROLL EATERS

JOHN QUAYLE WAS the son of an Anglican priest who had spent the first two decades of his life living in a vicarage in the tiny town of Manilla in northwest New South Wales. He'd exchanged only a few words with Jack Gibson before finding himself in the back seat of the coach's roomy El Dorado Cadillac: a red-and-white whale of a convertible with white leather seats and creases down each side like an expensive Italian suit.

Quayle had never laid eyes on anything like it: the car, let alone the man. Before that first Eastern Suburbs training session, held on a steaming February afternoon, Jack had asked in signature monotone: 'You're the kid from Manilla?' 'Yes,' replied Quayle. 'You fit?' 'Yes.' 'Good trainer?' 'Yes.' Jack sent him on a 5-kilometre road run the rest of the squad had half completed. When the coach saw him collapsed on a bench afterwards, he asked if he wanted to come to dinner with him and official Keith 'Clicker' Clark. Quayle was staying at a boarding house frequented by drunkards and loose men. He'd already missed the privilege of sharing the 7 p.m. dinner with them.

They ate at a little Italian restaurant tucked away at the end of Oxford Street in Bondi Junction and Quayle thought he'd stepped onto the set of a gangster movie. *Everyone* knew Jack; so many that Quayle figured he owned the place, but of course he didn't. They had a bottle of red wine with their meal, although that wasn't usually Jack's poison of choice—it was single malt scotch over ice. Whenever there was a break in conversation, Jack would casually look over at the young footballer, who wasn't saying a word. 'You okay, kid?'

When they dropped Quayle back at the boarding house on Bondi Road, Jack turned to Clicker. 'Son of a priest,' he said. 'Better get him somethin' better than this.' When Quayle jumped out of the Cadillac, Jack looked at him as the Cadillac drove off. 'We'll do this again.' Then he was gone.

The following week, after a punishing training session thanks to George Daldry, Quayle walked out of training a few paces behind Jack and Clicker, ready to demolish another plate of spaghetti. 'Um, where's the Cadillac?' Quayle quietly asked Clicker as they approached an EJ Holden. 'He lost it in a card game,' Clicker said from the corner of his mouth. 'It took a while,' remembers Judy Gibson. 'But he got it back.'

Within a week, Jack had arranged new accommodation for Quayle with Clicker's aunt in Clovelly, where he always found a meal on the table. Within a month, Jack was inviting Quayle to join him after he had finished his day job, which was collecting glasses at the leagues club, at a restaurant he had bought into at Rose Bay. When he learnt that Quayle had been a competitive go-kart driver, he made him his unofficial driver. Depending on the mood of Lady Luck, that would mean he was steering around a Valiant, a Holden or a Chevy.

One night, they headed to the Forbes Club just off the main strip of Kings Cross. On the outside, it looked like a standard inner-city two-storey terrace, but after Jack gave a subtle nod to the men out the front, the door opened onto another world. Quayle stood there wide-eyed: at the red carpet, the stunning cocktail waitresses and the chandelier that hung above the green baize of the black-jack, roulette and baccarat tables. Here were Sydney's well-to-do set, gambling and laughing and drinking and chain-smoking.

Once they were inside, a man in his late 50s greeted the pair with arms outstretched. His silver mane was slicked back and his dark brown skin glowed. It was Perce Galea, who was the equal and contemporary of Joe Taylor, but the 'Prince of Punters' was better known. About four years earlier, he'd nearly caused a riot at Rosehill racecourse when his boom colt Birthday Card had won the Golden Slipper and he'd thrown a wad of notes into the crowd.

'Kid from the bush,' Jack said to Galea as he made his way to the tables. 'You're living in Clovelly, aren't you?' Galea said. 'Come down to the surf club on Sunday.' So he did, as instructed. Easts players were often there. Kevin Junee, Jim Matthews and Larpa Stewart were this particular Sunday. 'Jack's told me all about you,' Galea told Quayle. 'If you ever have any problems, you come to me.' Then he planted a $50 note in Quayle's hand. It wasn't the first time he'd done it to an emerging Easts player.

Quayle had been invited into this exclusive, wide-reaching network, all thanks to his coach. Growing up, he'd seen followers of every kind come to his father seeking advice, yet those who followed Jack were equally devout. 'I'd never met anyone like him,' says Quayle. 'I'd never met anyone who could hold the room like him, whose company you wanted to be in. You wanted to impress him. And he only had to tell you to do something once.'

It was the man and not the coach in Jack that had made him so successful in his first season, with hope already bubbling about what could be achieved in his second. He was a strict disciplinarian—but no tyrant. The sense of larrikin in him was never far away. The players feared his reputation—but didn't respect him for that reason alone. He understood footballers and they understood that. He was never one of the boys, but his relationship with them was almost paternal.

What nearly stopped Jack from coaching beyond one season was that he was also a father at Nicholson Parade in Cronulla. Just before the 1967 season, Judy had given birth to their second boy, Matt. Easts officials had told him at the end of the year that the job was again his if he desired it. When Jack learnt that Judy was pregnant with their sixth child—they already had five under the age of eleven—he was undecided. Jack was only 39 himself. The travel and time were taking its toll. Easts officials were relieved when he finally agreed to coach again in '68.

It was a juggling act. His SP bookmaking operation was expanding, and he had other enterprises warming up. Trading under the name of The Jack Gibson Players' Agency, he established a unique employment service that would allow country clubs to sign up players and coaches from the city. Jack wouldn't take his percentage cut from the player but would take about 12 per cent from the club. New South Wales Rugby League president Bill Buckley welcomed the initiative, and Jack used his allies in the press to spruik the concept.

He may have been selective with the words he used, but Jack always fostered a tight relationship with the media—both as a player and as a coach. He saw reporters not as necessary evils, but as important parts of the machine. He knew the racing writers, especially Pat Farrell, from Thommo's. He wrote a column for

The Sun, and maintained a close relationship with Ernie Christensen. He posed for a photo for *The Daily Telegraph* in early 1968, clutching a telephone and looking industrious as he went about the business of scouting football talent. The accompanying story from Bill Mordey, a long-time friend, resembled a free advertisement.

Those favourable headlines evaporated after just six rounds of the season, and the blame couldn't be laid on the team's performance. After winning just one of the four pre-season matches, Easts swept aside St George, Wests, Balmain and Cronulla before losing by one point to Penrith. Yet trouble was brewing.

For all the 'square peg' talk before his initial appointment, Jack's relationship with officials was now cordial. He used to call the lazy ones the 'sausage-roll eaters'. Not any more. He even deflected much of the praise of the previous season their way. 'I rank the confidence between the players and in the selectors as the big reason for our success,' he wrote in a column for *The Sun*. 'I don't reckon the selectors have made one "blue" this season.' In January 1968, Jack had taken the unprecedented step of organising his players to meet with officials at his Nicholson Parade home to thrash out issues ahead of the season. They had talked for hours.

But it was always going to be an uneasy peace. In the days before the match against Canterbury, selectors Tom Fitzpatrick and Clicker Clark quit. Jack and third-grade coach Col Donohoe also said they wouldn't participate in team selections. It rocked the club. A report in *The Mirror*, which did not carry a byline, broke the news of the internal rift. The reporter phoned Jack for comment. 'Ask somebody else if you want to know what's happened,' he snorted before slamming down the receiver.

At the Thursday night training session, Easts secretary Jim Hunt was determined to sort out the problem. Instead, a blazing row erupted between Jack and president Doug Fry. Everyone at training saw it, or at least heard it. The coach refused to help in the selection of the side to play Canterbury, preferring to play touch football with some of his players while others chose his team.

The issue had nothing to do with the selections being made, but the manner in which they were being selected. During 1967, Gibson and lower grade coaches Jack Hampstead and Donohue had been joined by two selectors, Clicker Clark and Gerry Seymour, in selecting the teams. Easts officials had scrapped that system, with four selectors of their choosing joining the respective coach to decide the teams.

Confused? Jack was. He was angry that politics could prevent him having the system that had been so successful. That power meant more than common sense. He was bitter about an article suggesting that he had been cited for the argument with Doug Fry, but had heard nothing from the committee. It also elicited a feeling he expressed to Ernie Christensen that would characterise Jack's disdain for mulish officials for decades to come: 'I think I am useless to the organisation unless I can do the job my way.'

He was never forced to front a disciplinary committee, he was never censured, and his side beat Canterbury by a point at the Sportsground that Sunday. But after that episode the rugby league rumour mill spat and spluttered and started to churn out the line that Jack Gibson wouldn't be coaching at the club beyond that season. And it would be his decision—not the sausage-roll eaters'.

●

The imbroglio did not stop first grade's momentum. John Peard had recovered from his bout of glandular fever, and returned to five-eighth, with Jim Matthews shunted into the centres. Kevin Junee remained irrepressible at halfback, although pushed along by an emerging halfback called John 'Monkey' Mayes in the lower grades. As for the coach, he was continuing to look at other ways to skin the cat.

After a loss to Parramatta, he cancelled training and the team held a 'no-holds-barred debate' at the home of local publican and devout supporter Roley Pugh. 'I think the long talk will prove valuable,' Jack said. He nurtured his players with the right words. When Quayle was given his first start, because lock Bunny Reilly was out injured, Jack told him: 'You go out and do your best, kid.' Quayle missed three tackles, and was dropped the following week. 'You did good,' Jack told him. 'Bunny's back.'

His strict policy of no fighting in the heat of battle remained firmly in place. After leading Wests 22–0 at half-time one afternoon, he warned his men: 'Wests will turn it on in the second half. If anyone retaliates and gets sent off, they won't be paid.' When his front-rower John Walker was marched eighteen minutes into the second half for throwing a punch, Jack was furious. Then he learnt that his player had been bitten on the ear, and after full-time launched an impassioned defence. 'There is no doubt he was bitten. I saw the teeth marks.' Wests' captain that afternoon was Noel Kelly, Jack's close mate. 'Rubbish,' he said when told of the biting allegation. 'None of our blokes would ever do a thing like that.'

For the first half of that season, they traded the competition lead with Manly, but there was a pervading feeling with every defeat that their form could collapse at any moment. Jack complained about a 'staleness' falling over his side during training sessions. Geoff Prenter wrote in *The Sun*: 'The house that Jack built needs a fresh coat of paint.' Of most concern was how his side would only steal victory late in the game. Jack would sometimes send replacements on the sideline to the kiosk to buy a pack of Cravens as he chain-smoked through the nerves. His hands were often shaking for an hour after the match. 'I don't know if I can stand any more of these finishes,' he confided at training one day.

Yet he maintained his typical serenity at half-time. 'How do you think you're playing?' was all he might ask of his playmakers, Junee and Peard. He might bring up the run-around move they had practised at training all week. 'Have you forgotten it?'

Or sometimes he would do something to inspire them in a manner that embodied the style of the man. Trailing at half-time at the Sportsground, the team sat in the dressing-room in a circle, waiting for the coach to arrive. When Jack eventually fronted, he walked into the centre of the circle, took a deep, final drag of his cigarette and then dropped the butt at his feet. 'Gonna take your skirts off for the second half?' he asked calmly, stubbing out the cigarette with the toe of his shoe. Then he walked out. Peard only remembers him doing it once, and cannot recall the game, but insists they won.

Up until the final round in late August, Easts were considered serious premiership contenders. If they beat Souths in the Match of the Day at the SCG, they were likely to finish minor premiers—less than two years after finishing the season winless. The match was an epic, which the Rabbitohs only won when their winger Eric Simms landed a sideline conversion. While defence had been the cornerstone of their success last season, they had also found a way to score. But they still lacked size, and in the semi-final against St George the following Saturday they were steamrolled 17–10. The scoreboard flattered them. 'Big frames are needed to back up big hearts,' offered Mike Gibson in his report for *The Telegraph* the next day.

After full-time, Gibson—who was no relation—spotted Jack sitting in the dressing-room draining a beer like there was a nail in the bottom of the bottle. A year ago, Jack had said time had run out for his team. 'Time has run out for *me*,' he mumbled. Jack thought he would lose the position, even if he applied for it. He took another swig of the beer. 'Just say some people at the club don't see eye to eye with me.'

In the end, the club made the decision for him. After that storied debut season, he was handed a cheque for $1000. He'd achieved the same again and was handed a cheque for $800. 'That didn't inspire me to stay,' Jack said on reflection many years later. 'It didn't inspire me to leave either, but I did think the pay was a little light, so eventually I decided for 1969 that I'd sit up in the stand.' The job went to Lou Neumann, the big South African who would also be captain.

Of course, the money was irrelevant. Jack wasn't coaching for the cash, just as he had never played for it. To offer him less was an insult, especially when the club was about to embark on a rumoured $60 000 spending spree for players, including the signing of rugby union internationals Alan Cardy and John Brass. The brand-spanking-new $1.2 million leagues club in Spring Street was hauling in money. In charge was the indefatigable Ron Jones, a shrewd operator who was establishing himself as the king of the Eastern Suburbs castle.

When Jack said he didn't see eye to eye with certain individuals at the club, he meant Jones. 'I have no doubt that he left because of Ron Jones, because he started to interfere,' Quayle insists. 'Jack was getting too much authority. Jack was the guy all the reporters wanted to speak to. He was becoming more prominent. All the football committees loved Jack. But Jones wanted to be the boss. He destroyed all that Jack had built because he wanted to be the boss.' After Jack had left, Jones told the press: 'It's easy to lift a side off the bottom but not so easy to keep them on top.'

But that wasn't the end of it. At the football club annual general meeting early into the new year, Jack asked for the microphone. He prefaced what he was about to say by insisting: 'This isn't sour grapes.' He didn't rant. Nor did he take aim at the sausage-roll eaters who had forced him out. Just as he had done with his players when they were struggling at half-time, he challenged the members to make a change. 'Easts have been good to me during my ten years as a player with the club and two years as a coach,' he said. 'I was dead and buried as far as football was concerned when Easts gave me a chance to coach. But I am disappointed that here tonight we have only one member of the executive who is being opposed. To me this shows a lack of interest in the club by the members.'

The ones who should have cared most.

9 COACHING THE ENEMY

THE STORY GOES that the bet was $10 000. The man it belonged to was the Honourable Sir Robert William Askin, the Premier of New South Wales. He had a close relationship with Perce Galea and Joe Taylor, both of whom it has been said paid him large sums to keep their illegal casinos open. Askin regularly smoked a big fat cigar: when he was running the state, sitting at the tables at the Forbes Club or standing in the enclosure at Randwick racecourse. Askin loved a bet. He loved a bet almost as much as Jack never forgot one.

The story goes that this $10 000 bet, apparently laid with the football coach during the late 1960s, did not come off. Weeks passed and the Premier still hadn't settled. Finally, a member of the gambling fraternity put Jack straight. 'Don't you know?' Jack was told. 'Askin doesn't pay.'

Like hell he doesn't. Jack drove the Cadillac straight up to Macquarie Street, reefed on the hand brake in front of State

Parliament and marched up the stairs, straight into Askin's office. You can't see him, Askin's secretary told him. When Askin heard who it was, he invited him to take a seat. 'Jack, what can I do for you?' the Premier asked politely. 'I'm here for the $10 000,' Jack deadpanned.

The story goes that they sat in silence for a minute, staring down one another in the office of the Premier of New South Wales, before Askin finally ended the standoff. 'I'll allow you to get up and leave,' he told Jack. 'Or I'll charge you with extortion.' Jack rose to his feet, nodded, and left. That's how the story goes. 'I don't know that story,' says Judy Gibson. 'But it wouldn't surprise me. What I do know is if anyone welched on him, he would confront them. And he wouldn't have cared who it was.'

The story is unconfirmed, but it was a popular one in those days and remains so with some of the racing fraternity from those times. Like many anecdotes about Jack Gibson, especially those concerning the sacred ground of illegal SP wagering, they seem too vivid and wild to be true. As is the case with many anecdotes about Jack Gibson, few people will categorically deny them. Folklore of that scale wasn't beyond Jack, even if it places him in the Premier's office, eyeballing the leader of the state over an unpaid gambling debt. Askin was the most successful Liberal Premier of New South Wales, having won four elections, but since his death in 1981, aged 74, he has been recalled as a corrupt politician best forgotten.

A year spent away from football was never an opportunity for Jack to stop and smell the roses. His acrimonious departure from Easts gave him time to concentrate on the areas of his life he normally didn't have enough time to attend to. Bookmaking was one of them, and 1969 was the year when his operation grew wings.

He employed a handful of people to help him run it. One of those was Ron Massey, who he had met in the 1950s through Ron Taylor and who had become a close friend. Others would take bets over the phone—and then settle down the track—with a legion of punters. The biggest of those punters remained the Ingham brothers. Jack Ingham was a keen student of the gallops, while Bob's interest was the harness racing. They would bet on almost every race on a big racing day, usually about $4000 to $5000 at a time, and sometimes more.

Like all smart bookmakers, Jack would farm the bet around to other bookies, taking five cents in every dollar that was won. One of those bookies is believed to have been George Freeman, the handsome, white-haired, exceptionally groomed organised crime figure. Freeman lived at Yowie Bay, only a few bays around from where Jack and Judy had built a new three-storey house in Cowra Place, which had sweeping views over Port Hacking to the blue haze of the national park to the south. As he had done at Nicholson Parade, Jack had dug out the foundations on his own, often inflaming the troublesome disc in his back.

It is unclear where Jack's SP bookmaking operation took place. 'But he never did it from home,' Judy insists. 'Never, ever. I don't think it was even suggested that he would do it from home. If he had I would've said no. I can't remember ever having a conversation about it. He was respected in racing. He paid his bills.'

He had always kept those darker corners of his life separate to his marriage, including the days when they first dated when Jack worked at Thommo's. Judy didn't ask about what he'd seen beneath the swinging light bulbs of the two-up ring, and he certainly didn't offer it up. 'Maybe I was never inquisitive enough,' she says. 'Maybe I should've asked him more questions. He didn't like people asking questions. That never stopped me from asking him a question—but I probably never had a need to know, which sounds very naive.'

Maybe she didn't ask because she didn't want to know the answer. 'No ... Well, that's a question I could ask myself now. Did I not go there because I didn't want to be involved, so the less I knew the better? I'd say so. I'd say that's why he never talked about it. We both knew it was going on, but we never talked about it. It didn't worry me. I didn't see it as a criminal act at all.'

●

Bookmaking was never going to keep Jack away from rugby league for too long, or gently nudge him back up onto the hill to watch as a mere spectator as he had promised after the semi-final loss while coaching Easts. He'd declined an approach from Newtown secretary Frank Farrington to do for the sagging Bluebags what he had done for the Tricolours. But he persisted with his players' agency, which he predicted would become 'normal practice' for professional footballers years before the explosion of the now-ubiquitous player manager.

He also signed on to become Cronulla–Sutherland's public relations officer for the 1969 season. 'We couldn't let a personality like Jack, who lives in our district, sit idle,' said club vice-president Bob Abbott, a friend. Jack had established a strong bond with the pressmen during his two seasons at Easts, and knew how to use them to his advantage. But his role with Cronulla went much deeper than that. He advised on recruitment matters and promised to encourage the promotion of junior talent. 'I don't believe in buying players sight unseen,' he declared in one story. It was a clear backhander to Easts' committeemen, who had spent up for the 1969 season and still had Jack's detonation at the annual general meeting ringing in their ears.

All those dollars from the leagues club had seen Easts pinned as a glamour club, but this didn't translate into on-field success that year. If the seeds of the Gibson coaching legend were planted in those first two seasons, it was only enhanced by Easts' failure that first year after his departure. Come mid-season, with Easts having no chance of reaching the finals, the call to make big back-rower Louis Neumann captain-coach had come to nought.

It was a topic too tempting to ignore for Jack's new column in *The Sun*, called 'Jack Gibson's ... Hotline', which reproduced the photo taken of him holding the telephone receiver as he stared keenly into the distance through his horn-rimmed glasses. No longer answerable to officials, he now had the freedom to open the shoulder blades on whichever topic he desired—and he did so. One week, he took aim at the thuggery employed by some players. The next, he carpeted Penrith for signing players outside its own junior base.

He never specifically took aim at Easts' decision to appoint Neumann, but did write that the day of the captain-coach was over, and highlighted the success of Roy Francis at North Sydney that 1969 season as proof. Then he whacked the sausage-roll eaters in general by reaffirming his belief that the coach must always have complete autonomy over his side. 'I'd like to see coaches being able to decide who gets bought and who doesn't,' he wrote. 'After all, it's the coach who lives or dies on the results of his team. Don't you reckon he should have the last say on its composition?'

Internal politics—specifically interference from the leagues club—was tearing Easts apart, just as it had forced Jack out. While his former teammate Tony Paskins was the preferred option of the all-powerful leagues club to replace Neumann for the 1970 season, there was also a push to appoint the former Souths coach Bernie Purcell. Meanwhile, a reunion of past Easts players sparked the idea of an impossible dream: bringing back Jack. A decision was made that night late in the season to run a rebel ticket against the current football administration. Terry Fearnley would stand for president, but the coup d'état was all about Jack's reinstatement as coach.

The Easts fans certainly wanted it and most outside the club thought the club had made a grave error of judgement in letting him slip away. 'I gave the matter a great deal of thought before deciding to seek re-appointment,' Jack declared to reporters phoning him at Nicholson Parade the morning after the reunion. 'Most of the Easts committee, I feel, would think that I would not swallow my pride and attempt to regain the coaching job.'

The push ended before it even started. The stop press in *The Daily Mirror*, which could always be found in red ink on the top of the back page, told him a few days later there wasn't going to be a homecoming:

NEW COACH FOR EASTS: Don Furner, the former Kangaroo worward [sic] and Country Seconds coach, was appointed last night to coach Eastern Suburbs for the next three seasons. The appointment ends speculation that Tony Paskins, Bernie Purcell or Jack Gibson would be given the coaching job.

Easts had sprung a surprise. Jack cut out the stop press and glued it into one of his scrapbooks.

●

Unwanted by his old club, yet a free man for whoever wanted him. And he was wanted. He'd only been at it for two seasons, hadn't won a premiership, but applying for the Easts job had pricked ears across the league. Western Suburbs were the first to come knocking, but Jack said all along that he 'doubted' if he could take it. Noel Kelly, his good mate, was also a candidate. Would he be so inclined about the vacant St George job, then? 'I wouldn't say that,' he said with a slight grin.

Surely not. The Dragons had for years appointed coaches from within the Red V family, starting with Ken Kearney in the 1950s. After Killer, it was Norm Provan. After Sticks, it was Ian Walsh. After Abdul, it was Johnny Raper. But when Chook decided to depart at the end of the '69 season to play local footy in Newcastle, secretary Frank Facer was too astute to let the way things had been done in the past prevent him from rediscovering success for the future. The Dragons' exalted run of eleven premierships had ended three years earlier, at the same time as the four-tackle rule had been introduced.

Facer was determined to usher in a new era, and, as one unnamed committeeman confided to Geoff Prenter in *The Sun*, 'There has been a reluctance not to select a coach outside the club. But St George no longer walks with the drovers—and we are now with the sheep.' Jack's take on it went like this: 'It's funny when you look at it. When I took the job at Easts they were used to losing. If I get the job at St George the players I have will be used to winning.'

Provan's name was raised as a potential candidate, but his business interests stopped him from applying. The Dragons halfback, Billy Smith, was also said to be interested but withdrew from the race when he learnt of Jack Gibson's interest. Winger Johnny King and reserves coach Sid Ryan applied anyway, even if they knew from the start that the job was Jack's if he wanted it.

Upon his appointment in January 1970, Jack made something clear from the very start: he wouldn't be afraid to stamp his authority on a club he had sparred with for years as a player, and that hadn't been coached for decades by an apparent outsider. 'It's a job I wanted and a job I'm sure I can handle,' he told the *St George Leagues Club Journal*. 'As far as fitness is concerned, it's left to the individual players to do all the necessary early work. If they neglect it, we're not going to worry about them.' He was pampering nobody.

Those words about pre-season fitness, as much as his authoritarian reputation, had many of the Saints players feeling edgy before Jack had even placed one of his well-polished black shoes in the joint. The unwritten story about St George's unparalleled success during their eleven years of supremacy was that many of its superstars burnt the candle at both ends. Dragons folklore tells of their two best players, Graeme Langlands and Billy Smith, fronting the dressing-rooms before a match in three-piece suits, having attended a function the night before. Others would wander out of the Mandarin Club in the city and blink at the Saturday morning daylight and then be named man of the match at the SCG later that afternoon. Drinking sessions at the Carlton Hotel just down from Kogarah Oval were legendary. And sometimes the session would continue elsewhere. Would it remain this way under Coach Gibson?

Langlands was concerned for other reasons. He knew of Jack's unyielding policy of players fronting training on time, and as a driver of a brewery truck feared he would be disciplined. 'I knew we wouldn't want to be late,' Langlands says. But Jack had already identified the great Changa as the key man for his side. They had said goodbye to Raper, the greatest lock-forward in the history of the code. Other legendary figures had gone in previous seasons.

From the moment Jack gave Langlands the captaincy—ahead of Billy Smith and big Queensland front-rower John Wittenberg—they struck an instant rapport.

For the rest of his coaching career, Jack Gibson's reputation as a strict disciplinarian would precede him. Whichever club he signed with, there would be uneasiness among the players about what it would mean for them. In reality, the acid was on him when he came to St George. It was the side responsible for more heartache throughout his career than any other. He knew they had reached the semi-finals for the last seventeen seasons and continuing that was Frank Facer's bare requirement of him. As that season played out, as the Saints marched towards another semi-final appearance, the Gibson coaching philosophy wasn't so easy to define.

The case of Billy Smith proved he wasn't all hard-arse. Billy didn't burn the candle at both ends so much as take a flame-thrower to it. If anyone was going to kick on after the 10 p.m. closing time at the Royal Hotel, it would be him—and usually that meant heading to Mick Moylan's, a pub at Sans Souci only a short car ride from Kogarah. Because Jack had connections all over town, he usually knew when Billy was there and how much he'd drunk.

But Jack wasn't just concerned about Billy's schooner count. He knew what Billy Smith added to his side, something that went beyond the fact that Smith was the best halfback in the land. In those days, first-graders played injured until their body— or the coach—would allow them to play no more. Smith knew which of his teammates was injured, which man was struggling, and consequently would bob up alongside him to help him out if the play went that way. His teammates admired him for his selflessness—and that's why Jack was prepared to give him leeway should he so happen to bob up at Mick Moylan's two days before a match.

Two results midway through that 1970 season had the rest of the players eating out of the palm of Jack's hand. The first came against South Sydney at the SCG in early May. Having lost the grand final to Balmain as unbackable favourites the previous season, the Rabbitohs had started this one as overwhelming favourites and had not been beaten by the time they met the Dragons in round seven. Rabbitohs fullback Eric Simms kicked goals from anywhere, and the pack, including players like Ron Coote, Bob McCarthy, John O'Neill, John Sattler and hooker Elwyn Walters, was considered the best in the premiership.

That Saturday afternoon, Jack's side simply tackled them into the rock-hard turf of the cricket ground, and the result was hailed by the press as putting 'the kiss of life' into the premiership. In the rooms afterwards, a reporter asked the coach if he fed his players tackling pills before the 16–8 victory. 'Just be kind to them is the secret,' was his reply.

The star that day was Phil Hawthorne, the former Wallaby playmaker who had found form that year under Jack and after the triumph over Souths won the Australian five-eighth spot ahead of Manly's Bob Fulton. That had merely been an entrée to what he did in late July—this time against Manly and Fulton. They won that game 22–14, but it had deeper meaning: it showed them what was possible. They had been without Langlands and Smith because of injury. They were coming up against the competition leaders. But somehow Jack had infused them with enough self-belief. It started with Jack's call to make Hawthorne captain for that match.

The captaincy had done the same thing for Langlands, who realised quickly he could approach Jack about anything. 'He was a straight-shooter just like Frank Facer,' remembers Langlands. 'I could talk to him man to man whenever I needed to.'

Straight-shooter, perhaps, but definitely cunning and calculating. As the season climbed towards the finals, he publicly mused that he hadn't seen Souths play a 'clean match all year'. It riled Souths supporters, including president Denis Donoghue who challenged him to a $1000 bet before their match late in the season. 'They must have more money than sense,' Jack laughed. 'I don't bet on football matches, particularly when my own team is playing.' The obvious subtext was that Jack was trying to put pressure on referee Don Lancashire in the hope of swaying the penalty count his side's way. It didn't work: Souths won by a point.

The defeat didn't prevent Saints from finishing in the top four, and with one round to play they had already stitched up third position. Then they lost to Canterbury, meaning the Berries finished fourth and didn't have to play Eastern Suburbs in a sudden-death play-off, and there were immediate accusations that Saints had thrown the match. 'Well, did *you*?' dozens of fans asked Billy Smith as he stood at the bar in the leagues club afterwards. 'Don't be ridiculous,' Smith said.

Injury ruled Smith out of the following week's semi-final against Canterbury, but it didn't matter because Langlands was still there: his five goals were everything in the 12–7 win. Suddenly, Saints were eyeballing the two giants they had already slain that season: Manly in the preliminary final, and then potentially Souths in the grand final. 'We have a few little tricks up our sleeve,' Jack told Billy Mordey in *The Mirror*. Evidently, not enough: Saints lost 15–6. Just like his Easts sides, Jack's Saints were not able to make an impact in the semis when it mattered most.

It wasn't enough to spook Frank Facer, though. A month after the season had finished, he approached Jack about the 1971 season to sniff out if he wanted to apply. It was the committee's decision, but the boss was happy. Johnny King was the only other applicant.

Like the stop press from *The Mirror* a year earlier that had informed him that he had missed out on the Easts coaching job to Don Furner, the letterhead of the St George District Rugby League Football Club was inscribed in burning red ink:

M J Gibson,
2 Cowra Place
CRONULLA
13th November, 1970

Dear Jack

I have much pleasure in advising that you was [sic] the successful applicant in the ballot for First Grade coach with this Club for the 1971 season.

With kind regards, and trusting our association will be to our mutual benefit.

Yours faithfully
F Facer
Secretary

Jack cut out that one, too, and glued it into his scrapbook.

John Arthur Gibson. Born in
Kiama, 27 February 1929.
Here, he is aged four.
(Jack Gibson collection)

Florence Thompson, Jack's mum. (Jack Gibson collection)

Flo with Jack's father, John. Relatives say he was more like his mum than his dad. (Jack Gibson collection)

He hated the conformity of school, but he thrived on the camaraderie of St Gregory's at Campbelltown. Jack is second from the left in the second row in this photo from 1942—his first year.
(Photo courtesy of St Gregory's Campbelltown archives)

Meeting Joe Taylor—
The Boss—changed
everything. (Newspix)

From the moment
they met, Jack and
Ron Taylor were
like brothers.
(Jack Gibson
collection)

Early in his life, Jack
loved three things:
drinking, punting,
chasing skirt.
On this occasion,
it's drinking. (Jack
Gibson collection)

Then he met Judy Worrad and the chasing ended. They were married on 21 May 1955 at St Ann's Catholic Church, Bondi. (Newspix)

Family came first . . . With Judy daughters Joanne, Tracey and Sue.
(Jack Gibson collection)

And with eldest son Luke, behind the bar at their first home in Nicholson
Parade, Cronulla. (Jack Gibson collection)

As a front-rower for Easts
in the '50s, Big Jack feared
nobody. (Newspix)

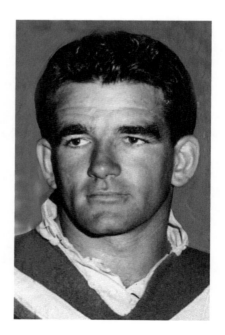

In 1960, he captained the
Tricolours all the way to the grand
final against St George. (Newspix)

Fending off Easts back-rower Don Fenton at Henson Park in 1962, despite a broken collarbone while playing for Newtown. His good mate Terry Fearnley is in the background. (Jack Gibson collection)

'We can't win,' Jack told his Western Suburbs teammates before the 1963 grand final against St George. He'd heard referee Darcy Lawler—flanked by Wests' Kel O'Shea and Saints' Norm Provan—had backed the Dragons. (Newspix)

A fast bowler for Waverley in the Sydney grade competition, Jack often bowled in the SCG nets at the likes of Test cricketers Neil Harvey and Alan Davidson . . . like it was a Test match. (Newspix)

Jack spent hours spearfishing in the waters near his home in Cronulla. His mates thought he was 6 foot 3 inches of moving shark bait. (Jack Gibson collection)

Some reckoned Ron Massey (far right) was Jack's right-hand man, although
as coaching co-ordinator he was more his eyes and ears ... when he could
bear to look. (Rugby League Week Magazine)

Champagne anyone? Jack quenches Johnny Peard's thirst after Easts had won the 1974 premiership, with Bunny Reilly and Arthur Beetson looking on. (Newspix)

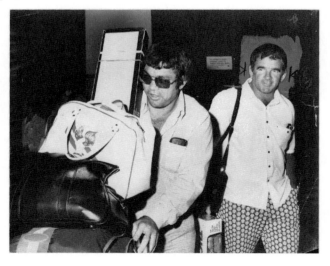

Arthur Beetson was concerned when Jack was appointed coach of Easts. Within a year, he considered him a 'coach, father and brother'. A trip to England and the US only cemented their lifelong bond. (Newspix)

The Roosters players chair Jack and Arthur from the SCG after claiming back-to-back titles, having won the 1975 premiership. (Newspix)

Celebrating with fans after winning the 1975 grand final. Jack had fallen out with Easts as a player and in his first stint as coach, but he could never get the red, white and blue out of his system. (Newspix)

Hugging Ron Coote and Arthur Beetson in the SCG dressing-room in '75. Russell Fairfax stands right behind Jack. He was still part of the team despite breaking his ankle before the finals. (Newspix)

Because the coach lived or died by the result, Jack wanted complete control of his football side. 'It's like Tommy Smith with horses,' he once said. 'You give him the horse—and he decides what race it runs.' (Rugby League Week Magazine)

GIBSON TO COACH PARRA

TWO-YEAR CONTRACT

By PETER FRILINGOS

Jack Gibson will coach Parramatta, rugby league's "sleeping giant," for the 1981 and 1982 seasons.

Jack Gibson . . . new hope for the Eels.

• Continued Page 2

JACK GIBSON TO COACH EELS

JACK GIBSON last night agreed to coach Parramatta for the 1981 season.

Gibson, who was one of three contenders for the job, last coached South Sydney in 1978.

He took Eastern Suburbs to a premiership victory in 1975.

Jack always made good copy. When he signed on to coach Parramatta for three seasons, it was front-page news that afternoon in *The Daily Mirror*. (Jack Gibson collection)

Training out of old Granville Park in 1982, first-grade team meetings were held on an old government bus. As Peter Sterling said: 'You just wanted to be on that bus.' (Newspix)

Throughout his career, Jack raised the ire of officials because he would cancel training and show the team inspirational films. He didn't particularly care what the officials thought. (Newspix)

10 SECOND EFFORT

THE TAIL OF the 8-millimetre film flew off the reel and flicked over and over and over, but the clicketty-clack couldn't break Jack's concentration. Epiphanies tend to do that.

When the lights came on, he leaned back in his chair and looked over his shoulder directly at Terry Fearnley, his former Easts front-row partner whose lounge-room he was now sitting in. Jack pushed the horn-rimmed glasses back with his index finger, but this time it didn't mean he was angry. He'd been mesmerised, and that was something not easily achieved.

'Brother,' he said, pausing. 'That's the hottest thing I've ever seen.'

Fearnley knew he'd be impressed. Now a car salesman for Holden, he had gone to Melbourne the year before for a General Motors management training conference and the last item on the agenda had been a 30-minute motivational film called *Second Effort*. It featured the legendary American football coach Vince Lombardi, who steered the Green Bay Packers to five National

Football League championships during the 1960s and the first two Super Bowls played in '66 and '67. Lombardi had been ravaged by cancer just two years later, and died suddenly at the age of 57 that September. His legend would never be as easily torn down.

While they may have been different personalities, and Lombardi would have disapproved of Jack's colourful background, there was an affinity. Lombardi had taken over the Packers in the late 1950s when they were a broken side and turned them around just as Jack had done with Easts. They also shared common beliefs when it came to running a football team. Discipline was tantamount to success. A player's skill amounted to nothing if he wasn't in command of the right attitude. Lombardi's method had always been about the self-empowerment of his players. Of prompting them to make the second effort on their own accord. And that was a hymn sheet Jack was already singing from.

The next night, the St George players fronted training and you can imagine their puzzlement when they were told there was no need to strap on their boots and begin the warm-up. The start to the season had been indifferent, at best. Despite winning the pre-season competition, they had won four of the first eight matches, and were still smarting from a 23–14 loss to Parramatta at Kogarah Oval the previous Sunday. But instead of a rigorous hit-out on the training field, all three grades and their coaching staff were squashed into the dressing-room, where Jack and Fearnley had set up the projector.

The officials present that night grumbled. No surprise there: Jack and the sausage-roll eaters were already on shaky ground. In his written application for the job that season, he had asked for increased powers in selection—and got them. Specifically, he wanted a voice in the selection of the reserve and third-grade sides and in which positions certain players played. Yet merely having a say didn't guarantee he got the team he wanted.

His troublesome back had, ironically, forced him to use ingenious methods to break the deadlock. Before the round-six game against Cronulla, he had strained it so badly while lifting a trailer at home that Judy had to drive him to training as he lay in the back of the family's wood-panelled station wagon because he couldn't sit upright. Later that week, the pain was so excruciating that Ron Massey rushed him to Waverley Hospital, with Jack screeching with pain every time the brakes were applied. He was placed in traction and told he would remain in hospital for days after the match at the SCG that Saturday.

He listened to the game on a transistor radio as Frank Hyde called the play on 2SM. Hyde's voice reached its crescendo when Brian 'Chicka' Norton, who had been called up from reserves, scored a runaway try of some 80 metres. After the Dragons won 24–20, Norton received Hyde's man of the match award of a Seiko watch even though winger Geoff Carr had scored three tries.

When Jack fronted training the following Tuesday, the selectors—headed by chairman Paul Broughton—were adamant Norton must remain in the side at the expense of Peter Fitzgerald. Jack liked Fitzgerald. He liked how he tackled the same blades of grass as Bunny Reilly did at Easts. He liked how he was as dirty as a coalminer at the end of every match. Knowing Broughton and the selectors would outvote him, Jack and Massey devised a cunning plan to ensure Fitzgerald was in their side.

'I don't want to pick Langlands,' Jack told the selectors, who laughed him off and outvoted him. 'I don't want Billy Smith,' he told the selectors, who this time were more astonished than amused. 'You can't leave Billy out.' When it came to the back row, the selectors gushed about Norton's try against Cronulla: 'I wish you had seen the try Chicka scored.' Jack responded angrily. 'I wish I'd seen the bloody try, too,' he snorted. 'I'm the coach. I let you get your way with Langlands and Smith, but I want Peter Fitzgerald.' After much debate, the selectors finally relented. Wisely, Massey advised Jack to tell Langlands and Smith what had transpired to avoid any confusion about his motives.

Jack's confrontations with officialdom weren't isolated to selection night. All-powerful president Len 'Deacon' Kelly strode into the rooms after a loss at Kogarah one Sunday and started to blowtorch the players about their performance. Jack ordered him from the room. Massey reckoned there and then that he had ruined any prospect of coaching the Red V beyond that season.

So with the relationship already strained, more than a few of the sausage-roll eaters tut-tutted in the dark when the lights went out and the 8-millimetre film brought one of the white walls in the dressing-room to life. Jack didn't care what they thought. He never did. He knew he wasn't showing his players a motivational film used by insurance companies and car dealers. This was the hottest thing he'd ever seen.

The premise of *Second Effort* was about a salesman, played by prominent US actor Ron Masak, being told the value of persistence by coach Lombardi. 'Why didn't you make the second effort?' Lombardi asks him in the opening scene after a sale falls through. Throughout the film, Lombardi detailed the pillars that brought the Packers their storied success of the 1960s. The message was spliced with grainy footage of his men in yellow and green sweeping to victory, as well as shots of the coach hoisted onto their shoulders with steam coming out of his mouth as he bellowed with joy into the cold winter air.

It was his unique phrasing that appealed to Jack. 'Confidence is contagious, and so is the lack of it.' 'Fatigue makes cowards of us all.' When he shows the salesman footage of a Packers touch-down, with the receiver juggling the ball to complete the play, Lombardi described it like this: 'He saw his chance to run to daylight and then he took it.' When the salesman dared suggest that winning isn't everything, the mastercoach rolled out the line that has echoed through professional sport ever since. 'You're absolutely right,' Lombardi said through his gap-toothed grin. 'Winning isn't everything, but it's the only thing.'

The scene that resonated loudest with the Dragons players—and certainly with their coach—came when the salesman asked Lombardi to pretend he was a player on his first day of training, sitting there in the sacred Packers dressing-room. What would the coach say to him? Lombardi rises, walks to the back of the room and delivers an oration with a piercing stare through his signature glasses—not horn-rimmed like Jack's, but the plastic-top, metal-rim eyeglasses he wore every day. So real was the speech delivered in Lombardi's rich Brooklyn accent, those in the Kogarah Oval dressing-rooms must have felt like they'd been transported to Lambeau Field in Green Bay, Wisconsin:

My name is Vince Lombardi. I want to welcome you to the Green Bay Packers. Last year, the Green Bay Packers won an unprecedented third successive world title. The Green Bay Packers have won five world championships in the last eight years. You have been selected, you have been invited here, because we believe you have the necessary talent and the ability to do the job. If you have the total commitment and pride necessary to become a part of this team that has been built on pride, you will stay here. This is also a team that has been built on confidence. You show us that you have the inner drive, and the competitive drive to make things happen, believe me, you will be a Packer.

And football is a Spartan game with its qualities of sacrifice and self-denial. It is also a game of violent contact. And because of that violent contact, there's a personal discipline required that is seldom found any other place in this modern world. We're hoping to make you work harder than you've ever worked in your life, because the history of the National Football League proves that most games are won in the last two minutes of the first half or the second half. It's usually the team that's best conditioned which usually wins the game. We're going to expect a one hundred percent effort at all times. Anything less than that is not good enough. It requires exhaustive hard work to the point of drudgery. It gives one hundred percent elation when you win, it gives you one hundred percent fun when you win, but exacts a one hundred percent resolution when you lose. The success of the individual is completely subjective to the satisfaction that he receives in being a part of the successful whole.

It's a game most like life in that it teaches that perseverance and dedication, hard work, competitive drive, selflessness and respect for authority is the price we all have to pay to achieve the goals that are worthwhile.

By the time the film had finished, and the 8-millimetre flew off the reel and started to go clicketty-clack, the players were awestruck, just as Jack had been in Terry Fearnley's lounge room the previous night. Jack quietly asked for the reel to be swapped over, and all three grades watched it again.

For the next seven weeks, none of them left the field with the empty feeling of defeat. Every grade won every match. By the end of that home-and-away season, only first grade had lost two games and St George had claimed the club championship. When all three grades swept into the grand final, the sausage-roll eaters shook their heads but this time in disbelief. They had no choice. It was the hottest thing they had ever seen.

●

Ian Walsh seemed to know something that everyone else did not. 'St George have no man of authority in their forwards like Kevin Ryan or Johnny Raper and that's where we'll beat them,' he told Ian Heads in *The Telegraph*. 'Our pack will murder them, we're specials,' he told Peter Peters in *The Sun*. 'We've won four games under referee Keith Page this season—and Saturday will make it five,' he told Tony Megahey in *The Daily Mirror*.

Walsh was no hack. He'd won five premierships playing hooker in the Red V jumper, including the last of St George's eleven successive premierships in 1966 when he was captain-coach. But he was convinced the Parramatta side he now coached was about to put these pretenders firmly back in their box.

And he had a point. St George appeared to be a two-trick pony and those tricks were named Langlands and Smith. Their pack was tiny compared to most, and especially so for that first semi-final against Parramatta, which featured a goliath in prop Bob O'Reilly. Saints lock Ted Walton and props Keith Maddison and Harry Eden had been thrown in for the sudden-death match, having played most of the season in reserves. Eden was supremely fit but so much of a lightweight some considered him a reserve-grade back-rower at best. But he was tough: when he wasn't playing, he was collecting money for Jack's SP business.

Centre Bob Clapham was also a shock selection in the centres, and while these manoeuvrings might have perplexed Walsh and other outsiders, Jack could not care less what they thought. For the past two seasons, he'd rumbled with selectors and consigned players to lower grades, or promoted players from those grades in spite of reputation. As he explained to Clapham as they stood in the middle of Kogarah Oval after the shock selection: 'It took four games to get into the firsts. It takes only one bad one to get you out.'

In terms of referee Page, that was a different matter. Jack had pounded his men about not conceding a solitary penalty. So disciplined had they been, so miserly had they become in conceding any advantage, some critics claimed Saints were receiving preferential treatment. Two nights before the semi-final, Bill Mordey fronted training at Kogarah and the mood was jocular. Jack's four-year-old son Matt drove a tractor around the field, and *The Mirror* photographer snapped Changa Langlands jokingly pointing a finger at him while taking him to task.

The image appeared on the back of the newspaper the next day, but the accompanying story wasn't so playful. Jack had unloaded. 'It's become a joke,' he fumed about claims of favourable treatment from the whistleblowers. 'For two years, we've been playing to the rules and we'll continue to do so.' Then he squared up Walsh. 'He's been bagging his players all through the year. I just wish he'd leave my men alone.' Jack defended his players like they were his own blood, and it was that belief that allowed them to ignore any suggestions their side did not extend beyond the names of Langlands and Smith.

That belief was there in the semi-final when they fluffed an 8–2 lead and allowed Parramatta to draw level and send the match into extra time. As the sides rallied themselves for another twenty minutes that afternoon, the feeling was that the match was there for the Eels to win, for they had the ascendancy. Instead, that little forward pack kept tackling and tackling, and then Billy Smith put in a high kick, Changa Langlands gobbled it up and scored the try that buried the result.

It was there in the preliminary final the following weekend against Manly, a club rumoured to have splurged $250 000 on building a premiership side that featured high-wattage players like Bobby Fulton, Great Britain international Malcolm Reilly and Australian hooker Fred Jones. The Sea Eagles were favourites and accordingly led 7–6 early into the second half, but then came two moments of brilliance from Langlands and Smith within three minutes: the first when Langlands pounced on a Smith cross-kick close to the tryline, the second when he supported the halfback after a break down field and then raced away to score. After that match, Johnny Raper lobbed in the rooms and slung his arms around Smith and Langlands, the latter having suffered a deep gash across the bridge of his prodigious nose after he was struck by an errant boot. 'Best game I've seen Billy play,' Raper said.

And it was there—this belief that the side went beyond the names Langlands and Smith—in the lead-up to the 1971 grand final. South Sydney were the defending premiers and their pack was the most feared in Sydney. Each of their players either had played for Australia or would in the near future. Prop John Sattler had played with a broken jaw in the grand-final win against Manly the year before, and fellow front-rower John 'Lurch' O'Neill was equally tough; George Piggins gave away plenty of penalties, but he was the most cunning hooker in the competition; back-rowers Ron Coote and Gary Stevens were relentless. But the man *nobody* could stop that season was Bob McCarthy, the mobile, quick-thinking forward who Souths coach Clive Churchill had described as 'the greatest second-rower in my time'. Meanwhile, Saints were about to go to war with the lightest grand final pack in the club's history.

As far as both captains were concerned, the key man seemed to be Piggins and the leather he could win—or concede. Saints hooker Col Rasmussen had humbled Manly's Fred Jones in the final, but could he do it against Piggins? 'Piggins will be giving away his usual number of penalties,' Langlands said. 'You can bet George Piggins will win the scrums and we'll be too hot to handle,' replied Sattler, before declaring: 'No doubt Jack Gibson has something special in store for us, but even he cannot produce a miracle.'

And as for coach Gibson, the whole thing just smacked of a hole about to be filled. This grand-final win would make up for all the times as a player when a premiership slipped by because of the men in the Red V. This one would make up for the sins of Darcy Lawler. And all this as coach of the side that had haunted him as a player, that had fallen away after its eleven years at the top, but was now rebuilding. And for the club he'd walked out of two decades earlier because of his lack of commitment. 'I'm lucky I wasn't dealing with myself then or I'd have been outed for ten weeks, not two,' he joked with Ernie Christensen about being suspended for failing to show up to third-grade training in 1950.

St George had lost only two of their last sixteen matches, and many of those matches had been without the 'firm' of Langlands and Smith. Jack was being lauded for the sense of *team* he'd instilled among a group of unfashionable and underrated players. 'That's rubbish,' he said to *Mirror* reporter Tom Ramsey. 'If you can't help yourself, how can you help the team? I preach to them to win for themselves.' Preach? 'Dammit, if they can't win for themselves, there's nothing left over for the team.' Then he thudded his right fist into the palm of his left hand. 'That's all bull about winnng for your club. I've never met the footballer yet who enjoyed having a poor game in a winning team.'

That applied on the field—off it was an entirely different matter. The night before the grand final, he invited the players to dinner at his home in Cowra Place. It wasn't the first time: for the last two years the side had bonded at several social nights, all of them dressed in coat and tie, at the Gibson residence. Jack may have been scrupulous when it came to football, but he was no square: he knew how to relax away from the game. He was also wise enough to know when his captain, Graeme Langlands, needed some leeway. Langlands was such a restless sleeper the night before the matches that mattered that he'd require half a dozen or so schooners of beer to make sure he didn't stir during the night. Just as Jack was prepared to loosen the leash for Billy Smith when required, so it was with the captain. Besides, Chang was high-beaming with confidence. Throughout that season, Jack had let him take control for the final fifteen minutes of every training session. That week had been no different.

To understand the twists and turns of that grand final, you shouldn't read about it in a book, or even watch old footage. You need to listen to how Graeme Langlands recalls it:

Keith Holman blew the whistle and from the very first scrum hooker Col Rasmussen had his eyes gouged. It wasn't the first time this happened against Souths but Rasso was prepared to cop it sweet. They threw everything but the grandstand at us in the first half but we held them out until Eric Simms banged over a field goal to give them a 1–0 lead at the break. Our prop Graeme Bowen couldn't come out for the second half because of a knee injury and young Russell Cox took over.

Gibbo kept our keenness razor sharp during the interval, talking to each one of us and the team as a whole. Every player was convinced we could beat Souths and we were determined to do it. But we'd been back on the field only about a minute when Gary Stevens and Ron Coote combined to send Ray Branighan over for a try.

For the next 15 minutes, Souths put tremendous pressure on us and I don't know, to this day, how we held them out. At one stage, we held them out for 18 successive tackles and on the 18th there were at least seven players stretched out suffering from exhaustion. Inevitably, the crack came after about 16 minutes and Sattler sent Coote crashing over in the corner. As soon as Simms hit the conversion attempt from the sideline I knew it was going between the sticks.

It wasn't long before we copped another king-hit when we were penalised right in front of the posts and Simms simply tapped the ball over to make it 11–0. So there they we were, with 15 minutes left to play, and down 11 blot. You wouldn't have backed us with counterfeit money. Nine months of gut-tearing training injuries and knock-down drag-out games all counted for nothing at this stage.

After that conversion I belted the ball deep downfield and we all charged after it like mad dogs. As quick as a flash we had the ball again and Billy Smith sent Barry Beath over wide out for a try and I booted the conversion.

In the next couple of rucks, we could all feel Souths were starting to falter. It couldn't have been more than a minute before Beath and Cox combined to send Teddy Walton spearing over in the corner. Again I kicked the conversion and the impossible had happened—we had pulled up to 10–11.

Souths were gone to Gowings, make no mistake about that. But a little bloke named George Piggins had other ideas and in those dying minutes, he alone broke our backs. Every time we were in possession there was Piggins marking the tackled player and raking the ball back to Souths. If he did it once, he did it half a dozen times, blast his hide.

There were two minutes to go—two lousy minutes. Coote was on the burst and I dived at him and down he went. I thought I had him but then I caught sight of Bobby McCarthy scooting over to score the winning try. 'That's it,' I told Coote. 'You're too good, mate.' 'Sorry mate,' he said, half apologetically.

In the Members' Bar afterwards, Langlands shared a beer with McCarthy and Sattler. They both admitted they thought Souths would've lost if not for their hooker. Langlands barely heard them. All he could notice was Georgie Piggins in the corner, grinning as he sipped a soft drink surrounded by an army of South Sydney supporters.

Jack didn't retire to the bar. He was driving back to Cowra Place with Judy, and they sat in complete silence for most of the journey. After they arrived home, he didn't seem terribly keen to leave again for the after-match function at the leagues club. 'I'm not goin',' he said. 'What do you mean you're not going?' she inquired, gently. Then she noticed the expression on his face—devastation. He never brought the emotion of footy home, and never impressed it on his wife and children. This was a rare unguarded moment. 'I can't believe how much I have let them down,' he said, quietly.

Judy finally convinced him to go. And while Langlands made a speech that night at the leagues club auditorium, Jack was too broken to say a word. Anyone who got close to him knew that no other football result, for the rest of his life, wounded him as much as that one. Before the grand final, a reporter had asked him to name his greatest moment in footy. 'I hope I'm coming to it,' he'd smiled. 'I hope it's not behind me.'

Now he didn't know.

•

Aside from how it had all ended, the revelation of *Second Effort* and its seemingly mystical hold on his Dragons that season is tightly affixed to the Gibson legend. Yet there's no reference to the film in a single newspaper story from those times, and those St George players who are still alive only vaguely remember the power of the message and its influence. They only remember Jack's coaching. *Second Effort* may not have necessarily lit a fire in them, but it lit one within the coach. The professionalism Lombardi was preaching had served as a revelation for his fellow Catholic.

Jack knew he had to move away from the way things had always been done, and it started with the little things. He had told his players and coaches they were now officially on Lombardi Time, meaning they had to turn up ten to fifteen minutes early, and advised them to set their watches accordingly. On game day, footballers normally ploughed through a steak in the morning, but Jack instructed them to instead drink Sustagen, a new sports drink being promoted by Australian Test fast bowler Dennis Lillee. 'I can't drink twenty schooners tonight if I only have Sustagen during the day,' centre-cum-forward Ken Maddison grinned to his winger, Geoff Carr, before one match. Veteran forwards considered the traditional nip of port in the rooms just before running on to constitute a warm-up. Jack scrapped that one, too, preferring his players do drills and stretching on the field just before kick-off. No more oranges at half-time, either. They were replaced with little plastic bottles of Orchy juice. As Carr recalls:

'The message from *Second Effort* for Jack was to start looking for the edge in everything he coached.' Lombardi helped him launch the search party.

But it went deeper than swapping Sustagen for steak. His coaching philosophies had now entwined with his life, such was the emotional investment. It had been the same for Lombardi. 'I don't know how else to live,' Lombardi said in *Second Effort*:

> Unless a man believes in himself, and makes a total commitment to his career, and puts everything he has into it—his mind, his body, his heart—what's life worth to him? Coaching is selling. Selling and teaching. When they join this team, I tell them there are only three things important in this life: their religion, their family and the Green Bay Packers.

The ironic part about it all was that Lombardi made the motivational film at the time when he was searching for motivation himself. When he left the Packers in 1968—his first year out of coaching—he was a lost soul. Insurance companies and sales organisations had gobbled up *Second Effort*, but he lamented upon its completion that it didn't come close to the sensation he felt stalking the sideline as Green Bay's NFL coach. 'I miss the fire on Sunday,' he told the famous American sportswriter WC Heinz.

Jack had an ability to walk away from the fire momentarily. But the hurt from that grand final defeat pushed him away. He almost seemed to run from it. When he told Frank Facer he didn't want to coach St George again, a sense of panic fell over the club. Len Kelly—the president he had ordered from the Kogarah dressing-rooms one time—pleaded with him to stay and described him as 'the best coach in Australia'. Jack reported to Facer's bedside as the ailing secretary recovered in hospital from major surgery, but it still didn't change his mind. Right down to the very night when they took the vote, when they appointed Graeme Langlands as captain-coach, the committeemen phoned Jack to see if he'd changed his mind.

It wasn't the money, as Facer said. It wasn't his sore back, as some speculated. It wasn't a dispute with the club, as whispered by others. 'I'm not interested in coaching next year and that's that,' Jack repeatedly told the pressmen.

And it was.

11   BONDI YANK

FOR AS LONG as anyone could remember, he was a figure of authority. As a footballer, he never had the physical talent, but he had the will. As a coach, he had come into the job needing to drag a team back from the edge of the abyss and identified defence as the best way to do this. Defence was about attitude, and that was a good starting point. Then he invested his faith in unfashionable players. Men who were unwanted but not washed up. As a man, he was handsome with dark hair and dark eyes. He had a solid, square chin. He filled out a suit like he was born in one. He was married with three boys and three girls, and had a silent respect for the man upstairs.

He was Dick Nolan, coach of the San Francisco 49ers, and his resemblance to Jack Gibson was spooky. So was the way they found each other.

Just because Jack had stopped coaching in the wake of St George's grand final defeat, it didn't mean he'd walked away forever. He couldn't get Vince Lombardi's voice out of his head, so at the end of March he travelled to America in search of more about the art of coaching. His travelling companion was Terry Fearnley. Fearnley had never held a strong desire to coach, but watching *Second Effort* enough times by now convinced him to pursue it. Like Jack, he couldn't win a premiership as a player— but maybe he could do it as a coach. This was his second effort.

Jack had long felt a connection with the United States, long before he eventually arrived there. His father's brother, Frank, had gone there in search of gold after the Boer War and was never sighted again. For years, Jack never doubted his family's belief that another great-uncle, Hugh Cooper Gibson, had been Secretary of State to President Woodrow Wilson during World War I. Only years later did they learn that Uncle Hugh had been a senior State Department official who became ambassador to Belgium and later Brazil.

Yet the American in Big Jack had less to do with bloodline and more to do with his sense of style and cool. He'd lived most of his life in the Sutherland Shire but was inescapably considered part of the eastern suburbs set. And if you were part of the eastern suburbs set, and you wore expensive suits or heavy dark coats, and spoke with a discerning drawl, and drove big ostentatious American cars like a Cadillac or Chevrolet or Pontiac, you were thought of as a 'Bondi Yank'. Jack Gibson was never a certain *type*. But the legend fitted that description perfectly.

This trip to the US was a pilgrimage and—typically—Jack had told Fearnley that all arrangements had been made prior to their departure and he needn't worry about a thing. They were set down to meet retired tennis players Jack Kramer and Ted Schroeder, who had skewered Australia in Davis Cup matches in the 1940s. Schroeder had formed his own professional tour during the 1950s, while Kramer had started to build his empire while promoting the game in the post–Open era from 1968 onwards. Both men were close friends and celebrities in their own right, and they were often sighted wagering large sums at Californian racetracks. While Fearnley was unsure how Jack had set up meetings with men of such influence, he put it down to his former front-row partner's vast network, which seemed to have few limitations.

They were due to meet Kramer in San Diego and Schroeder in Los Angeles, but their first stop was Honolulu, Hawaii, for a few days of relaxation. Jack had never been this far from home and was prepared to do it in style by making reservations at the lush Outrigger Reef Hotel located just metres from the sand and the dead calm waters of Waikiki Beach. Who knows what had drawn him there? Whatever the reason, Jack's stay was to have a profound effect. One of those quirks of fate that changes everything. A bit like meeting Joe Taylor.

The Reef Hotel in late March 1972 just happened to be the venue for the National Football League annual meeting, which involved the owners and coaches of every American football team in the country. That night in the bar, Jack and Fearnley struck up a conversation with one of the organisers, who said he would try to rustle up a coach to have a quick yarn with the rugby league coaches from Down Under.

Moments later, Dick Nolan strode into view. In the early 1960s, when Nolan was playing as a defensive back for the New York Giants, Camel cigarettes thought he was the right style of man to slap on a billboard overlooking Times Square. When injury ended his career in 1962 while playing for the Dallas Cowboys, legendary head coach Tom Landry made him his defensive coach. In 1968, he signed on as head coach of the

49ers, who had struggled to make any impression on the league in those seasons. Initially, they were listless years, but he kept his faith in under-appreciated quarterback John Brodie, bought solid defensive players, and by the time Jack and Terry Fearnley met him that night he had won three consecutive National Football Conference West Division titles, missed out on playing the last two Super Bowls by a game, and in 1971 was named coach of the year. He was also affable and charming. 'When you've finished your tour, come to San Francisco and I'll show you around,' Nolan told them following a brief conversation.

Within days, Jack and Fearnley were in Redwood City, on the San Francisco peninsula, sitting in Nolan's office at the 49ers base and training camp. Over the next four days, he gave them unfettered access to his team and its operations: training, facilities, all of it. They met the franchise's general manager and part-owner, Lou Spadia. And before they had left town they met Hank Greenwald, a play-by-play broadcaster of the San Francisco Warriors basketball team, later known as the Golden State Warriors.

Of course, when the business of football was done, the matter of pleasure wasn't far from Jack's thoughts. He had never been to America, let alone Las Vegas, and for someone whose life had been inexorably chained to the turn of the card, those neon delights were too hard to resist. He hired a Pontiac, threw Fearnley the keys and told him to drive. Within half a day they were parked outside the famous Caesar's Palace. Fearnley was mesmerised by the casino's glamorous appearance: its long line of fountains, and the statue of Caesar himself. 'There is no way we're getting in here,' he told Jack. 'I've got this note from an associate back in Australia,' Jack replied. 'This'll get us in.' Jack went to reception and returned minutes later. 'We're in,' he said. 'In the honeymoon suite.'

That evening, they went to the iconic Desert Sands further along the strip. The Sands had hosted the likes of Sinatra and Sammy Davis Junior, Dean Martin and Louis Armstrong. On this night, though, Don Lane was performing. Lane was the American performer who had made it big in Australia with his talkshow on Channel Nine, but was presently appearing at the Vegas showrooms. His schtick was that he was just a little Aussie battler, doing his best.

'You've got to have a bet,' Don suggested enthusiastically when he spotted two more little Aussie battlers, here in Sin City. No need to say it twice: Jack walked up to the blackjack table and a few hours later left with a thick wad. Estimated value: $3000. Fearnley, who was far thriftier with his cash than Jack, thought it terrific. That was enough to pay for the trip. That was until the next night when Jack hit the Sands again, lost all of it and then turned to Fearnley. 'How much money have you got?' he asked, needing more betting ammo. Fearnley gave him a couple of hundred. Then Jack lost that, too.

Upon their return to Australia, Jack and Fearnley set about writing a report on their trip to the US and specifically what they'd learnt from Dick Nolan. They leaked some of the report, written at the request of New South Wales Rugby League boss Bill Buckley, to the *Rugby League News,* and it highlighted the professionalism of American football across every part of its business: from the enormous value and weight of television broadcast rights to the importance of having leading officials, who were of 'no difference' to those of large companies, steering the league. The Americans didn't know what a sausage roll was, let alone why one of its leadings officials needed to eat one.

Jack and Fearnley reported that while the NFL was playing to an audience far bigger than rugby league's, it didn't mean the game here shouldn't pursue similar standards of professionalism. 'We have a young country with a rapidly increasing population and while gridiron is entirely different to rugby league, the administration, promotion and requirements of players and public are identical,' Jack wrote in the report.

What struck him deepest, though, was the autonomy that Nolan had at the 49ers. The head coach was responsible solely for the running of the team, and he was empowered with the responsibility of finding the assistant coaches and talent scouts to work with him. Meanwhile, the general manager and executive ran the club. That was the demarcation Jack had for years been fighting for. 'I'd probably be at Saints if they'd given me what I'd wanted,' he confided to those close to him. 'I might've still been with Easts for that matter. It's like Tommy Smith with his horses. You give him the horse—and he decides what race it runs in.'

What struck Fearnley deepest about their American experience was the instant connection between Jack and Nolan. They had conversed like kindred spirits during those four days at Redwood City. A lifelong relationship had dawned, and both their horizons unexpectedly expanded. As Fearnley once said of their union: 'Things are meant to be in some way, aren't they?'

•

The phone at Cowra Place kept ringing out. Frank Farrington was on one end, but Jack wasn't there to pick up the other. He and Judy were somewhere in Europe enjoying a long-overdue holiday. Farrington was desperate for him to return so he could offer him the coaching job at Newtown.

The Bluebags were still alive in the premiership when their president, Chicka Cahill, demanded their committee contact Gibson. It wasn't being disrespectful to the incumbent coach, the great Harry Bath, who had told them he wouldn't be coaching next season because of business commitments. Jack had only been back in the country for a handful of days in late August before Newtown tracked him down. He accepted the position without much thought.

What sold him so quickly was that he was promised control of selection and the running of his side. Selectors and lower-grade coaches still had a voice, but Jack's would be the loudest. He told them he would run the three grades like an American team, and appointed Terry Fearnley and lower-grade coaches Paul Cuneo and Clarrie Jeffries as assistants. It had to be on Jack's terms. He wasn't returning to coaching so soon if it was any other way.

Newtown were a young and honest team—they'd finished fifth that season, just one point out of the finals—but it was a team devoid of a genuine star. The good old Bluebags might have been one of the foundation clubs of the league from 1908, but it was one of the poorest. Cash was tight. Jack signed a one-year deal with a one-year option, and it was as much for his benefit as the inner-city club's. 'If they want to get rid of me at the end of the year or I want to go, I'm free,' Jack said. 'The option is not binding.'

He didn't just want autonomy when it came to running the side—he wanted to return to America. Within days of signing on for the 1973 season, Jack was on the phone to the Ingham brothers. He wanted them to sit at the back of the room at the Newtown Leagues Club as he addressed his players for the first time. 'I want you to tell me what you think,' he told them. Afterwards, as they ate dinner, the Inghams told their friend— and bookmaker—they would always back him, no matter what. They agreed to sponsor the club.

According to the daily newspapers, the Inghams were on board because they were 'thick and thin Bluebags supporters'.

The pressmen had got it wrong. The Inghams had only a passing interest in rugby league, let alone an allegiance to any club. They only supported a man. 'We weren't supporting rugby league or Newtown,' recalls Bob Ingham. 'We were supporting Jack Gibson. When a good mate asks you to support him, you support him—if you are a good mate.'

The Inghams were also prepared to fund another trip to the US—for Jack, Farrington and the club's new physical conditioner, Mick Souter. Jack had known Souter since he was fifteen. He was a Cronulla boy and member of the surf club where Jack would find himself each Sunday, often to settle up with punters who had wagered with him that weekend. Jack would tuck the dollars into his bathers. Sometimes he'd play shuttlecock and make Mick his doubles partner, teaming up to take on another senior member of the club—usually with $50 riding on the result. Souter had played a handful of seasons for Cronulla, but missed the 1972 season because of a broken rib that had punctured his lung. He was studying to become a physical education teacher at the Sydney Teachers' College when Jack convinced him to play for Newtown that season, as well as train them.

When Souter fronted 49ers training at Redwood City in early December, what first struck him was the unmistakable similarity between Jack and Dick Nolan. 'You could've transposed them,' Souter recalls. 'They were that similar.' Then he looked at the training paddock. The players. The *size* of them: 6-foot-3 human machines running as quick as rugby league outside backs. Souter pumped their conditioners for information about their training methods.

That Saturday afternoon, the trio watched the 49ers narrowly beat Minnesota from the comfort of Lou Spadia's owners' box at Candlestick Park. The spectacle of it effectively blew Farrington's head off. He had seen the future of professional football, and wanted his financially ailing club to be a part of it.

Jack relished that afternoon at The Stick, but his mind was also down the interstate highway at San Jose. That's where America's two leading sports psychologists, Thomas Tutko and Bruce Ogilvie, could be found. Jack had known for years, back to his playing days when he was considered the fittest in the club, that supreme physical conditioning was fundamental. Now he was keen to tap into the power of the mind.

Tutko and Ogilvie had written a book called *Problem Athletes and How to Handle Them* a few years earlier and it was being gobbled up by NFL coaches, including Dick Nolan. They had also devised a survey consisting of some 190 questions that could be fed through a computer to determine which players should be retained, which should be cut, and which ones could become useful footballers in the future. Armed with this survey, Jack promised to try it out on the Newtown players upon his return.

Before the trio left San Francisco, their study trip received column inches in the city's oldest newspaper, *The Examiner*. When they returned to Australia, they received plenty of intrigued coverage in the local press, yet privately there were sniggers from those within rugby league's old school who wondered what the hell American football had in common with their game. When Jack suggested publicly that representative teams should be selected by computer, it raised eyebrows.

He wasn't the only one. Soon after their return, Farrington convinced his committee to dump the Bluebags nickname Newtown had carried since inception and call themselves something more snappy—like the Jets. 'The name is pretty apt when you consider that our home ground Henson Park is right under the flight path to Mascot Airport,' Farrington advised the press upon their return to Australia. The New York Jets had earned their name because it was under the flight path of JFK Airport. If it's good enough for New York, why not Newtown?

As for Jack, he seemed happy with the shrill of the air traffic overhead as he conducted training sessions under lights at Henson Park. Leaning back against the fence, wearing the blue tracksuit, he was asked how he felt about his one-year deal. Was he here for the long term? Or was this just a fling?

'I'm 43 years of age now,' he said, drawing back on his cigarette. 'Newtown is going to be the last club I coach.'

12 JACK AND THE JETS

'TIME TO FEED the chooks,' he'd say when it came to speaking to the press, although Jack rarely refused an opportunity to talk to them. He was a cunning self-promoter; he knew that interviews publicised his club and the game. On this warm Monday morning in March, the chooks formed a semi-circle around him at the front of the Cronulla Surf Club. 'Jack, there's a story going round that your Newtown boys were wearing mascara against Canterbury last night.' Jack grinned. 'That's right.'

That's right? In America, the use of eye-black by professional athletes was nothing new. The greatest baseballer of them all, Babe Ruth, had rubbed grease under his eyes in the 1930s believing it eliminated the glare. In the 1940s, Washington Redskins fullback Andy Farkas would burn corks and rub the black ash under his eyes for the same purpose. By the time Jack went to the US, most American footballers lathered on the mascara for night matches. But in Sydney in March 1973, in the Wills Cup pre-season rugby league competition, it was just downright weird. 'It works all right,' Jack said. 'You don't think American gridiron players wear mascara for fun, do you?'

What else had he gleaned from his time in America? 'I learned plenty over there,' Jack replied. 'But I like to keep all that to myself for the present. The things we learned cost us a lot of money.' It cost Jack and Bob Ingham a lot of money. 'One last thing,' they asked. 'Who puts the mascara on?' Jack grinned again. 'I do.'

In truth, Jack hadn't returned from America with the secret of life. He hadn't come back with the identity of Colonel Sanders' eleven secret herbs and spices—although when Kentucky Fried Chicken came to Australia in the early 1970s it was one of his secret, guilty pleasures. A distinct professional approach to fitness is what Jack and Mick Souter, his conditioner, had learnt most from their time around Dick Nolan and the 49ers. Newtown became their guinea pig.

They ran fitness tests for the players in October, and the key indicator was the seven-lap run. Over the years, it became a legendary and fundamental part of Souter's regime. Not only did it tell him which players needed extra work, it told him which ones not to sign in the first place. Souter would hand all players a fitness program for the summer, and tell them which workouts and local gyms to attend. He then tested them when they returned in January. It was basic stuff, but at the time rugby league had never seen anything like it.

Supreme fitness, of course, was the cornerstone of defence. *Stop them scoring tries.* It had been Jack's mantra since his first day on the job with Easts in 1967 and he wasn't changing now— especially now—that he had found his way to Henson Park again, just as he had during his playing career. Newtown had few gamebreakers. No Graeme Langlands. No Billy Smith. Lionel

Williamson was the captain and an Australian winger—but many thought at the age of 29 his best years were behind him. They had an ageing legend in centre Brian 'Chicka' Moore, but Jack was convinced about his value. Lock Neil Pringle was on the rise, but that's about where the envy of other clubs ended when they ran an eye over the old Bluebags.

It changed nothing. *Stop them scoring tries.* Standing next to Dick Nolan, Jack had seen the 49ers players running into tackling bags held by support staff and instantly knew he needed to find something similar. One morning, he and Souter trawled the truck depots and at the next training session had a couple of inflated inner tubes from the huge tyres. 'Like downing a greased pig,' Jack smirked when he rolled one away and told Pringle to chase it down and tackle it like it was a runaway centre.

Jack appreciated a defender who hit so hard it unsettled the dust on the grandstand rafters. The textbook way to tackle was to hit with your shoulder, then use your feet to drive against the momentum of the player carrying the ball. Jack had no regard for the textbook. 'Leave the ground,' he'd tell his men, over and over and over, as they hunted down the inner tube. He wanted his Jets to be *launching* into tackles, not standing still.

Stop them scoring tries. They couldn't do that in the first half of the Wills Cup final against St George under floodlights at the old Sydney Sportsground on St Patrick's Day, wearing the mascara Jack had carefully put on. When half-time arrived, they trailed 15–2. It was a steamy night and Jack didn't want them sitting in the furnace of the Sportsground rooms, so he asked them to drop a knee in the middle of the field. Hundreds of children gathered round them as the coach took his position before them, and he had to shout above the din to deliver one sentence: 'Stop them scoring tries.'

Newtown won 17–15. When Chicka Moore scored the match-winner, the coach—positively sparkling in a bright blue tracksuit on the sidelines—jumped from the white wooden bench and into the air. He'd never been so animated at a football match; possibly ever.

•

Rugby league was in love with Newtown then. It was a foundation club but starting to struggle financially, a fight for its very existence looming. Lifelong Bluebags fans were fast being replaced by Greek soccer supporters as multiculturalism took a grip on the inner west. Nobody wanted to see a rugby league club from 1908 wither on the vine. In Jack Gibson they trusted to ensure that didn't happen. After the Wills Cup victory, an anonymous Newtown player confided to *Rugby League Week* editor Geoff Prenter that he was ready to back his own side to make the five, such was the belief since coach Gibson's arrival. 'Jack treats men as men,' he told Prenter. 'That's why he gets results … If you can get me $9000 to $2000 the Jets for the five, I'll be very happy.'

As the warm weather abated and the season settled into its inevitable grind through the colder months, the Jets won matches and admiration with their courageous defence, but the truth was inescapable: they were punishing to watch. They were tackling their way to victory and it hardly appealed to the masses. When they upset premiership favourites Manly 20–10 at the SCG through nothing more than mind-numbing tackling, there were barely 10 000 fans dotted around the ground for the Match of the Day.

Jack didn't care how they won. They could do it in field goals if he thought it guaranteed victory. He'd remained true to the NFL philosophy of all three grades preparing together, and when they remained unbeaten for five consecutive weeks he arranged for all of them—including wives and girlfriends—to go out for a night at the Chevron Hotel in Potts Point to watch actor Ronnie Frazer in the stage production *Some of My Best Friends Aren't*. This was a reward. 'And if the players continue to show such keenness and dedication to the game there'll be plenty more nights in the nightclubs,' Jack said.

American football and its emphasis on defence remained a guiding influence for the coach. He and Nolan nattered on the phone at least once a week and compared notes through regular written correspondence. Early into the season, Nolan flew to Sydney. Jack had to calm down the talk that he was going to head-hunt players to join the 49ers. Nolan, sitting next to Jack at the SCG against Easts, was gobsmacked at the fitness of the players. 'I would say your players are in better physical condition for running because of the speed of your game,' he said. Newtown lost 11–9, but the real difference wasn't in the scoreline. The Jets players were on about $2000 worth of match payments, Easts on about $7500.

That's why Newtown had to stop teams from scoring tries. Jack didn't have strike players across the park. He didn't have any at all. Defence was about heart and attitude, and that was something he could teach them. Weeks later, before the match against St George, he set up a projector at Henson Park just as he'd done at Kogarah Oval two years earlier and showed his players *Second Effort*, as well as footage from a handful of NFL matches.

Lombardi's message crept into them as it had the St George players. They were so scrupulous with their defence in the first half it killed the match as a spectacle. As they walked from the field at half-time, the Jets players were oblivious to the drone of boos bouncing around the SCG. With eleven minutes remaining, the scoreboard attendant still unmoved from his seat with the score 0–0, Jack made the match-winning move on the chessboard.

Ken Wilson had played in third grade earlier that day, and had sat in the dressing-room for reserves and most of first grade. Out of nowhere, the coach hooked five-eighth Kevin Fiddock from the field. He had faith in Ken's kicking. Wilson had been on the ground for only two plays when the ball swung back and he slotted the field goal. Newtown held on to win 1–0. League had never seen a scoreline like it. The game was blasted by the press and public as a joke. The Newtown players posed in the SCG dressing-rooms like they'd won the grand final.

Stop them from scoring tries. Newtown didn't stray from that game plan all the way to the end of the regular season. First grade finished fourth on the ladder, reserve grade had finished second, while third grade were minor premiers. It meant Newtown, founded in 1908, had won the club championship for the first time in their history. Years later, many considered it Jack's greatest coaching achievement. Not Ron Casey, the outspoken 2KY broadcaster and *Mirror* columnist. 'It is inescapable that Newtown plays dull percentage football and the public just doesn't want to watch them in action,' he wrote. 'And the sooner they and their dull football are eliminated the better for my taste.'

Jack couldn't care less. Winning was all that mattered, just as Vince Lombardi had said in *Second Effort*. He had maintained his strict policy of his men turning the other cheek when confronted with on-field thuggery, and not one Jets player had been sent off. 'I'm very proud of that,' he said as the finals loomed. Then he grinned. 'Don't get me wrong. I'd send them out with a bloody axe each if I thought it would do any good.'

It was that way of thinking, and certainly the way he articulated it, that intrigued Sydney's sporting cognoscenti. Nobody knows who first said it, nobody knows where it came from, but the description of 'supercoach' was being attached to his name consistently as that season drew to its conclusion. Supercoach. Jack had yet to win a premiership, but in six seasons he had picked up conventional coaching wisdom and dumped it on its arse.

He was a revolutionary, and while many privately smirked at the inflatable tyres and mascara and seven-lap testing there was no dispute about what he was achieving. He had taken middling teams at Easts and St George and elevated them to the finals and almost the title. And now he was taking Newtown by the hand and taking them down a familiar path. The Jets were playing dog-ugly football. Everyone could see that. But they had heart and spirit and Jack loved that about them. By the end of that September, the rugby league public was right there with him.

When they beat Canterbury 13–2 in their first sudden-death semi-final, Mike Gibson rushed back from the Sportsground to offices of *The Daily Telegraph* in Holt Street in Surry Hills and started bashing out his copy. 'It was, without doubt, the worst major match of rugby league I have ever seen,' he wrote. But his venom wasn't directed at the Jets. They had to play like that. *Stop them scoring tries*. And they had.

Throughout that season, Jack had let slip to those close to him that he had never coached a quieter group of footballers. Fact was they were in awe of the coach. So it was that there was complete silence at half-time in the minor semi-final against St George at the SCG the following weekend. They led 7–4, but nobody would make a sound until Jack's deep voice broke it. 'Listen, I want another 40 minutes of concentration,' he said. 'You all saw the reaction after that bad kick.' He was talking about prop Col Casey's inexplicable shot at goal and the 60 metres the Dragons gained off the miss. 'Forget that now. Remember, if you stand flat-footed you are bludging.'

In the second half, none of his Jets bludged. Not for Jack. They kept losing every second scrum, losing possession, but they kept tackling for him, all the way with a minute remaining in extra time when they trailed 10–12 after Graeme Langlands had landed a penalty goal. That's when Jack figured the season was over. He stood at the urinal in the Members' Pavilion, waiting for the inevitable loss signified by the full-time siren. What he didn't see were his boys kicking deep into St George territory, chasing down field in the hundredth minute of play like it was the first, and then goading a penalty out of Dragons forward Graeme Sams, who handled the ball in the ruck right on the siren. Jack was still in the men's when he heard referee Keith Page's whistle and missed five-eighth John Bonham's penalty goal that deadlocked it at 12 all.

Afterwards, Jack wasn't in the mood for hyperbole. He looked across the dressing-room and it was strewn with broken and battered players. He was seething about how hard the SCG surface had been. Word reached him that the replay on Tuesday night would be played at the Sportsground. 'Thought they may have played it on one of the runways at Mascot,' he said dryly. 'It'd be no harder out there than here.'

Come Tuesday night, nobody cared how Newtown played. They were a team worth about $60000—only a fraction of what the other clubs were shelling out for their talent. They were the underdogs and that was a role Jack was more than familiar with. He'd been one as a player, and thus far as a coach. He was nearing the top of the mountain again, with a side that had never been taken seriously all season. The public sensed it, too. Thousands converged on the Sportsground and the entire Moore

Park precinct was chaos. Officials had been expecting a crowd of 15 000—double that number turned up. 'Jetomania', as the *Rugby League Week* front-page screamed that week, had set in.

Again, everything went against them. They lost the early scrums, they trailed at half-time, and in the second half the wind swung around to the south, up Driver Avenue and right behind the Red V, but in the end none of it mattered. Since he'd started coaching, Jack had kept tackle counts to gauge the workload of his players. Gerry Seymour was his statistical genius. And at the end of that semi-final replay, Jack's men had made no fewer than 248 tackles. Newtown won 8–5.

Afterwards, Jack could barely speak. 'Few teams would appreciate winning more than these blokes do,' he said, the hands shaking like they had in his first season of coaching. Johnny Peard, who had played under Jack at Easts during those first two years, had moved to St George and he was making predictions about the final against Cronulla before he'd left the field: 'They will beat them if they tackle like they did today.'

They didn't. Cronulla won 20–11. Then Cronulla lost to Manly, in perhaps the most brutal grand final played the following week. Jack Gibson was named coach of the year.

Shortly after the travails of the season, Jack phoned Frank Farrington. He had snapped up an offer to rejoin Eastern Suburbs. The leagues club was swimming with money, and its boss Ron Jones knew only one man could deliver the premiership it had not won since 1945.

Yet surely the Jets felt like he was abandoning them. 'How could we have felt like that?' says Farrington. 'He'd done so much for us.'

13 ARTHUR

THE GEORGE HOTEL is an imposing and elegant Victorian dwelling in Huddersfield in the north of England. It was here, on 28 August 1895, that officials from 21 clubs voted to break away from the Rugby Football Union and set up a new league, a new code. And it was here, in late 1973 during the Kangaroo rugby league tour of England and France, that Arthur Beetson was about to demolish a plate of eggs and bacon when Alf Richards rushed into the dining room. And if we're being truthful about this whole episode, it was a pound of bacon. Arthur was hungry.

'They just gave Jack the Roosters job,' Alf declared.

Arthur had met Jack only once: in the Tricolour Bar at Easts Leagues Club in 1967, when Jack was in his first year as coach and Beetson his second with Balmain, having arrived in Sydney from Brisbane the year before on the first air flight of his life with just $50 in his wallet. Jack stood tall in the middle of the dark cave of the bar that evening, resplendent in tweed sportscoat, and the room orbited around him like he was the sun.

Beetson had never forgotten that. Nor had he forgotten Jack's shrewd gaze through the horn-rimmed glasses, and it was that lingering image as much as that authoritarian reputation that concerned him on this morning at the George. He respected Jack but knew of the high demands he placed on his players. So Beetson ate the eggs—but not the pound of bacon.

When Beetson returned to Australia from the Kangaroo tour, he was spent—playing in sixteen of the nineteen matches had drained the big fella—but when he turned up at Easts training in late December just to watch, the coach walked over, muttered a few words, and Beetson promptly rounded up some gear and joined the session. When he didn't turn up for the next training run the following Thursday night, firm in the belief he was entitled to a break, Jack was on the phone the next day: 'Where were you last night? If you hadn't turned up for a month, I would've accepted it. But now you've come I expect you there every week.' Beetson never missed another session.

This prickly beginning belied the alchemy that would follow. By the time they found each other, Beetson was the front-row forward Jack had always wanted to be. He'd hit the defensive line and then stand tall after impact, towering above the opposition defenders clutching at his legs. He'd look left, then right, the leather in both hands as he waited for a support player to carry on the attack. He read the play ahead of everyone else, and would become frustrated when his teammates couldn't keep up. He'd absorbed criticism for years about his ballooning weight and limited game time. Oh how they laughed. He was 'Half-time Artie' and 'Meat-pie Artie' and he hated it because he knew—*he knew*—he was at training an hour before everyone else, even if many never seemed to notice.

Jack had returned to the Roosters, as they had now come to be known, on one fundamental condition: the unwritten clause he had been seeking his entire coaching career. He wanted the run of the team. 'Some of Gibson's requirements were that he would be in sole charge of the discipline of the three grades, that he would bring one other coach to the club, and that he would have a major say in the purchase of new players,' wrote Alan Clarkson in *The Sydney Morning Herald*.

Ron Jones had driven Jack out of the club in the first place. Now he wanted assurances, and Jones was prepared to make them. This was the year for those in the eastern suburbs to believe again. This was their year. Since his cranky departure at the end of 1968, Jack's old joint had almost climbed the mountain in 1972 under Don Furner, but rolled back down under Tony Paskins when they missed the finals the following season.

As agreed, Jack brought in a platoon of assistants like he was head coach commandeering an NFL franchise. Ron Massey was his co-ordinator. Mick Souter remained his conditioner. Alf Richards—the best on-field medico in the business—had ended a 27-year association with Newtown to follow Jack across town. Jack appointed his old front-row partner Terry Fearnley as reserve-grade coach.

Everyone was climbing aboard. Five-eighth John Peard had returned to Bondi after two seasons with St George—just in time to line up with halfback Johnny Mayes, who had been wooed back from Manly. Centre Mark Harris had dabbled with American football and quickly realised which side his bread was buttered on. Jack wanted Bunny Reilly to return from Cronulla and he did. Bunny was still tackling the same blades of grass as he had when Jack was there the first time. He was still Jack's gun for hire, the Axe, as he was known, because of his ability to lop down opposition trees no matter how big they were.

The final piece in the puzzle was the hooker. Ron Jones had managed to lure Kangaroo hooker Elwyn Walters across from Souths, and of course it hit a nerve with their foundation club rivals. The Bunnies were struggling financially. Many clubs were. And while nobody could ever prove it, few in the game doubted that the deep pockets of the leagues club had helped the Roosters form a team worthy of winning the premiership.

For a moment there, they almost looked like losing one of their best forwards. The towering, gifted Ron Coote had left Souths to join Easts in 1972 on the promise from Don Furner that he would be captain. Then Jack took it from him, gave it to Peard for two games, and asked all of the team to sit his 190-question aptitude test. The results were sent to the US, and when they came back the computer had spat out the most remarkable of results: Beetson had recorded a perfect score for leadership, which no athlete in America had ever achieved. 'How long am I captain for, coach?' Beetson asked Jack when told of his appointment. 'Till you lose it,' Jack replied. Coote considered asking for a release but bit down on his lip and stayed.

During those warm pre-season months of 1974, Russell Fairfax received a phone call on a Friday night. 'This is Jack Gibson,' said the emotionless tone on the other end. Fairfax was having a rare quiet night in before playing a trial match for St George. He had won a Sydney rugby union premiership with Randwick the previous September, and played the last of a handful of internationals for the Wallabies at fullback against England at Twickenham in November. Training, let alone *playing*, with a league side was tantamount to treason. If rugby union officials had heard about it, Fairfax would have been banished for life.

It just so happened that Jack had heard the whispers. He didn't miss much. The word about Fairfax was that with a bony frame and long flowing blond hair, he looked more surfer than fullback. But he could run and step and was lethal when he returned the ball. That mail had come from the rugby union men he knew around town. How he came to learn of Fairfax training in secrecy with St George forever remains a mystery. 'This is Jack Gibson. I want you to play for Easts.'

Fairfax phoned St George officials the next morning and told them he would not be signing. The next morning, he signed with Easts. Fairfax was only vaguely familiar with Jack's reputation as a coach, but as a 22-year-old who trawled the city's nightclubs, he knew of his reputation from the two-up ring and within the racing fraternity. 'I wasn't scared of him,' says Fairfax. 'But I was scared of what he knew.'

Because Jack knew. Jack knew it all. His network had no bounds. Jack knew if Fairfax's Friday night had started at the Golden Sheaf on New South Head Road at Double Bay, before moving on to a nightclub at Kings Cross. Jack knew if Fairfax had caught a cab home but had deviated at the last minute and stopped outside the Bondi Lifesaver, the jumping nightclub next to Easts Leagues. Jack knew if he had stumbled out of the cab and through his front door at 3.45 a.m.

Fairfax loved Friday night. He owned the city on Friday night. He was a young PE teacher during the week, and Friday night was the night he lashed out. Of course, it was problematic with 8 a.m. training on a Saturday. That was Easts' final hit-out before playing on a Sunday. After the session, the team had a barbeque together. As had been the case since the start of his coaching career, Jack demanded punctuality. He was still running on Lombardi Time, with his watch wound forward ten minutes. When Fairfax turned up with the session already started, Jack asked him where it would be more convenient for him. 'Pioneer Park,' Fairfax said, knowing that old suburban ground was close to where he lived. 'Right son,' said Jack. 'We'll be there.'

The following Saturday, Fairfax stumbled out of bed after another big night and drove like a maniac to the ground. He knew it was close to 8 a.m. and when Pioneer Park came closer into view he could see his teammates already on the field. In a panic, Fairfax jumped out and covered his hands in motor engine grease. 'Sorry I'm late, Jack,' he said as he approached the coach, raising his dirty hands in the air. 'I couldn't get the car started.' Jack's reply: 'That's fine, son. Go introduce yourself to the second-grade coach, Terry Fearnley. He's a mechanic.'

Because Jack knew. Jack knew it all. His players were patently aware of the Gibson legend. They could see it in the gold Cadillac he was driving in those days. When the coach threw a short remark their way, they didn't know whether he was being serious or not. And hell knows they weren't going to ask. It was how they reacted that mattered. And if they took his jibe with good humour, but listened to and obeyed its message, their stocks rose in his eyes.

Lying to him was not an option. Because Jack knew. He imposed a strict midweek curfew of 9.50 p.m.—ten minutes before closing time—for his players to be out of the pub and on the way home. When two of his forwards, Ian Baker and Kenny Jones, had a skinful and then started to fight each other on the footpath outside the Phoenix Hotel in Woollhara like old props do, Johnny Peard high-tailed it out of there but was nabbed by the police for speeding on the way home. Peard phoned Jack straightaway, knowing the coach would rather hear it from him than his network.

'Jack, I got done for speeding tonight.' 'Were you breathalysed?' Jack asked. 'Yes, but I wasn't over the limit.' 'Good, I'll see you at training on Thursday night.' A pause, just before the receiver was clunked down. 'By the way, Peardy,' Jack said. 'Who won the fight?'

●

Ron Massey wasn't scared of Jack Gibson. Family rarely is. Fifty years after their first meeting, when Massey was lying in a hospital bed believing his final hours were evaporating with every breath, Jack tried to walk into his room. 'Family only,' the doctor said. 'I am family,' Jack said bluntly, pushing him aside.

For as long as anyone could remember, Massey had been standing alongside Jack, or was at least in the vicinity. They'd met in the 1950s, and Massey had watched from the sidelines as his friend brutalised defences, knowing what others did not: that the extra sting in the tackle could be attributed to Jack's raw-boned body—or the leather shin pads Jack had snuck under the sleeve of his jumper.

They fished together. They went to the races together. They worked as SP bookies on the races together. And they watched football together. Hours of football. 'Right-hand man' is how many have described Massey, and he would always snap back that Jack was *his* right-hand man. By the time 1974 rolled around and Massey was working on the coaching staff full-time, Jack fumbled around and came up with 'coaching co-ordinator'. The term had come from the States, of course.

The simple fact was it didn't matter what Massey was called—it's what he did for Jack that counted. And what Massey did for Jack was that he never said yes. 'We're going to use this player on Sunday,' Jack would tell him, pointing to a team list, days before a match. 'Well, I wouldn't,' Massey would say, and leave it at that.

Hours later, Jack would insist he would be selecting the player. 'I think you should use somebody else,' Massey would deadpan.

They would muse and mull and bounce and rumble like this for hours, and they loved that the most about each other. As Jack said of Massey years later: 'If you want to know your faults, go and talk to your enemies for a while. They'll tell you. Ron was like my "enemy".' And after all that, in the twilight of their lives, neither believed they'd ever had an argument with one another.

'Mass' was also Jack's eyes. Over time, Jack's vision worsened and the play out in the middle became harder to see no matter how strong the horn-rimmed glasses were. 'He was Jack's seeing eye dog,' says Mick Souter. 'His vision was so acute.'

And sometimes Mass saw other things. He'd stand back when Jack talked at training to his players, with them scattered around him, as he discussed the coming match. Their eyes would be trained on Big Jack, never moving from him, as he moved around them. Massey would be watching them watching him. They were mesmerised.

If the players hadn't understood something Jack had mumbled to them, if they had not completely absorbed his instructions, they would corner Massey in private and ask for an explanation. Jack once considered bringing in psychiatrists to talk to his players, another pursuit for a winning edge. 'Why?' Massey asked him. 'The players already listen to every word you say.'

That season, they were listening well before the premiership even started. Manly had entered that season as undisputed favourites. They had won the last two titles and had triumphed the previous year with mesmerising back-line players like Bob Fulton and Graham Eadie, and brutal forwards like John O'Neill, Mal Reilly and Terry Randall. That 1973 grand final against Cronulla was the most violent match anyone had ever laid eyes on. Later that year, Jack had shown coaches from the San Francisco 49ers a tape of the match. The Americans watched aghast, as if they were seeing a horror movie.

Yet it took only until the end of March for Manly and the rest of the rugby league chitterati to learn and realise that their status as favourites was not sacrosanct. Jack was never one to get ahead of himself, but after watching his side punish South Sydney 43–0 in the final of the pre-season Wills Cup, he broke into a half smile. 'This side could be the best I've coached,' he said.

Fairfax had signalled his arrival as a key player that night. He had glided around defenders and linked with winger Bill Mullins so efficiently it seemed like they'd played alongside each other for years. Yet reputations meant nothing. Ron Coote, who was still wounded from losing the captaincy to Peard then Beetson, was the best cover defender in Sydney, stalking the area behind the first line of defence then swooping on any rival player that happened to sneak through. Sorry, but that wasn't good enough for the coach. He wanted Coote standing in the front line, closer to the ruck. 'Jack wanted him making 30 tackles—not eight,' Massey recalls.

Jack was still carrying the public baggage of turning Newtown into tackling androids the previous season, but he was unrepentant about it at Easts. He knew they could attack, but he wasn't moving from the belief that defence remained the cornerstone of a winning team. He wasn't budging on this, even if his approach had drawn criticism, as well as the cold fact that he had not yet summited the mountain with *any* team he had coached.

'I want all Easts players to tackle more—they are a great attacking side but they can't defend,' he told the press. 'If my style doesn't suit the side and players like Coote then I will have to alter my tactics.' It was a rare concession that he might actually be wrong. Then he swiftly added: 'But we'll do it my way for a start.'

As it turned out, Jack's way turned out to be the right way. Favouritism for the premiership swung from Manly to Easts in May when the two sides met at the SCG. Before that match, he was at it again, using his friends in the press to his advantage. He had fed the chooks a line about his fears that referee Keith Page would allow Manly to dominate the ruck, mauling the attacking players. Manly boss Ken Arthurson, who was gaining influence on the New South Wales Rugby League board and had known Jack for years, lashed out. 'I've never seen anything more blatant in my life—Gibson has definitely attempted to inluence Page,' Arthurson told Bill Mordey in *The Mirror*. 'He ought to stick to getting his own place in order and let Mr Page look after the refereeing. Gibson is always being quoted as saying everyone should look after their own house but he doesn't stick to this himself.'

The SCG heaved with more than 50 000 fans that Saturday, but the whistleblower didn't turn out to be the difference between the two premiership heavyweights. It was Beetson who did that, slipping balls in tackles and dominating for the entire match. The captaincy that Jack had given him via computer had prompted him to thrive. The respect from the players was palpable. Before the match, centre John Brass had told his teammates: 'Let's give Artie a big one, he has a chance of captaining Australia and we can help him out.' As Jack said after the 15–5 win: 'Arthur Beetson has more ability as a captain than any other player I have been associated with in rugby league.' Beetson was named captain of the Kangaroos days later.

Yet the growing respect between the two was tested as the Roosters rampaged towards an inevitable minor premiership. There was a Spartan attitude to their football, but Jack had not forgotten the importance of a happy, social unit. After Thursday night training, the players would head to the old Dunbar Hotel in Paddington near the Sportsground. By about 8 p.m., they would head to the leagues club. Not Russell Fairfax. He couldn't get in because of the rule that forbade men with hair longer than their collar to come into the licensed premises—star fullback or not.

So when the players parked out the back of the club, they would all deviate to the left while Fairfax veered right and into the Bondi Lifesaver next door. Over the next month, more players tended to veer to the right with him, preferring the nightclub with the stunning female clientele to the leagues club. Sensing a division, Jack convinced Ron Jones to turn one of the function rooms downstairs at the leagues club into a private bar for the players, who could bring girlfriends and a mate. 'From then on,' says Fairfax, 'nobody ever strayed. Jack didn't mind us having a drink—but he liked to have control of it.'

Like previous clubs, all grades trained together. They were divided into teams of four, playing spirited games of touch footy and volleyball against one another on Tuesday nights. Occasionally, they would hold Red Faces variety nights in one of the large rooms under the grandstand at the Sportsground when Johnny Peard would assume the role of MC and players would perform skits to be judged by Jack and Massey. They both saw those nights as crucial to the spirit of the club.

Even if one night almost broke it in half. Beetson was captain of one of the four teams, Archie and the Piledrivers. And there inside the room at the Sportsground, where the team would normally trawl through video of their matches, he decided one night to put on an X-rated movie and provide running commentary in rugby league style to accompany the explicit images on the screen. The players erupted with laughter. When the lights came on, though, there was stunned silence.

Where was Jack? His seat was empty. They sat there in silence for a minute, before sheepishly cleaning up and leaving. It was clear that Jack had been deeply offended.

The response was one of those incongruous parts of the Gibson legend. Here he was, this Runyonesque character who had knuckled his way out of trouble for much of his life, who had been a part of Sydney's dark underbelly for decades, offended by a blue movie. But he was a family man with daughters—and a devout Catholic devoted to the rosary. He had made it very clear early into his tenure at the Roosters that if another player had even flirted with a teammate's girlfriend or wife then he would be sacked.

'And he was a bit of a prude,' Beetson admitted years later. 'He was one of the straight backs. The old committeemen tried to knock people over to get front-row seats that night. The prawn and porn nights were standard back then. I nearly lost the captaincy over it. When he explained it to me later, it didn't make sense. I think he underestimated the integrity of a lot of the players. But, in his own opinion, he thought I might incite some of the players to run amok.'

There were murmurs that week that Jack was ready to quit as coach. He stayed on … and the Roosters won the minor premiership by eight points.

●

Jack was oh so close to the premiership that had always eluded him that he could almost reach out and touch it. He reckoned he liked the smell of footballers. Now he could smell a grand final win. Finally.

Yet he feared that referee Keith Page was dragging it away from him, keeping it just out of his embrace. He had maintained his strict policy of disciplined football from his players, no matter how much the opposition baited them with illegal tactics. In one match against Canterbury that season, flamboyant referee Greg Hartley had told the Belmore boys: 'This is your last warning. Any more of it and I'm going to send someone off.' As the players ran back onside, Beetson overheard one of the Canterbury players say: 'Don't worry what he says. Just keep bashing them!' In the rooms afterwards, Ron Massey pulled Beetson aside. 'You know what, Arthur?' Massey said. 'I'd like to see Jack turn you blokes loose for just one game when it's on like that.'

Jack never did and never would. But there was a belief among some at Easts that he was paying the price of trying to remove violence from the game—or at the very least from his team. His edict of clean football was treated with suspicion, and by the time the major semi-final against Canterbury came around, Jack's meticulously kept statistics showed they had been beaten 85–53 in the nine games officiated by Page.

Before that game, Canterbury's secretary Peter 'Bullfrog' Moore launched into Jack in the papers just as Arthurson had done earlier in the season after Jack had declared their forward Phil Charlton would try to take Beetson out of the game with illegal tactics. He had also enlivened the Berries with claims that three reserve graders in the club had been acting like spies and rattling off coach Mal Clift's moves. 'Easts claims are nothing more than a gigantic confidence trick on Mr Page.'

When Easts lost that match 19–17, Jack blamed Mr Page solely for the loss. Jack was furious that Page had come into the Roosters rooms before the match to lecture his players about the rules he would be cracking down on during the next 80 minutes. But what had really cut was the match-winning try awarded to Canterbury lock-forward John Peek, who had clearly scored from a kick from Garry Hughes which the replays showed was clearly off-side. Winger Stan Cutler had slotted the winning conversion after the full-time hooter. 'If Page has the final, I may as well not send a team out,' Jack fumed. 'If we want to win the ball from the scrums I'm going to have to start teaching them bad habits and it's too late for that.'

What had equally angered Jack that afternoon was that second-rower Greg Bandiera had sparked a huge brawl for hitting Canterbury's Brian Lockwood high. Bandiera had been cautioned twice during the match, but Jack had not forgotten that he had been sent off in a pre-season match. So Jack dropped him for the preliminary final against Wests, who had swept into the grand-final qualifier by upstaging Manly.

Bandiera wasn't the only one missing against Wests. Protestations against the bad call on Peek's try had echoed all the way down to Phillip Street and the New South Wales Leagues Club. Page was gone and referee Laurie Bruyeres was ushered in to control them against Wests. The Roosters breezed home 25–2. Wests captain Tom Raudonikis made his way into the rooms. 'It's impossible to see you losing the premiership after that,' he told the Roosters players.

During the lead-up to the grand final, the players took their position in the back of convertible cars for a street procession through Bondi Junction, where 20 000 people or more jammed Oxford Street. The players were armed with Ingham frozen chickens and threw them to the masses. The Inghams had followed Jack from Newtown back to Easts. 'When he went to Easts, we followed him there,' says Bob Ingham. 'I didn't support football. But I supported Jack. When I say I was that close to him, I mean it … But that day I thought we were going to get put in jail. Do you know how much damage a frozen chicken can do?'

For the grand final against Canterbury, Jack pulled a typical selection surprise. He had alternated Beetson between the front and second row all season. He could've brought Bandiera back from his one-week lay-off for his short temper against Canterbury the first time. He could've called up the experienced Laurie Freier. But instead he 'done' something typically Gibson-esque. He picked Ian Mackay, a 21-year-old who had played a handful of first-grade matches that season. 'This is no gamble,' Jack declared. 'I don't gamble in grand finals. Laurie Freier would've been a gamble. He has missed fifteen games and can play a lot better than he did against Wests last week.'

There was so much at stake. Eastern Suburbs had not won the title since 1945. Yet the confidence before the decider could not be quashed. Jack had put a media ban on his players, but it hadn't stopped Beetson from taking one almighty swipe in his regular *Rugby League Week* column:

> I'd like to extend an open invitation to Canterbury to attend our victory dance celebrations on Saturday night. I don't expect us to win by a wide margin. It will be very tough, but I know we can hold them in the forwards and our backs will do the rest.

While Peard and Coote and Harris and Fairfax did the rest, it was Beetson who *owned* the 1974 grand final. Referee Bruyeres had canned them with penalties early on, but it had not stopped Beetson from latching onto a pass from Fairfax to score the first try, then setting up the second, or from simply outsmarting Canterbury around the ruck. They eventually triumphed 19–4 despite the referee's whistle constantly being blown against them.

Afterwards, Jack hardly said a word to the press. He stood in the dressing-room and poured champagne into the mouths of the likes of Peard and Bunny Reilly while the rest looked on and laughed. This was about them, not his premiership drought that had just been snapped in half. The reality of it was that while premierships were the gauge of his coaching success, his ability to make his players better men was judged in other ways.

It was written all over Beetson's face. The image that stood out, though, in all the press the next day was that of the captain being lifted onto the shoulders of his teammates just after full-time, his right fist punching the air in triumph. A year ago, he had sat in the George Hotel and been put off his breakfast at the thought of Jack Gibson joining the club.

Like Jack, he had won his first premiership but had become something more than a premiership-winner. He was the leader of men. Someone for others to believe in. A bit like the coach.

14   THE HOUSE THAT JACK BUILT

Fuck.

Jack rarely let the word slip from his mouth. Never in front of his family. Never in front of women. Rarely in front of his staff or players. But he was prepared to say it to Kerry Francis Bullmore Packer, the richest man in the country.

It was Monday morning when the phone call came from leagues club boss Ron Jones. Jack and Massey were at Cowra Place, trawling through the videotape as they did the morning after every match. Massey would compile the statistics and record them in his big green book.

'Jack, it's Ron here,' Jones said down the line. 'I've got Kerry on speakerphone. We've got a team here that's going to be playing at the weekend. 'Good idea,' Jack said. 'Can you hold on one moment?' He pushed the receiver to one side of his mouth and signalled to Massey to pick up the second phone in the room.

'Yes Jack,' Jones continued. 'Kerry and I have been having a talk and we think this is the team that should go on the paddock this weekend.' 'Oh yeah?' Jack deadpanned. 'What's the team you've got there?' Jones read out the team. Silence. 'That's a good team,' Jack said. A long pause. 'But I can tell you it won't be the fucking team going on the paddock.' *Clunk!* He slammed down the phone.

John Quayle was sitting in Ron Jones' office, listening on the other end. 'That's the first time I'd ever heard him swear like that,' Quayle recalled years later.

Jack had rumbled with Packer before. In 1960, he had been part of Rupert Murdoch's hired muscle in the bruising confrontation for the Anglican Press that ended in young Kerry being badly bashed. The images of it were splashed all over the front page of Murdoch's *Daily Mirror* the same day. By the mid–1970s, though, Kerry Packer had evolved into the richest and most influential man in the country. When his cantankerous father Sir Frank Packer died in 1974, Kerry inherited the family's media empire. Like Sir Frank, Kerry Packer did not understand the meaning of certain words. Like 'no'.

Early the following year, Packer was shifting his gaze from television and magazines to another deep passion: sport. He was still a year or so away from his World Series Cricket revolution, which he sparked when he fronted the Australian Cricket Board and famously asked: 'There is a little bit of the whore in all of us, gentlemen. What's your price?'

Before dumping the genteel game of cricket on its arse, Packer was rubbing his big thick-fingered hands all over the Roosters. He lived in the posh suburb of Bellevue Hill, and while it emerged decades later that he was actually a South Sydney fan, he could see greater potential in the Bondi club. He convinced Ron Jones to allow him to erect a Channel Nine transmission tower atop the leagues club premises in Spring Street, and there was a growing belief that he wanted to buy the club entirely—something that he and Jones eventually fell out over years later, ironically.

Jack had enjoyed Packer's company throughout the '70s. They had played several rounds at The Australian Golf Club, where Packer was a member. They had traversed different paths but were similar men. They didn't tolerate fools. The difference was that Packer was more inclined to pick up the telephone from his desk and throw it at a fool's head while Jack would walk away.

The issue for Packer was that there wasn't the slightest bit of whore in Jack Gibson. He had no price. And he did not care who Kerry Packer was. Six days after Jack had essentially told the richest man in the country to go fuck himself, the Roosters fielded the team Jack Gibson wanted against Manly at Brookvale Oval. They won 22–16.

The press never got wind of the incident but they certainly smelled growing tension between Gibson and Jones. The autonomy that had seen Jack return to the club—that had delivered a premiership—had been undermined. Jack had to apply a smother. 'What everyone is waiting for is a blow-up between Ronnie Jones and me,' Jack said. 'I'd advise anyone waiting for that not to hold their breath because there is complete harmony between us and it will stay that way.'

•

Jack knew how to play the press, but he relished hosing down internal politics as much as he enjoyed playing it—especially when he had more pressing issues at hand. The Roosters had been so dominant the previous year that there was unbridled expectation the second time around. The truly great sides climb the mountain and stay there. It had taken so much work to get here. He wasn't leaving in a hurry.

Yet the New South Wales Rugby League had seemingly gone out of its way to bring them back down with the introduction of a controversial new rule. It limited Sydney clubs to signing only thirteen players who had played their junior footy outside the club's boundaries. Kerry Packer and the leagues club had deep pockets but the junior ranks of the eastern suburbs were shallow. Consequently, fifteen fringe first-graders were squeezed out. Jack's reserve-grade side from the previous season had effectively vanished.

Jack didn't help matters by thinking his men could prepare for the season on their own. Training programs were planned and prepared and handed to each of them for the pre-season. He thought he was empowering them, but it was a rare misjudgement. After they were bundled out of the Wills Cup pre-season competition by Wests in the first round it was clear some of them had betrayed his trust.

They met Balmain—last year's wooden spooners—in the opening round of the premiership and only snuck home in the dying minutes when winger Bruce Pickett scored. Against St George at Kogarah Oval the following week, Jack couldn't hide his frustration as hooker Elwyn Walters was outplayed by his opposite, Steve Edge. 'He wore a frown as furrowed as the Bondi sands,' wrote respected journalist Phil Tressider.

After they lost to Cronulla the following week, Arthur Beetson was adamant the sickness in his side was complacency. 'The sooner Eastern Suburbs forget they won the premiership last year the better,' he wrote in his *Rugby League Week* column. 'We are walking around with our heads in the clouds and if we don't wake up this competition will get right away from us.'

Jack was having no truck with it, either. He demanded a return to the fundamentals. Defence. Tireless work from the forwards. It was a deviation from the flamboyant style that halves Johnny Mayes and John Peard had displayed the previous season. A deviation from the sweeping runs of Russell Fairfax from the back. He'd been branded a defensive coach, but Jack had always maintained he merely coached the strengths of his side. Easts had shown flair last season because they had it in them. Not now. He was pulling down the shutters, applying the handbrake. Against Manly that following Sunday, his Roosters won 22–16.

They didn't know it then but something special was sparked in that result. From then on the Roosters could not seem to lose. Jack's preparation became meticulous. The advent of video had made it easier to break down a player's game. Missed tackles. Dropped balls. Bad passes. His vision might have been impaired, but the crackling black-and-white video that he and Massey pored over every Monday morning always allowed him to see who deserved to be picked and who did not.

He was smart enough, though, to loosen the leash for those who deserved it. Because Beetson handled the ball more than most players, because he was constantly asking the question of the opposition defence, the captain was allowed some latitude. Jack could let him know, in his own way, if he was overplaying his hand. 'Beetson,' Jack would mumble, 'don't be afraid to play the ball.'

The video analysis meant that Jack found it harder to tolerate mistakes from players, and, much more so, from his dear old friend, the referee. It only took until round five, after a match against Wests, for him to lower the crosshairs over Keith Page. 'It is time referees shouldered the blame for a poor display of football and stopped trying to exonerate themselves by throwing the blame on the coaches,' Jack said.

Here we go again. Another war with the bloke holding the whistle. Page fired off a letter of complaint to the New South Wales Rugby League, which tried to muzzle Jack from making his criticism of refs public. NSWRL boss Kevin Humphreys wanted him hauled before the league's executive. 'If you can't control him as a member of your club, we will,' Humphreys told Easts official Roy Flynn. 'He is not cited, he is not gagged. And no action will be taken. But we want to sit down and explain to Jack what damage he can do.'

Jack would not be fronting the executive and was less inclined to explain his actions. Besides, he and Judy had ducked up to his farm just out of Wauchope on the North Coast which he'd purchased a few years earlier. Ernie Christensen from *The Sun* tracked him down. 'I do not want to be controlled by Easts nor by the League and I don't seek to control Easts or the League. I'm not fussy whether or not I talk to the League executive but if they feel it is desirable I'll go along.'

The meeting was postponed, but the following weekend, against Penrith, he inflamed the situation. Greg Hartley was a diminutive man with slicked-down hair who paraded about the field like a matador might command the middle of the bullring. Hartley had a whistle instead of a red cape and he was the antithesis of Jack Gibson. 'Just don't talk to him—at all,' Jack told Beetson before that game. 'I don't want you to query his decisions. When he's putting you down, he'll be hurting that you don't question his decisions and just walk away.'

Jack boiled over at Hartley's control of the match, even though Easts won. When it was suggested to him that he was going to be cited again he detonated in the press.

'Cite me? For what, the silly looking things? What have I said that they could cite me for?' he told *The Australian*.

I'm not a ratbag. I've got a referee's ticket and I know what I saw. I criticise my own blokes for breaking the rules. And in the first place I wasn't criticising refereeing, I was criticising one referee who had an outstandingly bad display. I've been watching the video of the game since 2pm. We were penalised eight times in a row.

In the end, Jack did not front the league, although he had offered to march into Phillip Street with the same damning video evidence he and Massey were looking at every Monday morning. He was prepared to go through it, minute by minute, mistake by mistake. As for the notion of him being 'gagged' from criticising referees, he wasn't wavering. 'I'll keep on saying what I have been saying if I think it's necessary,' he said.

Big Jack … If you didn't know any better, you'd think he took pleasure in the pantomime of it all. There was certainly more to it than taking the Establishment head-on. If anything, it showed the players that the coach was prepared to go to war for them and at the same time put pressure on the referees and the league's officials to give his side a fair go. Years later, it became the oldest trick in the book.

It wasn't just league referees Jack rumbled with that season. His devotion to American football and its philosophies still rankled with other coaches. He was changing the vernacular of the game. Players no longer crossed the line for a try, they 'crossed the stripe'. Players no longer dropped the ball, they 'coughed it up'. If the Roosters had prevented their opposition from scoring it was considered a 'shutout'. To the outsider, it sounded like they were speaking another language.

There was some nagging doubt within the Roosters' ranks about the US influence, although they were rarely aired too loudly. At training he'd trial a play where centre Mark Harris, who had dabbled in gridiron, gripped the ball in one of his huge hands and threw a long spiral passes across the field like he was a quarterback. Sometimes, Jack would ask Johnny Peard to consider drop-punting the ball across the field instead of sending it along the back line. 'This is ridiculous,' Peard confided to centre John Brass one night. 'This'll never work.' But they kept toying with it—if only because of their faith in the coach.

That was the season when Peard was refining his kicking game into a dangerous weapon. Jack had identified among his mound of statistics that more points seemed to be scored from kicks than before. He'd brought in Peter Phipps, a kicking coach from Aussie Rules, to work with him on how to drop-punt the ball. Peard would spend hours in the local park alone, practising his high kicks to the point where he *knew* where they would fall. The more his kicks confused opposition fullbacks and wingers, the more the Roosters won. The Bomb had arrived.

The Bomb confounded teams, but it was the Wall that angered them. Looking like a move copied straight out of an NFL team's playbook, the Wall involved a line of players standing shoulder to shoulder from a tap restart with decoy runners charging from different directions. First, the press called it the Screen. Then it was the Wedge. Then it was the Wall.

Call it what you will, but rival coaches and players were convinced it was illegal. Under the rules of the game, defending players cannot be obstructed by other players from tackling the man with the ball. In one match against Wests at the Sportsground, four Easts players formed a wall from a tap restart, with Beetson charging through an opening. Referee Kevin Roberts allowed the play to continue, but when Easts scored later in the set the Magpies players were furious. 'It isn't a decoy but a deliberate obstruction and the sooner it's stopped the better it will be for the game,' Wests coach Don Parish said afterwards.

Jack kept quiet on the subject. More pantomime. But Beetson launched a passionate defence. 'The incident causing some people not familiar with the rules to howl concerns a type of shield we erect when the tap is taken. I am not going to reveal any details of our moves. But I can assure you we are not obstructing tackles.' The closer the finals neared, the more referees cracked down on the practice.

Once again, Jack didn't care about the criticism. He knew he didn't need the Wall to crack defences. The players just needed to be unleashed. With six rounds remaining, the restrictions he'd applied since round three—the last time they had sat in a losing dressing-room—were suddenly released for the match against St George. 'Righto,' Jack told them just before the game. 'I'm taking the clamps off you now. You've done enough.' The payoff: his side won 41–7. Saints' defenders struggled to bring down Mark Harris that afternoon, but it was Beetson who turned in the game of the season thus far.

The captain and his side were the freight train of the competition. Their golden stretch had thrown up the inevitable question: who would stop them? Jack had been around football long enough to know they could stop themselves.

He remained unrepentant about not retaliating to any foul play. Grant Hedger was an honest prop who was getting the job done up front. He'd watched the grand final from the SCG hill the previous year, cheering on Mark Harris. Now he was in their front row.

Easts were playing at Penrith one afternoon when Terry Geary landed a flock of uppercuts on Hedger's chin. Hedger obeyed Jack's instruction: he didn't retaliate. Later in the match, though,

Geary wanted another piece of him but his punch missed and inadvertently landed on Bunny Reilly. 'Shit, sorry Bunny,' Geary said. 'I meant to hit the other guy.' That was enough for Grant Hedger, and he started to defend his own honour.

In the rooms afterwards, Jack gave Hedger a fearful dressing-down before Beetson interjected and explained what had happened. Jack calmed down. 'You ever done any boxing, kid?' he asked Hedger. 'No, Jack.' 'Didn't think so.'

Jack knew of the quality within his side and would never take away from their skills. Russell Fairfax was in his second year of top-grade rugby league, but could never recall the coach trying to tell him how to attack. There were specific words about defence, but he never blunted the brilliance in his players. What Jack would do was to curb a toxic attitude as soon as he smelled one.

Confidence was coursing through the club. 'We know we are the best side in the competition but we know we still have to produce on grand final day,' Beetson had boldly declared mid-season. 'I honestly think without boasting that Easts could beat England.'

On a wet and miserable afternoon at the Sportsground during their unbeaten run, his side had struggled and trailed at half-time when they came into the sheds and slumped into their seats. They wouldn't be there for long.

Jack was never keen on half-time speeches, but on this day he was so furious he could barely talk. He paced around the room, sucking back on a Craven A and the smoke from it filled the gloomy room. He finally walked up to one player, looked him in the eye and beyond, and then moved on without uttering a word. He looked the next player in the eye and beyond, said nothing, and then moved on … When he'd stared down every one of them, he finally had his say. 'You've got no right sitting here in this dressing-room. Get your arses back out there.' His players waited in the driving rain for their opponents to come out for the second half.

To know Jack was filthy meant more than a thousand words, and slightly more than his intimidating stare. 'I can't tell you the match,' says Massey. 'But I know they won the game.'

As it turned out, they won nineteen matches in a row that season. No side in the history of the Sydney premiership had done that before. The game had never seen a coach like Jack before.

●

Russell Fairfax pulled his red-white-and-blue sock down to his boot and the blood spurted out and hit him the face. He was lying in agony in the middle of Leichhardt Oval during a midweek Amco Cup match against Auckland. Mark Harris had fallen on him among the tangle of arms and legs in a tackle and his ankle had snapped. The bone had severed his artery and now the blood was spitting out like an erupting volcano.

After he was stretchered to the rooms, the long-time Roosters doctor Bill Buckingham was there to greet him. Bill stood over the fullback with one eye opened, ash falling from the cigarette in his mouth as he stitched up the wound without any anaesthetic. Fairfax's season, with the finals so close, was over and it was the cruellest blow. When Jack visited him in hospital, he took one look at the food on his bedside table and shook his head. From then on, Fairfax would call the kitchen at Easts Leagues Club and they would bring him whatever he wanted for each meal of the day.

'I reckon I could still play first grade as Easts' fullback,' declared Clive Churchill, the great South Sydney fullback from the 1950s. 'The Roosters are so strong up front it doesn't really matter who plays there.' Jack did have someone. He had a kid called Ian Schubert.

The Shoe was one of those rare finds and it was Jack who found him. He was from Comboyne, a speck of a town near Jack's farm around Wauchope, and Jack had seen enough of him playing for the local side to know he might have been eighteen but had the physique and skills of a player well beyond those years. He had played in the back row for Australian Schoolboys on their 1973 tour of England before Jack convinced him to come to Sydney, but he'd excelled on the wing for most of that season. Jack had staked his reputation on bringing this kid down from the bush and Schubert had not let him down. After playing some minor trial matches for Easts, he'd told the coach he was going back home. Jack picked him in first grade.

'Jack's a persuasive talker,' Schubert told *Rugby League Week*. 'He's a man who can make you feel very good about how you went—or very bad.' He was often confused with Fairfax because of his long blond hair, and when Fairfax went down, Schubert slotted seamlessly into his jumper.

In the lead-up to the major semi-final against St George, Schubert had feared he would be bombarded with kicks from the great Graeme Langlands. He was right: St George won 8–5, thanks to an unsettling kicking game form Changa as well as Billy Smith. It was the Roosters' first loss in five months, and suddenly they were confronted with the sobering reality of needing to beat Manly to cash in on everything they had achieved throughout the year.

That's when Jack threw another of those selection curveballs. Centre John Brass had come down with bronchitis and was ruled out early in the week. Jack had spotted his replacement not in reserve grade, and not in thirds. He had kept his eye on the lanky flame-haired twenty-year-old running around for Bondi Royals in the final of the Easts' A-Grade competition. He liked what he saw. Reg Clough was in.

Clough broke down with an ankle injury against Manly, but the damage had already been inflicted. Easts won 28–13 —Beetson had been, like he was in all headline matches, unstoppable—to reach the grand final. But there was a fresh injury crisis in the centres that Jack had to deal with. He'd been named Coach of the Year that week, but he was more concerned about the fact that Mark Harris had suffered a broken leg in the second half.

Constable John Rheinberger was a twenty-year-old policeman who had excelled at all sports but had played mostly in the under-23s that season. He had played the final fourteen minutes of that final against the Sea Eagles and Jack had—again—liked what he saw. He considered him no gamble. 'He can do the job we want,' Jack said. The philosophy of training all three grades at the one time had been a blessing. 'We're like one big happy family,' Rheinberger said.

Before the grand final, the family sat down in the rooms at the Sportsground and put on an American football documentary. It wasn't *Second Effort*. Those messages from Lombardi had become entrenched in the Gibson way of coaching already. Instead, he showed a film about NFL defending champions the Cleveland Browns and how the San Francisco 49ers aspired to replace them as the best team in the US. The Roosters were the Browns. The Dragons were the 49ers. The film's name: *Mayhem on a Sunday Afternoon*.

The mayhem came in the grand final. It is a match remembered for the death threat directed at John Brass before the game, forcing the team photo to be taken inside the dressing-room.

It is remembered by Bunny Reilly as the match Jack put him on the bench even though he had a leg injury that effectively meant he couldn't walk. Jack still brought him on with minutes to play so he was a part of the win. It is remembered by some for the white boots worn by Graeme Langlands and the pain-killing injection in Changa's leg that had missed the mark and made him almost completely useless on the field. It is remembered by some for the performance of Johnny Mayes and Ian Schubert and the 38–0 scoreline at the end of it—the largest winning margin in the game's history until then.

And now here they were, sardined into the SCG rooms again. Same place as last year. Same result. Beetson asked for some quiet because he had something to say about the coach.

Jack and Arthur: they had become so tight. Their bond had grown tighter before that season had even started. Jack had convinced the captain to come with him on a fifteen-day study tour—just the two of them—that led them to Wigan in the north of England in an attempt to sign Great Britain forward John Gray, who had discovered the round-the-corner style of kicking. Wigan had asked for $40 000 for a transfer deal. 'No deal,' Jack bluntly told the club's full board.

It didn't matter. The rest of the tour had been a hoot. They went to the States, taking in Dallas and Miami and of course a trip to San Francisco to watch the 49ers. Beetson shook his head in disbelief at the money dripping from the over-muscled Afro-American players wearing top hats and 4-inch heels and some of them carrying canes. One night, they ran into Dick Butkus, one of the NFL's great linebackers, and Jack told him that Beetson was a pimp. He sat back and chuckled as desperate man after desperate man approached Beetson, asking: 'Hey man, where are all the broads?' Now they had combined, coach and captain, to win the Eastern Suburbs Rugby League Football Club back-to-back premierships.

Yet Beetson would never allow himself to take the credit for the grandeur of what had just happened at Easts. He knew the score. Jack had come home in 1967 when Easts were broken and started piecing them together again. He'd returned to deliver them not just one title but consecutive titles. Now everyone involved at the club from where the sun rises stood here, beneath the roof that he had provided, in the house that Jack had built.

As Beetson said within the hallowed walls of the SCG dressing-room that Saturday afternoon in 1975: 'Jack. You're a coach, a father and a brother rolled into one.'

15   THE SUPERCOACH

You knew when Big Jack had entered The Big House. The standing ovation gave it away.

The guards would turn the key, the gate would click open, and the Easts players would wait for Jack to lead them in. 'Hello, Mr Gibson,' the screws would utter quietly. 'What's doin', kid?' he'd say as he passed by.

His Roosters had become celebrities by 1976 and not even the sandstone walls of Long Bay Jail could block out that fact. And while the prisoners would ask Big Artie and Monkey and Bunny about their deeds on the field, it was the coach who attracted most of their worship. When he entered the assembly hall, it only took one of them to spy him, declare 'Jack's here' and everyone would stop dead in their tracks. Even the muscle boys would stop punching out the curls and bench presses, drop the heavy weights to the floor. Then they'd clap as one.

The Big House made the players squeamish. The prisoners would wolf-whistle at Russell Fairfax and say unspeakable things. He didn't like The Big House. Not one bit. But Jack felt at ease with these people. He was never one of them, had never walked in their shoes, but his colourful history of two-up rings and bookmaking meant he was familiar with those who had walked a fine line with the law and fallen the wrong way. He was tolerant of those who had made a mistake. He never judged them. What mattered is that they learnt from it. Consequently, he never felt a need to watch his back in The Big House, or for someone to watch it for him.

The jail visits had started two years earlier in 1974, when Lionel Potter was halfway through a stretch of seven years and two weeks for a crime he does not want to talk about. A crime a young bloke might commit because he is a young bloke. He was sitting in Parramatta Jail, wondering how he would reach freedom on the last day of 1976 without the boredom sending him mad. Through the newspapers allowed into the jail, and the black-and-white television the screws would set up in the exercise yard every Sunday, he had learnt to appreciate teams on the watch of Jack Gibson.

Potter was on the jail's sports committee and wrote a letter to the supercoach asking for the world: for the Easts players and coaching staff to conduct a training session on the tiny field they had in the exercise yard. 'It would break up the monotony of life,' says Potter now. One Sunday morning a few weeks after Potter had sent the letter, Jack and his assistant Stan Bottles arrived with the inflatable tyre tubes.

Before leaving, Jack had made a vow to Potter: while he couldn't bring the side in during the season, he'd do so when the next pre-season arrived. When the warmer months finally came, Potter was dubious about whether Gibson would honour the agreement, so he asked one of the prison officers to call the club. 'I gave my word,' Jack said. 'So I'm comin'.' That pre-season, Jack turned up with his side as promised.

The newspapers would lap up these stories, but there were countless times when the press never knew. By the mid-70s, John Quayle was playing at Parramatta, but he was still an Easts man in so many respects. He was second in charge to Ron Jones at the leagues club. 'We're goin' to see a mate of mine at Long Bay,' Jack would say to Quayle. 'Doin' it a bit tough.' Jack would never reveal what his mate was in for. 'You can come with me.' If Quayle couldn't make it, the coach would ask which of his players working at the leagues club could go. 'Who can you give me?' Usually, it was the purchasing officer, Arthur.

Quayle would meet Jack and Arthur afterwards at the Regent Hotel in Kingsford, or the Charing Cross Hotel in Waverley, and it would be miracle if they weren't playing cards when he arrived. Jack loved cards. He loved playing it with Beetson. *Against* Beetson. They would play an old Jewish card game called Clobyosh, which could best be described as a mix of gin rummy and euchre. The captain and coach would play it for hours, long into the night. Sometimes they'd ask Quayle to unlock the boardroom at the leagues club and they'd keep playing and playing and playing before Quayle grew tired of watching and went home to bed.

If it wasn't cards, it was golf. Jack loved golf. He loved playing it with Beetson. *Against* Beetson. The longer he played down the big fairway of life, the more golf he played. He'd become a scratch golfer by the '70s. He putted with a two-iron and believed it gave him more control, but his bread-and-butter shot was the driver off the tee. One year, when he was a member of City Tattersall's, he was the longest driver at the club. Yet nothing seemed to matter if he hadn't won against Beetson. If he'd lost after eighteen holes, they'd play another eighteen, just so he could beat him.

About the only time they weren't niggling at each other, when they weren't challenging each other in some way, was each Anzac Day when they were handed control of the two-up ring at the leagues club. Jack had some idea about that business, of course. One year, word went around that Kerry Packer was about to arrive and get involved. When the news found its way to the ring, Jack's eyebrows lifted, then he looked at Beetson. 'Time to pack this up.'

●

'Take Michelangelo. He took a lump of rock, chipped away the rubbish and came up with a masterpiece. Now, as coach, I like to see a player in action before trying to chip away his errors.'

Jack was in Brisbane, speaking at a Northern Suburbs Devils lunch to a room of Queenslanders, and the comparison with the sixteenth-century artist was apt, for Jack was rugby league's renaissance man. He was the coach of the year for 1975. He was the supercoach and his status extended beyond his own code. He was invited to a net session at the SCG for the ailing New South Wales cricket team, bowled as quick as he could at its best players for over an hour, and then took aim at their attitude. 'There was a complete lack of respect for one another and their own ability,' he said.

Supercoach. He hated the word. He never said it publicly but would ask the two reporters he trusted most—Ernie Christensen and Peter Frilingos—not to use the term. 'But that's what you are, Jack,' Frilingos would tell him.

Jack had not stopped looking for an edge. Within weeks of

winning the 1975 premiership, he and the rest of the team were flying to the US for a two-week study trip and of course they gravitated to Dick Nolan and the 49ers. Once again, it was the *size* of their footballers that intrigued the coaching staff, and in particular Mick Souter. Since the 1960s, most professional NFL clubs had used the Nautilus system: revolutionary power training machines perfect for high-intensity weight programs. Souter had been intrigued about it since travelling to the US with Jack in 1972. By coincidence, fitness instructor Tony Markham had set up a carpeted gym in Bondi Junction with six Nautilus machines and before the '76 season every Roosters player was given a three-month program.

Like Michelangelo chipping away at a block of marble, Jack and Souter wanted each of his players to be statues of David. 'We will be stronger,' Jack promised. 'There is pressure in staying ahead of everyone, but that's the best way to perform.' Stronger perhaps, but not necessarily better. When the Roosters floundered in the early months of the season, for the first time in a long time a question was posed: had Jack got it wrong?

The blame was laid squarely at the feet of the Nautilus system. Critics outside the club reckoned it was too much for part-time professional players to bear on the body. Jack never cared what others thought. But it was the doubts of his men that stung.

There had been quiet dissension for weeks. When Ian Schubert —whose body had ballooned with the extra work—was quoted in the newspapers claiming Nautilus had slowed his pace by as much as *10 metres*, Jack was furious. The coach eventually convened a 90-minute meeting to discuss the situation. The solution was that his players now had the choice of using the Nautilus machines or not. The payback was that he replaced Schubert during a midweek Amco Cup match against North Sydney.

'When a player suddenly loses all speed overnight, what can you expect?' Jack said.

The remark smacked of sarcasm; it was not like Jack at all. He'd believed wholeheartedly that the Nautilus system would make them a redoubtable unit late in the season—when it mattered, as it always did. Yet there had been talk of a player revolt, and tension began to bubble. He couldn't settle on a team and he grew impatient. In an early match against Balmain, he dumped Test hooker Elwyn Walters and brought in his gun for hire, Bunny Reilly. When they lost, Jack said afterwards: 'I apparently made a mistake on the hooking spot.' Only Beetson, Ron Coote, Kevin Stevens, John Brass and Bunny Reilly survived an introduction to the reserve-grade coach that season.

The weaknesses in his side ensured that Jack dug in further against officialdom. Against Manly one afternoon, Coote suffered a suspected broken arm and there were immediate fears that the career of one of the all-time great players was over. Meanwhile, in the same match, Beetson suffered a suspected broken cheekbone. After that match, Jack seemed less concerned about injuries and more about the double-movement call from referee Gary Cook on Reilly that cost the game. 'I might as well turn it up,' Jack steamed. 'This is on every week and we have lost a try in a particularly close game.'

•

Amid the clamour of criticism, the rumours started, grew legs, began to walk. Had Jack Gibson lost his desire?

'No coach in Sydney is putting more into his team than Gibson,' Ron Jones publicly declared in an attempt to bury the speculation. 'I have spent a lot of time with him in recent months and you would be amazed at the number of hours he's devoting to the team. In his three years with Easts I haven't seen him as determined. Don't you worry: Easts will be king-pin again this year and it will be thanks to Jack Gibson. It will be Easts first and daylight next.'

It sounded like a politician's speech and it was. Jack had not lost his passion for the game, the club, and certainly not his players. He was still their coach, brother and father. That would never change. But a devastating truth lay just beneath the surface and only a few knew about it. The players had a suspicion all was not right on the homefront for Jack, but he was never the type to divulge such things and they were too respectful and too petrified of him to ever ask.

Luke was Jack and Judy's eldest son. He was a pleasant, smiling kid, but by the time he was fourteen his behaviour had become erratic. He took Jack's big four-wheel drive for a joyride, crashed it and seemed angry, rather than remorseful, about the entire episode. 'You'll have to pay for that,' Jack told his son. Jack arranged for Luke to mow lawns and clean up properties to earn the cash. It was a life lesson.

They took him to a counsellor and the verdict was that the boy just needed some love. Jack and Judy couldn't understand that. Yes, Jack had been a father to his players—but it had never stopped him from being a father to his six children. He might've been busy coaching, and with his SP business, but he was no stranger at Cowra Place. He was the king of the castle there.

His three sons—Luke, Matt and John—would spend hours fishing off his boat on Port Hacking or watching from the rocks as Jack spear-fished. All of his children relished the water like their dad. While Jack's players knew of his understated sense of humour, the kids knew it better. He was strict with them, but they knew he was no tyrant. How could they think so when he would take them up to a busy road, place a wallet with a piece of fishing line attached to it and then sit off in the bushes, yanking it away from any motorist who pulled up and tried to take it?

What he never joked about was his family's protection. One time, a nudist sunbather laid out a towel on the beach right in front of the Gibson home and began soaking up the rays. 'What do you think you're doing?' Jack asked. 'Sunbathing.' 'Not here you're not. Get your clothes and piss off.' 'But there's nothing wrong with the human body.' 'There will be with yours after you've had a size 12 foot up your arse.'

'I don't feel I have any resentment that Jack wasn't putting in enough time,' Judy recalls.

Then, one morning, Luke was gone. Judy's night-time ritual had been to check on her children before she went to bed, but around that time she was doing a spirituality course and had forgotten to pop her head in before going to bed. It was only when Luke hadn't surfaced with the rest of his brothers and sisters in the morning that she realised he had vanished.

She frantically phoned around the neighbourhood—nothing. She went to his school and asked the headmaster if there'd been any problems—not a thing. He had disappeared and they had no clue where he'd gone. 'And after that he was gone for a month,' says Judy. 'It was a nightmare.'

A lead eventually emerged. A friend of the family had heard Luke talking about travelling to Coolangatta near the Queensland border. Jack caught the next plane there, went straight to the police station and explained the situation. They took down his phone number and said they'd be in touch. That was never going to be enough for Jack.

Every Wednesday morning, having trained the Easts players

the night before, he would catch a plane to the Gold Coast, hire a car and hunt the streets in search of his son. He'd fly back late Thursday afternoon for training that night, stay until after the game and then fly back again. For the next month, that was his life: nurturing the family of his football club while desperately trying to keep together the family that mattered the most.

Only a handful of people knew of the burden, because the Gibsons had wanted it that way. 'We didn't want it known because we wanted to protect the rest of our family,' Judy says. 'Both of us were absolutely struggling. There was nothing. Who he spoke to about it I have no idea.'

The breakthrough came when the police phoned to tell him a boy matching Luke's description had come into the station— although he had made no sense. 'I think I've got a lead for you,' the officer told him. 'I'm sure it's your boy who came in here. He was with someone who'd said he'd shot his father. He had another kid with him and I think it was your boy.' Jack and the officer drove to the address the boys had provided. Luke was there, squatting with complete strangers.

Jack and Luke flew back to Sydney that night. Standing at the foot of the escalator of the domestic terminal at the airport in Sydney, Judy watched them descending towards her, and when Luke's face came into sharper focus she knew.

'He's not the same,' she said to herself. 'He's gone. That's not Luke.'

●

Life went on for the Gibsons, and so did the footy. Jack settled on a line-up and Easts eventually snuck into the top four, and many put their late-season burst down to the weights system they had been using.

'Anyone for Nautilus?' Ron Coote wrote in *Rugby League Week*. It didn't stop Canterbury from barrelling them out of the premiership race in the opening weekend of the finals. Jack sat on the bench for that match and caught everyone's eye wearing an orange kangaroo fur coat for the first time. For five minutes after the siren he stared blankly at the turf in front of him through his horn-rimmed glasses.

A fortnight later, he told Ron Jones he was standing down and recommended Beetson be appointed as captain-coach. At the time, the players figured Jack's departure came down to nothing more than the fact that he never stayed at a club for too long. Only now, when you reveal to some of the old Roosters about the cross he had to bear in silence that season, do they understand why.

16 'I'M AN SP BOOKMAKER'

THE STEPS OF St Mary's Cathedral were flooded in dozens of wreaths the day they farewelled The Boss. More than a thousand mourners crammed the church, the throng spilling outside onto the steps and beyond, and later a procession of cars stretching a kilometre long clogged the Harbour Bridge as the hearse carrying Joe Taylor's 68-year-old body made its way to the crematorium on the north side of the city.

The biggest wreath was formed in a horseshoe, almost 2 metres high, and in the middle Joe's name was outlined with red roses. There was a card attached ... *Dearly loved and never forgotten. Rest in Peace, Joe.—Thommo's.*

Jack had stood that day in August 1976 alongside the underworld figures and distinguished politicians, the colourful racing identities and show business starlets and Sinatra wannabes. They had all known The Boss. He had shaped all of them in some way. But it was Jack who had the deeper connection. It was

Jack who had lost a father figure. Because meeting Joe Taylor had changed everything.

Jack hadn't acquired Joe's legendary disregard for money, although he wasn't troubled about handing it over. A year after the funeral, he collared Terry Fearnley and dragged him to the Forbes Club. That dark side of the city's underbelly wasn't Fearnley's scene. He felt edgy doing something that wasn't legit. Not Jack. He seemed as comfortable in those surroundings as his own living room. 'We've got no money,' Jack mumbled after a bad run on the roulette table. He was given instant and unlimited credit and it took him only a handful of games to be holding a fistful of dollars. As they left later that night, Jack divided up the winnings and discreetly handed it all over to the men at the door. He'd walked, and stood, in their shoes.

His attitude to gambling was just another one of those Gibson contradictions that others viewed as hypocrisy. He never trusted a gambler, even if he'd always been one, even if he profited from gamblers through his SP bookmaking business. 'Never trust a man who bets,' he would instruct his mates. During those days beneath the swinging light bulbs at Thommo's, he'd seen the decline first hand. A young upstart would strut in wearing a tailored suit, but within a matter of weeks he'd be looking a shade scruffy. He was on the slide. A few weeks later, that bloke in the tailored suit would be standing at the back of the crowd in a place known as the 'loose box'. That's where the broke punters stood. They were *loose*. 'When it gets to that stage, people will pawn anything,' Jack once said. 'And they don't care who they bite.'

Jack knew these types. He'd been around them before. He'd been one himself, to some degree. Those trips to the pawnbrokers were a distant memory now but he'd never forgotten them. 'Yeah,

I was a gambler,' he wrote years later. 'I gambled a lot. But I hated losing, probably more than I liked winning, and that was my saviour.'

That indescribable spasm of euphoria that comes when you find a winner: it never left him. During the 1970s and beyond, it was nothing for him to charter a Cessna and fly anywhere along the east coast midweek so he could drop into a country racetrack if he *knew* there was a good thing worth backing. While he was instantly identifiable—he was Jack Gibson, for crying out loud—the coterie of golfing buddies and other associates that accompanied him were not. They laid the bets. They led the plunge. Before they got off the plane, Jack handed them massive chunks of cash, which they'd judiciously lay with the rails bookmakers in the betting ring. When he was older, Jack's son Matt would watch it all first hand. 'You thought money was grown on trees,' he says. 'There was that much going around.'

If not on trees, in the surf. On most Sunday mornings, Jack would meet his regular circle of mates at the Cronulla Surf Club. That's where he settled up from the weekend's betting. Those who owed him from the previous day's racing would hand him the cash, and he'd tuck the wads into his swimming bathers. The only problem with that system arose when Jack forgot about it when he went for a swim, and the $20 and $50 paper notes would wash up onto the sand.

How vast was Jack Gibson's bookmaking operation? Not as big as the legend would have it. Not the biggest in the city, as some claimed. But big enough. In the 1970s, bookies like Jackie Lind, 'Melbourne' Mick Bartley and Nick Bodkin were the biggest fish in Sydney when it came to SP wagering. Jack could be best described as a bookie operating on the second tier below those men, with a phone operation hauling in the bets or men working for him out of various pubs around the city and in the far reaches of the state. It is said that his network extended as far as pubs in the Riverina.

From the start to the end of his time as a bookmaker, Jack's greatest clients were Bob and Jack Ingham. Like their business and their horse and trotting investments, Bob and Jack split their punting right down the middle: Jack on the gallops, Bob on the trots. When he was taking bets for the Inghams, Jack was wading into the grey area of being a commission agent. The commission agent would farm the bet around with other bookmakers and take his 5 per cent commission. Or he would take the bet himself. A mark of all three men is that the arrangement never stopped them from being mates.

While this dark side of the Gibson legend was illegal, he was never ashamed of it. That's how Sydney rolled back then. A few years earlier, in 1972, he'd been sitting alone at the end of the horseshoe bar at the Innes Tavern in Port Macquarie, sipping a schooner of Toohey's Old. Jack was living at his property at Beechwood, and Peter Kogoy was a young league reporter for the *Port Macquarie News*. When Kogoy spotted Gibson, it was an opportunity to strike up a conversation with a living legend. 'What do you do these days?' Kogoy asked innocently. 'I'm an SP bookmaker,' Jack replied. His business outside of footy was rarely spoken about among his coaching staff and players, but it was never hidden.

It was around 1977 when George Freeman, the organised crime figure, began to earn wide notoriety. A Crime Intelligence Unit report tabled in New South Wales State Parliament in March that year had named him as one of the city's biggest SP bookmakers. Yes, Jack knew him. They would regularly 'lay off' with one another. ('Laying off' is where a bookmaker bets with another bookmaker in an effort to reduce his liability to other punters.) One afternoon, Freeman came knocking at the door at Cowra Place. 'Can you take these to St Vincent's for me?' he asked Jack, handing him a big bag of clothes he wanted donated to charity. Freeman was noted for his acute fashion sense, especially white jackets. 'Jack didn't know why he just didn't want to do it himself,' recalls Judy Gibson. 'They were just acquaintances. I just think there was an understood respect between them. Jack treated people as he found them. He didn't go into their area. He didn't cross the line.'

Freeman was no pussycat. The CIU report alleged that Freeman had connections to US organised crime bosses and operated no fewer than twenty illegal betting outlets. Freeman claimed he was nothing more than a commission agent, just as Jack had been for the Inghams.

While Freeman attracted so much heat from the law, Jack escaped such scrutiny. By the early 1980s, with the State Government's TAB battling the illegal SP trade for business, the party was coming to a close. Superintendent Merv Beck was appointed head of a new Special Gaming Squad and, acting like Sydney's version of Elliott Ness, he cut a swathe through the SP network and illegal casinos that had been the lifeblood of the city since the end of World War II. Usually that swathe was cut with a sledgehammer crashing through a front door.

Jack never got the sledgehammer treatment, but Harry Eden did. He was one of the fittest men Jack had coached when he was in control of St George, and had worked as a bookie and collected money for Jack for a time. Beck's Raiders, as they came to be known, crashed through Eden's door one morning. 'Thank Christ for that,' exclaimed Harry, opening what was left of the door. 'I thought it was Superman.'

Why Jack had never received such scrutiny from the law is anyone's guess. What Judy Gibson knows is that it would never have mattered if Beck's Raiders had come tapping on her door at Cowra Place. 'If the police had come here asking what he was doing, I couldn't tell them anything,' she says. 'Because he never let me know.'

●

In 1977, Kevin Humphreys was into his fourth year as boss of the league. He was also a man in deep trouble. 'He's got so much shit in his boots it's not funny,' Jack often said whenever his name was raised.

Humphreys was a Balmain Tiger to the core. He'd played in the front row for them. He'd been their secretary, and his skills as a persuasive orator had come to the fore every Monday night at the New South Wales Leagues Club when he stared down the formidable league boss Bill Buckley and took him on. Humphreys sounded like a politician, although everyone was convinced that he would one day warm Buckley's chair. In 1973, he became chairman of the Australian Rugby League.

Kevin Humphreys was also a man who had no control over that indescribable spasm of euphoria that came when he found a winner. He was a mate of several SP bookmakers, including and especially George Freeman. Jack had known that Humphreys was in trouble midway through 1976 when the phone rang at Cowra Place and Humphreys was on the other end. Jack could hear it in his voice. He needed money to pay back Balmain Leagues Club, from which he had taken money to cover his own gambling debts. 'He was a man in trouble,' Jack recalled of that conversation years later.

When Humphreys and Jack met, the supercoach told the

chairman precisely why he was lending his support. Not because he particularly liked him. Certainly not because he felt sympathy for him. It had nothing to do with his SP business, either, because Humphreys had never wagered with him.

'I'm not giving you this money,' Jack said. 'I'm *lending* you this money for the game of rugby league. And I'm *lending* you this money on one condition: that you never bet again.' Humphreys agreed. Jack pulled out his chequebook and signed away $34 000 in his slow, elegant, loping hand. He did not reveal to Humphreys that he'd borrowed money himself to cover the loan.

Come the August of 1977, the shit in Humphrey's boots hit the proverbial fan. He fronted the New South Wales Central Court of Petty Sessions and it was alleged that between November 1974 and January 1977 the boss of the game had helped himself to no less than $52 219 from Balmain Leagues Club, of which he was secretary-manager. Jack Arthur Gibson appeared before the court and testified that he had lent Humphreys $34 000. Manly powerbroker and New South Wales Rugby League director Ken Arthurson had given him $5000. Jack had told the court that he would not have helped Humphreys had he 'not known what a man of integrity Humphreys was'. Humphreys was cleared on 12 August of any indictable offence.

Jack was livid that he had been dragged into the entire episode. But that wasn't the main issue. A man's word had been broken. It had taken three months for the $34 000 he had lent to Humphreys to find its way back to him—but it took Humphreys less than a day to break his word. Jack's network didn't miss a beat. The night after meeting Jack at Cowra Place and making his solemn oath, Humphreys was beneath the swinging light bulbs at Thommo's. Come Saturday, he was at Randwick, standing in the betting ring.

•

The Jet Set Lounge, high in the grandstand at Henson Park, was pumping. Waiters in black ties poured champagne for the beautiful people, for the politicians, for television executives. Colourful advertising man John Singleton was the life of the party. He always was. Jack was less animated. He always was. He was more interested in watching his prized recruit out there on the field.

Jack had been responsible for one of the biggest coups in league history: signing Oakland Raiders running back Manfred Moore. Jack had spotted him while in San Francisco, and had acted as an unofficial agent in procuring him on loan from the NFL franchise. Moore had played in the Super Bowl that year, but many league experts scoffed about whether the experiment would work. 'He hasn't come here for his health,' Jack snorted at Sydney Airport when he walked through Customs with the star footballer, who was snapped with Jack's sons Matt and John. That's why Jack merely smiled watching from the back of the Jet Set Lounge when Moore leapt high and scored a try just twenty minutes into his debut match. Four matches later, he received a head knock and he returned to the US.

A year away from club football was never enough to keep Jack far from the game. Apart from talent scouting for Newtown, he had been keen to coach New South Wales in its interstate series against Queensland. He had also declared an interest in coaching Australia in the 1977 World Cup that year. In the end, he was overlooked for both jobs. When Terry Fearnley was announced as New South Wales coach, and Jack accepted a one-off job coaching Queensland Country, it sparked rumours about a falling-out with his former assistant coach and long-time friend.

Of course, Jack was never afraid to disagree with a friend. But there was no falling-out this time. He took the extraordinary step of releasing an open letter for Bill Mordey to publish in *The Mirror.* 'There is no feud between Terry Fearnley and myself,' Jack declared. He had applied for the New South Wales job the day before applications closed. It had annoyed some of the suits at board level that he had dallied for so long. He was beaten in the vote 20–18.

There had certainly been animosity between the two the year before. Jack wasn't angry with Fearnley for leaving his coaching staff and taking over at Parramatta. The desire to coach had been sparked in Fearnley during that watershed trip to the US in 1971, which had been sparked by that watershed moment when they watched *Second Effort* together. But when Fearnley had signed Johnny Peard from the Roosters, there had been acrimony.

'So you've gone to Parramatta for the big paper bag of money, eh?' Jack had said to Peard. It wounded Peard. It wounded Fearnley. The simple fact was that Jack had not offered the 30-year-old Peard, who had suffered a knee injury and concussion while playing for Australia, a contract.

Senator Ron McAuliffe, the chairman of the Queensland Rugby League, had gone after Jack to coach Country against Brisbane and had got his man. A few weeks before the annual match, Jack and Ron Massey had flown to Rockhampton to watch a trial between Northern and Southern zones.

Massey and Jack were separated for the match, with Massey finding the last seat in the press box. Throughout the match he heard two men near him making their feelings about certain players known. 'Poor old Platzy,' they said in reference to back-rower Greg Platz. 'He can't play.' Massey thought they must've been watching a different game. Platz—who went on to represent Australia the next year—was the best player on the field, he thought. Sitting elsewhere in the crowd, Jack was thinking along the same lines. After full-time, McAuliffe approached Jack. The two men Massey had seen were with the Senator. They were selectors. 'Jack, do you want to sit in on our selection meeting,' McAuliffe asked him. 'No. I'll let you people decide,' Jack replied.

As they walked away, Massey relayed what he'd heard during the game. That was enough for Jack. He raced after McAuliffe and handed him a piece of paper. 'I'm not telling you how to pick your team,' Jack said. 'But if those six blokes on that piece of paper aren't in the team, you can find a new coach tomorrow.'

Jack's side was considered no chance of beating City, who were coached by legendary Queenslander Barry Muir. Jack didn't care. 'They smell okay to me,' he said at a reception days before the game. The *smell* of footballers. He loved saying that. It was a typically unique way of saying he liked being around them. That he understood them. Shortly afterwards, he tapped his players on the shoulder to get back to their South Brisbane hotel to watch a series of gridiron films he had brought with him.

'We've got five days to blow up the bridge,' he told them. 'That's the time we got, so that's the time we use.' It was never going to be easy. Souter had taken time off to help train the side, and put them through his seven-lap time trial at Lang Park to assess their level of fitness. Only three players finished it.

Then Souter hauled out the inflatable tyres and they started working on their tackles. One of the Lang Park groundsmen pulled Massey aside and asked if he could speak to a gentleman who had been watching from the stands. 'That is the first time I have seen someone *teach* defence,' the man told Massey. 'I want to congratulate you and your coaching staff for doing it.' The man was Duncan Thompson, who had been a legendary halfback in the 1920s before becoming one of the state's most respected coaches.

Jack was leaving nothing to chance, either. 'You'd be surprised what we know about them,' Jack said, sounding like M from a James Bond movie when fronting the press. 'We know a lot more about these players than they think we do.'

Jack was talking up a game that he knew he could not win. Country lost 41–12. Jack never coached them again and confided in those around him that representative football wasn't for him. It made sense. It was hard enough to blow up the bridge in five days, let alone make them better men.

17   SACKED

HERE HE WAS, back between the dank walls at Henson Park again. These suburban grounds had become his weekend church. This time, he was sitting next to Bob McCarthy at half-time. 'You can split them in eight minutes, Macca. Just concentrate on making a bust.'

He'd been around footballers long enough to know when their bodies were running on empty, almost down to the minute. McCarthy was an ageing giant of the game. He'd returned home to the Rabbitohs that season after two years with the Canterbury Bulldogs. On this miserable March afternoon, in the 1978 Craven Mild Cup final against his former side, he was lacking condition and carrying a rib injury. He couldn't make it through the second half. Jack knew it. Knew what he was going through because he'd been there himself. Eight minutes.

Shortly after the resumption of play, McCarthy charged onto a short ball from Darryl Bampton. *Kaboom!* That was the bust.

Then came McCarthy's pass to John Berne. He scored and Souths led 5–3. They won 10–3. Jack had miscalculated: it took five minutes, not eight.

George Piggins—the Rabbitohs' redoubtable hooker—walked from the bog of Henson Park and punched one fist into the air and held the pre-season cup in the other. Like McCarthy, Piggins was nearing the end of his career. He'd broken Jack's heart in 1971 when he commanded the scrum for Souths in their grand final win over St George, but those glory days were long gone. Souths had won just three matches last season and trundled in stone-cold last. But this win at Henson suddenly provided hope that the so-called Pride of the League could rise again.

Jack's very presence had done that. Usually those Souths types viewed anyone from Easts with deep suspicion, but Jack Gibson was seen as a club on his own. That he had decided to coach Souths and nobody else was a stunning show of faith. He'd done some work with them the previous year at the request of coach John O'Neill, a club legend, but Jack had also fielded offers from Penrith, Canterbury and North Sydney for big money. Much more money than Souths could afford.

Jack was never about the money, of course. That came from other sources. He often reckoned that coaching cost him cash anyway, so it wasn't going to decide where he landed. Coaching Souths brought a significant challenge. Besides, those other big-spending clubs had voted against him in the ballot for the New South Wales job the previous year. Jack hadn't forgotten it.

Before one of their pre-season matches against Easts, Jack had set up a video in the sheds and pressed play just minutes before kick-off. It was the closing stages of the 1971 grand final. McCarthy went plunging over for the final try, and their theme song echoed around the SCG as they completed a lap of honour of the SCG. *Glory Glory to South Sydney*. 'That's what it's all about,' Jack said softly, even if watching it again wrenched at his own heart.

The beast started to stir. At a luncheon at Souths Leagues Club before the season kicked off, Jack commanded the microphone for 45 minutes. 'Gentlemen,' he said, poker-faced, 'we are going to win some football games this year.' The room roared.

Yet it was across Chalmers Street at Redfern Oval where Jack held the most important pre-season gathering. In normal circumstances, he might hold a black-tie event with all the players and their partners at his home in Cowra Place. Surely the auditorium at the leagues club would be more comfortable. Instead, he squashed them into the home dressing-room and it was so tight that it was impossible for every person in the room to not know one another by the end of the evening. Which, of course, had been Jack's intention in the first place.

Watching from the sidelines that season, snug in his now-trademark kangaroo fur coat during the winter months, Jack again proved to himself the value of motivation and self-belief. Those two meant as much as talent. On Tuesday nights, he'd usher his players into the leagues club and they'd watch old reels of NFL matches. Or a compilation of American football's greatest tackles. Or *The Longest Yard*, the hit movie from 1974 featuring Burt Reynolds in which a team of prison inmates takes on a team of prison guards.

Souths ducked in and out of the top five all season, and Redfern Oval swelled with optimism. They were exceeding all expectations, and the proof was right there in the *Big League* match-day program. There was no constellation of stars in this side. Hard-running winger Terry Fahey was an Australian representative and their best player.

It was men like Paul Sait who embodied the revolution. He was a fading star nearing the end of his career, but the news Jack was coming had prompted him to rip 6 kilograms off his body in pre-season training. He could've become a slob trudging around reserve grade but come mid-season he was making bolshie predictions: 'We can win the grand final this year.'

George Piggins, the captain, was another who had enjoyed the arrival of the new coach. He'd warmed to Jack instantly. As Piggins once said of their rapport: 'Jack liked my head—and I liked his.' Both hard men, both devout followers of the game, both unlikely to suffer a fool gladly. While Jack was still drinking scotch over ice and middies of Toohey's Old, he admired the resolve of men like Piggins who abstained from alcohol. It showed their dedication to the jumper.

Midway through that season, Piggins was at training one night, casually talking to his teammates, when he took a step back and felt the cartilage in his knee give way. It required surgery and he was sidelined for most of the season. When he made an inglorious return in reserve grade against Wests, he was benched before full-time. That trampled the enormous pride within a man like George Piggins.

At the leagues club later that night, he fronted Jack. 'If I'm going to get pulled off in second-grade games, tell me,' he demanded. 'I'll retire.' 'This isn't the place to talk,' Jack replied. 'Jack, if I don't talk about it, I'm not going to sleep,' Piggins shot back.

The matter was dropped, but when the pair met the next day it flared up again. 'I never slept last night over your comment,' Jack said. 'I'd rather you not sleep than me, Jack,' said Piggins. Silence. The coach then said he'd made a decision. Good. Piggins said he'd live with it either way. That weekend, Piggins was named first-grade hooker and captain and he finished the season there.

A month out from the finals, the dream of Souths at least playing some post-season football was very real. Then they fumbled their way out of the premiership race. When Parramatta did a 50–10 demolition on them in the second-last round it was over. Because Jack had dragged them beyond anyone's expectations, though, nobody considered their season a failure.

A few weeks later, Jack approached Piggins to talk about his future. 'You've got one more season left in you,' he told him. Piggins' knee throbbed at the mere suggestion. 'Jack,' Piggins said, 'I couldn't play if Jesus Christ asked me.'

So revered had he become around Redfern, Jack must have fought the temptation to say he just had.

●

It only took a year for the divine intervention of Jack Gibson to turn cold. Not among the players. Not among the fans. The committee. A familiar theme.

So here Jack was, thumping on the front door and when George Piggins opened it three words came out that he'd never said before and would never say again: 'I've been sacked.'

'Yes, I know,' Piggins said. 'What d'you mean you know?' Jack asked. 'Who's got the job?'

Piggins delivered the news: Bill Anderson, the reserves coach, had been appointed to the top job. Brian Smith, the reserve-grade halfback and captain, had been appointed his assistant. Ron Massey was also there that morning at Piggins' home in South Coogee. He was incredulous at the suggestion. 'You shouldn't go around saying things like that,' Massey said.

Surely not. Surely not Bill Anderson. Jack had taken him from teaching at Gymea High School and given him the under-23s at Easts. Then he gave him the reserve-grade gig at Souths. Like all of his lower-grade coaches, Anderson was a fundamental part of the Gibson machine. And now Anderson had apparently knifed him. Surely not. Surely not Bill Anderson.

Jack and Massey thumped on Piggins' front door the next morning. 'You're right,' Jack said. 'The bastards.'

Piggins had for months sensed a plot to bring down the super-coach. Because he hadn't declared he was a Gibson ally, he'd heard the whispers around the club. First grade had gone backwards by the end of the season, finishing in ninth position. But the lower grades had made the finals, and Jack knew that was a sign that this was a club on the rise, such was his holistic approach. He just needed time.

A year or two earlier, Jack had watched *The Club*, a satirical play by playwright David Williamson that exposed the cut-throat nature of running an Aussie Rules club and the falling-out between president and coach. Now life was imitating art. Jack had told president Norm 'Nipper' Nilson to leave the dressing-rooms during a match one afternoon, as he had at other clubs. Ron Massey was watching that day and believed he was blackballed there and then.

The relationship between Jack and the Souths board had started to tear during the 1978 finals series, even though the Bunnies were playing no part. That month, a dark cloud formed over the game and referee Greg Hartley was in the eye of it. Terry Fearnley had left Jack at Easts to take on the first-grade job at Parramatta, and he was steaming after losing a minor semi-final replay to Manly and pointed the finger squarely at Hartley's mistakes after the winning try had come on the seventh tackle. When Wests lost the final to Manly after Hartley had awarded another try off a seventh tackle, then another off a suspected forward pass, coach Roy Masters did the same. Jack's criticism the year before had already helped convince Richie Humphries to retire from refereeing.

Never one to back away from a streetfight with officialdom, Jack felt it necessary to take a strong stand—and they don't come any stronger. 'I don't want the man refereeing my team and I'm sure plenty of other coaches feel the same,' he said of Hartley. 'And I'd expect the backing of the committee.'

When the 1979 season started, the referees' appointments panel wisely kept Hartley away from Souths and Wests matches, but what concerned Jack was that his own board hadn't been prepared to back his stance. When Ernie Christensen from *The Sun* phoned him for comment in late February, Jack delivered an ultimatum: 'Souths' committee have to decide whether I am more important to them than Greg Hartley. It appears there are a lot of frightened people in the club.'

But his falling-out with Souths went deeper. When their heads hit the pillow at night, South Sydney fans and officials alike would slip into grand dreams about the glory days. They believed Jack could return them to the time when the leather was speared out along the back line with Clive Churchill chiming in from fullback and then dishing off to winger Johnny Graves to score another glorious South Sydney try in the corner. 'But the traditional South Sydney style of football seems to have vanished forever under the coaching of Jack Gibson,' former Souths centre Bernie Purcell wrote.

Jack had little time for romanticism. He was about winning football games, and his philosophy on that score never wavered: he'd do it in field goals if he had to, if the roster he had dictated as such. He'd signed a young raw-boned kid from Roma in Queensland, and when Charlie Frith hit Bill Cloughessy so hard it put the Wests prop in hospital, that signalled the coach's intentions. A few rounds into the premiership, back-page headlines in *The Sun* screamed of Jack's desire to turn his forwards into 'hit men' with a legal yet lethal head-on tackle where defenders launched their shoulder at the chest of ball-carriers. 'I don't use cheap shot players because there's no place for them in our game,' he said in response. 'And there's no place for cheap shot reporting.'

Then Bob McCarthy took a few cheap shots of his own. McCarthy had retired with a crook shoulder the previous season after just five matches, but in an interview with *The Mirror's* Jack Darmody—a hard-drinking, hard-talking legend of the newspaper industry—he proffered new reasons. 'There were club parties I wasn't invited to,' McCarthy revealed. 'I wasn't even told they were on. It wasn't hard to feel that some people didn't want me around.' It wasn't a direct attack on Gibson, but given how the coach seemed to organise every social event it may as well have been.

Then McCarthy waded into an area where few souls had been brave to go before: he questioned the supercoach's wisdom.

He wouldn't use me properly. I like to move the ball around and open up the play, but he was intent on a close tackling defence. I can tackle as well as anyone but I believed that the job is to break through and attack. At Souths, they were so intent on defence that players were being queried and criticised about their tackle count at halftime. There was no encouragement to move the ball and the style of play is the same this season.

Clearly, that admiration from the previous season had vanished. Darmody gave Jack his right of reply, and it was laced with subtle sarcasm: 'Everyone wants to score but the tackle load has to be shared equally. When Bob was coaching for Souths [in 1975] he did not score a try in five games and during that period they had 158 points scored to their 42.'

During his two seasons at Redfern, Jack was convinced that they did not have the back line to play attacking football. They had the hard-running Terry Fahey—'The Redfern Express'—out wide, but it was the tiny matter of getting the ball to him that was a concern for the coaching staff. 'We didn't have the players to play the sort of football they wanted,' recalls Massey. 'Billy Anderson told them he would get Souths playing the way the committee wanted them to play.'

At training on Tuesday night after his dismissal, Jack assembled the three grades in a room at Souths Leagues Club. He told club secretary Terry Parker he wanted him in the room. He should hear this. 'I want to make it clear that I am not getting out by way of resignation,' he told them. 'I was stone cold sacked.' It emerged the next day that Jack had asked for pay rises for his staff—including Bill Anderson—plus a confirmed agreement he would coach for the next two seasons. He had not asked for more money for himself. He also rejected the Souths board's desire to abandon his policy of not using a full selection committee. 'It's a great pity,' Jack said. 'I believe Souths have the most disciplined outfit I have been associated with.'

That week, there was a knock on the front door at Cowra Place and Judy Gibson opened it to find a distraught Bill Anderson. Jack had had deep concerns about the young coach's personal welfare, and confided to others at the club that he feared Anderson could've done something to himself. Anderson might not have campaigned for Jack's job, but he didn't tell him that the Souths board had approached him about it. 'In hindsight, it would've been sensible to speak to him about it,' Anderson says with regret now. 'When they wanted to replace an icon of the game with a 32-year-old untried coach like myself I should have asked more questions. But I wouldn't contend that I undermined Jack.'

'He undermined Jack,' says Massey. Whatever view Jack took on that, he believed a man's life was bigger than footy. So he drove Anderson to South Coogee and thumped on George Piggins' front door one last time. 'Billy wants to see you,' Jack said. 'He wants to apologise.' 'He's got nothin' to apologise to me for, Jack,' said Piggins. 'He's done it to you.' Jack pulled Piggins aside and said: 'Go easy. He's not holding up that well. He's having a nervous breakdown.'

Decades after the fact, Souths president Norm Nilson doesn't recall being ordered from a dressing-room or any dispute over pay, even though the club was not flush with funds in those times. 'There were a few members of the board who didn't like him. Jack had to be the boss.' No surprise there: a power struggle between Jack and the sausage-roll eaters over the running of the football team. He'd fought that battle before. In deference to Jack, Piggins ran for president at the next football club elections but narrowly lost the vote to Nilson. 'But I never went into Billy Anderson's dressing-room,' Piggins says firmly.

The Souths players were mystified and angry about the coach's sacking. A farewell party was hastily arranged at the Maroubra Seals, the sports club across the road from the famous stretch of beach in Sydney's south, and they approached him one by one to pump his hand and thank him. As the beers went down, Lionel Potter sidled up to him at the bar and picked his brain on all matters football.

Potter had finished his time at Parramatta Jail. Now he was a part of the furniture as a trainer at Souths. Jack had given him a chance in life, although Potter was needling him with a question he had always skirted: who was his favourite player? They were all equal in his eyes. But Potter was relentless and wanted to know. 'Bunny,' Jack said, 'was the toughest.' Bunny Reilly: his gun for hire.

What surprised the players most that evening was the respect Jack afforded Bill Anderson and Brian Smith. He wished them no ill will, even if his estimation of both men had plummeted and would never be the same again. Because Jack also never forgot. A few seasons later, when he'd moved on and Anderson had left coaching to work as a sideline commentator for Network Ten, they would still talk and even share the occasional beer.

But the first time Anderson approached him and thrust a microphone under his nose, Jack casually brushed it aside. 'Your time's not up yet, son.'

18   FIRED WITH ENTHUSIASM

'YOU'RE GONNA WIN. You *have* to win, mate.' The rangy eighteen-year-old kid is squinting into the midday sun. This is not a training session, for there is no team for Jack to coach right now. The teenager is battling heroin addiction, and the supercoach sees the filthy drug as tougher opposition than anything he might coach against on a rugby league field.

He'd bought the two-storey house in Gunyah Street, just off Nicholson Parade in Cronulla, three years earlier and loaned it to the We Help Ourselves (WHOS) organisation. Drugs frightened Jack when nothing else really did. He was now 48, and he'd spent so much of his adult life building up young men. Drugs were tearing them down. He became involved because he had seen children of friends destroyed by this growing menace.

Then drugs hit much closer to home. Judy was in the bedroom when the phone rang. It was Luke, who was now eighteen. 'Mum, I'm at the police station,' he said. 'They've arrested me for drugs.'

Judy collapsed on the bed. 'What do you mean you've been arrested for drugs?' Jack and Judy had suspected he was smoking marijuana. Jack had come in to the kitchen one day and grumbled: 'Someone's pinching this hose. It's getting shorter.' Susan, Tracey and Joanne were of an age to inform him someone was using the hose to make a bong to smoke cannabis.

Jack and Judy were naive about drug use, and when Luke fronted court and it was revealed he had been injecting heroin, the *St George and Sutherland Shire Leader*—the local newspaper— splashed it across their front page. Jack handled the situation just as he had done when Luke had gone missing four years earlier. 'Quietly,' recalls Judy. 'Always quietly.'

From the moment he had filled his black Pontiac with flowers to the windows and picked up his wife to be, Jack had made those closest to him feel secure. His status as the best football coach in the game never went unnoticed when he was in public with them. 'Good on you, Jack,' a punter would call out, but rarely did they hassle him for his time. Yet at home he was an ordinary father and husband.

He was still a man of few words, but there was always an underlying sense of humour about his manner. And he was always there for Judy and his children. They knew that. They would holiday down south at Mollymook or up north at Greenmount on the Gold Coast. The three boys would watch their old man trim hedges and rake up leaves and then set it all alight, much to the chagrin of the neighbours and the fire brigade. He was the larger than life character of their household, just as he was out there in the community, or on the rugby league scene.

And Jack missed nothing. He would open everyone's mail, and one day intercepted a letter from a friend of a friend of Joanne's who had been sent to jail for armed robbery. Jack wrote him back: 'This is Joanne's father. Don't ever contact her or any member of my family again. I know plenty of people in that jail at the moment and they are busting to do me a favour. Don't make me call one in.'

Somehow, though, Luke slipped through the net and fell into the mire of heroin; it wounded Jack deeply. Luke's behaviour became increasingly unpredictable after he had faced court. He could be obsessed with cleanliness, hanging his clothes on the clothesline before hosing them down, maddening Judy. Sometimes she would sit and patiently listen as he talked for hours about heaven and earth and sin. 'And I used to think that was my role,' she says. 'To listen to all that.'

Meanwhile, a year away from coaching hadn't diminished Jack's standing and influence. When he signed on as *The Daily Mirror's* new rugby league columnist, posters outside newsagents declared it as the 'SPORTING SCOOP OF THE YEAR'. Jack never typed out his own columns. While he would often wake up at 3 a.m. and trudge out of bed to write down the random thought that had woken him, he would use Peter Frilingos to ghost write his words.

Over time Frilingos—known universally as 'Chippy'—had replaced Ernie Christensen as the leading rugby league reporter of the day. Jack had known Frilingos for years. He trusted him. And Frilingos had known of the Gibson legend better than most, having been exposed to Sydney's underbelly while on police rounds as a young reporter. With the shackles of officialdom released, Jack would intone his thoughts down the line, and he never missed his mark. The byline accompanying his photo read: 'Jack Gibson: the man they can't gag.'

His first column was an evocative open letter to Jim Comans, the new chairman of the judiciary, asking for him to 'hit the hoodlums' running wild on the weekend. 'The greatest game of all should only be administered by the greatest administrators of all,' he wrote. He took aim at St George and their coach Harry Bath for his side's roughhouse tactics. 'Harry Bath, can you see the light at the end of the tunnel? Just make sure there's not a train coming at you.'

So much for a year off. On 14 April, at the Crest Hotel in Kings Cross, more than 100 players met for the first meeting of the players' association. Jack was voted as president unopposed, and his chief concern was the taxation structure that slugged footballers heavily.

Even when they weren't coaching, Jack and Mass were never far from one another. They had no team to dote on but instead ran a book on the rugby league season. Kerry Packer laid the biggest bet with them, naming three teams to finish the season as minor premiers, but come mid-season it was apparent the biggest whale of them all had done his cash. As Massey confided years later: 'It was a bookmaker's dream. We couldn't lose.'

In terms of all the other bets taken, their best result was Eastern Suburbs to win the title under coach Bob Fulton. Massey was already helping another former Easts player, Ron Coote, who was coach of the struggling reserve-grade side. Each week, Massey would trawl through video footage at Coote's Maroubra home.

Nobody in the game commanded the play-pause-rewind of the video like Massey. His ability to read and assess and identify the Roosters' strengths and weaknesses had been fundamental to their premiership success. When Fulton learnt about Massey doing video for Coote, he asked if he could do it for him, too.

Because Easts loomed as the best result, Massey obliged. Then Jack found out about it. He'd read about it in a newspaper column written by Arthur Beetson, who'd spotted Massey and

Fulton sharing a lift at Easts Leagues Club. 'Why are you helping Easts?' Jack asked Massey. 'Easts is our best result,' Massey replied. 'It helps us.'

Jack respected Fulton as a coach, but he was angry that no Easts players had been allowed to attend the players' association meeting at the Crest Hotel. So Jack laid a massive bet on Canterbury to win the title and suddenly Massey's perspective on helping Easts swung. 'What are you going to do now?' Jack said. 'I won't be helping Easts,' Massey laughed.

●

Ron McAuliffe had unlocked the idea—now he had to find the right men to follow it through. The Queensland senator had flagged the audacious notion of a State of Origin series for 1980, and New South Wales Rugby League boss Kevin Humphreys had agreed to it.

McAuliffe had convinced himself that the very future of the game in Queensland depended on the state side beating New South Wales at Lang Park in this solitary match. Jack had coached the Queensland Country side in 1977, so McAuliffe picked up the phone and asked for advice. 'I need fellows who you'd want in the trenches with you when the going gets tough,' McAuliffe said.

Jack knew of such a man. He was 35 and in the twilight of his career. He was carrying too many kilos, had lost the captaincy at Parramatta and was fighting to keep his position in first grade. Arthur Beetson was perfect. 'If you get a commitment from him he'll give you the greatest game of his life,' Jack told the Senator.

Beetson was named captain, and when he trotted out onto the turf the cathedral of Queensland rugby league bubbled and frothed before erupting with approval. Before, Jack would never have approved of a bloodied Beetson throwing wild punches at anything in a sky blue jumper, but he did this time. He understood the passion. Beetson turned in the game of his life, as Jack promised. The legend of State of Origin football had been born.

Jack was in the stands that night of 8 July and he relished the ferocity of it all. What he didn't approve of was dour English referee Billy Thompson, who allowed the game to degenerate into a slugfest. Thompson had been imported because he had no affiliation to either side. 'I thought they were all supposed to be impartial,' Jack mumbled.

By now, the tentacles of Gibson's influence were reaching far and wide. He was a man without equal in the coaching ranks of rugby league, even when he didn't have a job. Elsewhere he was seen in the same light as Rale Rasic, the giant of soccer who had led the Socceroos to their first appearance in the World Cup finals in 1974, and Ron Barassi, the pre-eminent coach in Australian Rules who had won premierships with Carlton and North Melbourne.

Yet even Barassi would confide to others about Jack's influence. It had been the rugby league coach who had been at the vanguard of telling club officials that a football team was best left in the hands of the man who lives or dies on the result. The coach. Until then, coaches had been second-class citizens. Jack had elevated their status above and beyond the best player in the side.

During a trip to Melbourne in 1976, Jack was invited into the dressing-rooms at the Richmond Football Club at the invitation of coach Tom Hafey, who had done to the Tigers in the late 1960s what Jack had done to Easts at the same time. One of the key men in Hafey's side was Kevin Sheedy, a theatrical little back-pocket who had designs on coaching after he retired. In 1980, he was an assistant coach at Richmond but was examining every detail of the coaching science in microscopic detail. When Sheedy was appointed coach of Essendon for the 1981 VFL season, one of the first men he called was Jack Gibson. He remembered the rugby league coach, whose demeanour had reminded him of Detective Columbo, in the Punt Road dressing-room that day.

Jack was never forthcoming in handing over his secrets and philosophies, even if he had liberally lifted them from other sources himself. Yet he could see Sheedy's approach for what it was: a young coach yearning for knowledge. He liked that. He'd been like that himself and was still looking for that edge. When Sheedy and his wife Geraldine flew to Sydney, and then caught the train to Cronulla, Jack spent the entire day with him and not just two hours as arranged. 'There was a touch of genius about him,' Sheedy recalls. 'And he trusted that what he told me wouldn't be shared with anyone else—just my players.'

It wasn't just young coaches wanting Jack's ear. Inevitably, he was courted by Sydney clubs and regularly linked to them. 'They want to hire my ability but not my personality,' he told friends, and if they didn't know any better they would've thought he enjoyed all the interest. At Redfern Oval, a civil war was brewing: a group of players wanted Jack parachuted into the place to replace Bill Anderson. In the first week of the finals, *Rugby League Week* boss Geoff Prenter was so confident that Jack was heading to Cronulla that he declared it. On the front-page. He was wrong.

The idea of Parramatta joining the race for Jack Gibson started with Ray Sheargold, the secretary-manager of the Parramatta Leagues Club. The Eels had never won a premiership since entering the competition in 1947, but it had been right ... *there*. They had lost grand finals in 1976 and 1977—the last one in a replay against St George.

Then came the dark days of losing those finals matches with Greg Hartley in the middle. By 1980, they were under Jack's former playmaker at the Roosters, Johnny Peard, and there were fears that a grand final win just wasn't in the woodwork of the club. Parramatta was a sleeping giant. They just needed the right man to wake him up.

Denis Fitzgerald, by his own admission years later, had 'serious apprehensions' when Sheargold raised the idea of Jack Gibson. He was wary of the baggage: the run-ins with officials; his failures at Souths; the way he had left Redfern. If only he'd known that down Cronulla way Gibson and Massey admired Fitzgerald, who had been a tall and lean prop for the Eels but was now the fresh-faced 30-year-old boss of the club. They admired how he stood up and fought the administration at the New South Wales Rugby League's fortnightly meetings at Phillip Street. He would be outvoted 40–2 on any issue. They liked that.

Sheargold and Fitzgerald went to visit Jack at Cowra Place, and when they left both parties knew where this was heading. Soon after, they agreed to terms, and those terms specifically meant Jack had complete autonomy over the football club. No selectors. As Jack often joked: 'Selectors? That's what Americans call the gears on their car.' It had taken fifteen seasons, but he finally had absolute control of his football team.

Jack also had another triumph. Before he had revolutionised the role of the rugby league coach, before he had brought a sense of Lombardi to it all, the coach not only lacked the status he deserved but the pay he deserved. His belief was that the first-grade coach should receive the same amount as the highest-paid player in the club. He didn't need the cash. It was a matter of principle. For the 1981 season, the highest-paid players at the Eels were lock Ray Price and centre Mick Cronin, who were set to receive about $30 000 each. When Fitzgerald told Jack he would be earning that too, the coach signed for two years.

Peter Frilingos broke the story on the front page of *The Mirror* on the afternoon of 12 September. 'GIBSON TO COACH PARRA' screeched the headline, which devoured the entire page. The city hummed all day about the news. Later in the week, Jack joked in his weekly column about the 86-kilometre round trip between his home and Cumberland Oval, the Eels' home ground. 'I will have my friend Ron Massey riding shotgun—that will be my only insurance against foul-ups.' Then he added this: 'I haven't spoken to any players who I consider would be an asset to Parramatta—but I will be. So for the time being I will leave any future players with this quote that coach Lombardi has been given credit for: "If you aren't fired with enthusiasm, you'll be fired with enthusiasm."'

The day after Frilingos broke the story, Jack was at the SCG to watch Canterbury play Easts in the major semi-final. The winner would go straight through to the grand final. After the Bulldogs won 13–7, Jack found his way into their rooms and plonked down next to second-row forward Graeme Hughes.

'Can you win it?' Jack asked him. 'Yeah, Jack,' Hughes said softly. 'I think we can.' Jack slowly rose from the bench, walked to the middle of the room and took a breath so deep his nostrils flared. 'Yep,' he said. 'Smells like a premiership to me.' He then left the room.

A fortnight later, Jack was watching from the Members' Bar as the same teams played out the grand final. Canterbury led 12–4 with five minutes remaining. Jack had tipped them in his column in *The Mirror*. Then Bulldogs fullback Greg Brentnall raced down field and put up a speculative kick, and winger Steve Gearin reached out, latched on to it and scored a miracle try. Jack wasn't so fussed about the try as the result. He and Massey had won their cash.

Hours after full-time, Mick Cronin was in the Members' Bar sharing a beer with John Lang, who had played hooker for Easts that afternoon. Cronin, the Parramatta and Australian centre, first met Jack in 1974 when they shared a game of golf with Arthur Beetson, Bob Fulton and Ron Coote at The Australian. He was impressed with the big gold Cadillac Jack had arrived in, and intrigued as the supercoach struggled around the greens using a two-iron as a putter. 'You don't say much, do you?' Jack said to Cronin that day. He had been thinking the same thing of Jack.

Now they were about to come together as player and coach. Cronin had scar tissue. In 1977, Parramatta had won their first minor premiership and Cronin had won the Rothman's Medal as the game's best player. With three minutes remaining in the grand final against St George, he had generated a try for Ed Sulkowicz that levelled the scores with minutes remaining. He then had a conversion kick from the sideline. It was the most important kick in the club's history and easily his career. He moved in, poked at it with his toe … and missed.

'What do you want out of football,' Jack asked him. Cronin could not have made it any clearer: 'I want to win a premiership.'

Good as gold, thought Jack. 'I think I've found myself a centre.'

During the pre-season, Jack prepared his Parramatta players on his farm at Wauchope. The short-term reward was watermelon. The long-term reward was three premierships. (Jack Gibson collection)

Laying down the law before a pre-season match . . . 'When Jack spoke, you listened,' says Mick Cronin. (Newspix)

In 1981, Jack Gibson went to war with Greg Hartley, Kevin Humphreys and the NSW Rugby League. The tabloids couldn't get enough. (Jack Gibson collection)

Hell-bent on muzzling Jack and Parramatta, the game's officials threatened a record fine. (Jack Gibson collection)

Until Jack came along, Parramatta just wanted to win a premiership.
Then they won three. Here they hold the Winfield Cup after winning the
1983 grand final against Manly. (Jack Gibson collection)

An iconic image of Peter Sterling, Jack and the famous kangaroo fur coat
that weighed as much as the Winfield Cup. (Newspix)

Jack talked as easily to Prime Ministers as the man on the SCG gate. He and Bob Hawke had healthy respect for each other—even if he voted Liberal. (Newspix)

Holding the Winfield Cup with Eels chief executive Denis Fitzgerald, who had initially taken some convincing to sign him as coach. (Jack Gibson collection)

Kevin Humphreys faces a District Court in Sydney on 29 April 1983, to answer fraud charges. 'He's got so much shit in his boots it's not funny,' Jack often said of the former leader of the game. (Newspix)

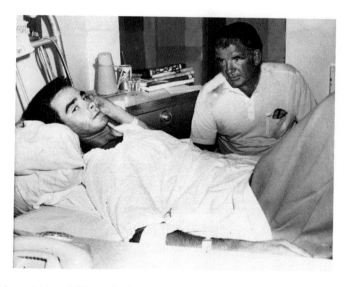

Jack blamed himself for a freak accident in which son Matt had his leg bitten by a horse on the farm at Wauchope. (Newspix)

As much as he tried, the supercoach could not win a breakthrough premiership for Cronulla as he had for Parramatta. (Rugby League Week Magazine)

When Jack walked into the Big House, the inmates would stop and applaud. This image from his private collection was taken at Parramatta Jail. (Jack Gibson collection)

They hated being there but some of the biggest names in sport went with him—because Jack had asked them. (Jack Gibson collection)

Luke Gibson was a beautiful kid torn down by schizophrenia. Jack shaped the lives of generations of young men, and it broke him when he couldn't save the life of his own son. (Jack Gibson collection)

They had lived a public life for years. Three weeks after Luke's death from a drug overdose, Jack and Judy agreed to this photo for *The Mirror*. (Newspix)

Jack thought he held all the aces as NSW coach for the 1989 State of Origin
series. Despite a wealth of baby-faced stars in Bradley Clyde, Laurie Daley,
Mario Fenech and John Cartwright, the Blues lost comprehensively to
Queensland. (Newspix)

Jack Gibson was introduced to a whole new generation of fans as a commentator for Channel Nine. (Jack Gibson collection)

Right to the end, Jack and Ron Massey considered each other family. (Newspix)

Wayne Bennett was given the job as coach of the Broncos on Jack's recommendation. Now, only Bennett has won more premierships. (Newspix)

Running a leg of the torch relay for the Athens Olympics in 2004. It was around then that Judy noticed the start of his decline. (Newspix)

One of the last photos of the supercoach. With Judy and children (from left) John, Joanne, Matt and Sue. (Jack Gibson collection)

The Team of the Century observed a minute's silence after Jack passed away less than two hours before kick-off in the Centenary Test in 2008. 'That's Jack,' Noel Kelly laughed. (Newspix)

Thousands of mourners, from all corners of his life, converged on St Aloysius Church, Cronulla, for Big Jack's funeral on 14 May 2008. (Newspix)

The Roosters players of the day formed a guard of honour as the hearse was driven away. Fittingly, the late coach was wearing a Roosters tracksuit. (Newspix)

19 SEAGULLS

THEY HAD BEEN so close to catching her. They had been on this witch-hunt all year, but somewhere in that first half they had let her slip away.

'There's not much I can do now,' Jack told his boys. None of them raised their heads. 'It's up to you. You've got 40 minutes to do something about this grand final ... and a lifetime to think about the result.' Then he walked out.

The witch was the 1981 premiership.

They'd been thinking about it for a year already, ever since they'd met him for the first time at the leagues club that past November and he'd laid it all out, every detail of what he expected. 'My commitment to you is this. We'll have no selfish players, no players who attend discos on Thursday nights playing for this club. I don't intend to compete with discos or any similar diversions as coach of Parramatta. If you cheat on yourself and your teammates it naturally follows that I'll be next and I won't have that.'

Not one eye moved from him. He sounded like a general marshalling his troops for battle, although he wasn't wearing khakis but a white shirt and fetching chequered pants. 'It's most important that everybody here realises that we are not going to like or agree with each other at all times. But we must all have enough respect in each other to know we'll come up with the right solution. Stay solid and have respect for each other and you will be winners.'

Jack's reputation had waltzed through the door at Parramatta long before he had. Some players were concerned, not least those who often waded into the downstairs bar better known as the Swamp at the leagues club on Thursday nights. Such things didn't concern Mick Cronin, who was still making the 300-kilometre round trip from his home at Gerringong on the South Coast to Parramatta for each training session. But he did pause during that first meeting and thought: 'Well, this is going to be an interesting year.'

Bob O'Reilly had been sitting in one of the bars at the leagues club before that night when he'd felt a tap on his shoulder. It was Jack. Would he play for him next season? The Bear had made his debut in 1967. Now, this ageing Test prop (and bricklayer) had done the medial ligament in his knee with five matches to go in the shadows of the 1980 season; he figured it was all over. In his mind, he'd retired. He'd also heard about Jack's unshakable regime of tackle counts and inner tubes. 'He wasn't the bloke I wanted to be bumping into at my age,' O'Reilly joked. 'It won't be easy,' Jack said to him. 'We'll need to get some of that puddin' off you—but I'll look after you.'

The Bear stayed. So did centre Steve Ella, the Zip Zip man. He had been offered *four times* as much money to sign with Souths under Billy Anderson. He waved it away to stay at Parramatta.

Ron Hilditch, a Kangaroos representative, admitted he was sour when first told he was making a permanent moved to the front row, but he accepted it with time.

They all did. It was only a matter of months into the new year before they discovered, like every other player coached by him, that he cared for them as men as much as footballers. They received his trust if they trusted him. The first step was returning from their six-week off-season fit and ready to play. If a player didn't have the discipline to get himself fit, how could Jack trust him on the field?

Steve Edge knew about Jack already. He'd seen it a decade earlier as a young hooker playing under-23s for St George. Jack was coaching first grade and Edge had marvelled at how there was no distinction between the three grades on grand final day in 1971. Despite losing their matches, Jack brought the two lower grades into the famed SCG dressing-rooms before the firsts played their decider against Souths. There was no class divide in football, just as there was none in life, as far as Jack could see. Edge always remembered that grand final day, not for the losses but for the respect shown by the coach.

The little hooker had shocked the game when he'd left the Dragons to play for the Eels in 1980, but he simply saw it as moving from one Sydney powerhouse to another. Soon after arriving at Parramatta, Jack made his players do the same aptitude test that had delivered Arthur Beetson the captaincy at the Roosters. This time, the results were fed into a computer somewhere in America and it spat out the name Steve Edge.

Nothing had changed in the Gibson approach. Mass was still by his side. Alf Richards, the best on-field medico in the game, too. Mick Souter had almost rejected the offer to be the strength and conditioning coach because of the commute from Cronulla, but the thought of what was possible drew him back into Gibson's staff, and into the driver's seat of Jack's Cadillac—he would drive while Jack and Mass baited him with their playful sledging, as was their way.

The new addition to the Gibson coaching machine was John Monie. He'd won titles with Woy Woy on the Central Coast. Jack's network had informed him that some of those had been with inferior sides. 'I'm not offering you security,' he told Monie. 'I'm giving you an opportunity to be my reserve-grade coach.'

Monie climbed aboard. Parramatta were ripe for a premiership. They just needed to be led to it.

Raymond Price was the bearded lock-forward, his thatch of scraggly hair pinned back with electrical tape. He would work as a carpenter during the day before dropping his tools and training with the same intensity he displayed on the field. Jack admired that. He also sympathised with those who played *against* Price. 'It's a hard way to make a living,' he said. 'He doesn't know the meaning of the word fear. He doesn't know the meaning of a few other words, too.'

Price formed the cornerstone of a dour forward pack, but it was the back line that oozed glamour. Peter Sterling was the halfback. Blond and wiry, he was an emerging pin-up of the game with a passing, running and kicking game that was just as pretty as he was.

Brett Kenny was the five-eighth. He had vision and rubbery ankles that enabled him to swerve and step like a Ducati rounding a hairpin corner. Should Ella and Cronin make the bust out wide, they had a long-haired winger called Eric Grothe. He had a sidestep: straight ahead. Whether the defender in front of him wanted to stop him was another matter.

Right on queue, the concerns about the defensive coach in Jack Gibson blunting the gorgeous attack on offer at the Eels started to whir. It was a fallacy. He never muzzled attack, despite what the sausage-roll eaters at Souths reckoned. He just believed and maintained that defence was the heart of winning football games. As he would tell them: 'Viv Richards: he can hit a six but still has immaculate defence. Muhammad Ali: He can knock a bloke out, but he is a magnificent defender. You can score all the points you want—but the best defensive side wins.'

But perhaps for the first time Jack realised it took more than that. Instead of running against officialdom, it was best to have them running with you. Denis Fitzgerald had backed him in sacking fullback Garry Dowling and former Test second-rower Lew Platz, and backed him in signing thirty-two-year-old Kevin 'Stumpy' Stevens, who had played in Jack's premiership side at the Roosters in 1975 but was now unwanted and unloved at Bondi.

But how long before the relationship soured and eventually snapped? There is a well-worn line attached to the Gibson legend that premierships were built in the front office. He never believed that, but he'd been at enough clubs to know he needed the Parramatta board fighting with him, not against him, if they were to catch the witch. It was during their darkest period that season that Jack knew they could do it.

After nine rounds they led the competition, but then they lost three games straight. Easts. Manly. Newtown. Three big guns had dragged them down and Jack was subsequently hauled before the board. He didn't appreciate the summons notice. 'Hello, they've got a problem with my coaching methods,' he thought. Instead, all Fitzgerald and his executive wanted to ask was if he wanted more players. They were concerned he didn't have the right ones to win the premiership.

Respect and common ground had been reached between the board and the coach. They were with him, not against him.

But it was the alchemy between player and coach that stirred the atmosphere at Cumberland Oval. The ground had been built in 1847 and if you didn't know any better you would've thought it hadn't been touched since. Plans were afoot to demolish it and build a new multi-purpose stadium. But Jack's presence had brought the weather-beaten old joint to life.

It was his charm. The players' mutual love and respect quickly came to include the coach and his staff. All three grades trained together, just like the Roosters and Souths, and they were split into four teams on Tuesday nights and played off-side touch and volleyball against each other.

What they liked most, though, was how he talked to them. The boy Grothe. The boy Kenny. The boy Sterling. Mick Cronin often thought Jack gave the impression he was thinking of something else. 'Where's the boy with the beard?' Jack would mumble. 'Where is he?' He was looking for Ella but staring at Cronin.

Then Jack would start explaining an intricate play before someone would break his concentration and call him away. 'Where was I again?' he'd say when he returned. 'You better start fresh, Jack, because we're all confused,' Cronin would say. They didn't know whether he was joking, confused or deadly serious. Nobody was game to ask, of course.

And then, sometimes, his message came to them through other means, and it was during these moments that they found them- selves tucked right up in the palm of one of those big hands of his.

Peter Sterling. Sterlo. The little halfback with the blond hair was in rare form, gathering pace as the season rolled along but his kicking game wasn't coming with him. Was it his timing? Was he holding it wrong? Maybe the coach would know. When you have a problem with your game, you speak to the coach. What am I doing wrong, Coach?

'Kick to the seagulls,' Jack mumbled. He walked away. Sterling walked away, scratching his head.

Come Sunday afternoon, the SCG was bathed in sunlight as Parramatta's forwards rattled through their tackles on the first set of the match. Sterling wasn't thinking of what Jack had told him earlier in the week. He was focusing on catching the leather and then kicking it as hard as his right foot would allow.

Sterling is set deep. Steve Edge spears the ball back to him. The ball thuds into the halfback's outstretched hands. He looks up at the open space at the other end of the field and that is when it happens. No angelic choir. No parting of the clouds. No shaft of light beaming down from Heaven. Just a flock of seagulls, picking at the hard turf, deep in opposition territory.

It was an epiphany for Sterling then, and the story became the stuff of rugby league folklore. This was Jack's true Lombardi moment. The Packers' head coach had made famous the term 'run to daylight'. It meant his running backs should look for a hole, any hole, and exploit it. Lombardi named his 1963 memoir after it. It was beautiful because of its simplicity.

Sterling regrets that the story has become so well known. He wished he had kept it locked inside. 'I'm glad people know because it gives them an insight into Jack,' he says now. 'But I never intended it to become a part of the game's folklore. It was an intimate thing. Just Jack and me.'

●

Inside the white-picket fence at Cumberland Oval it was always about Jack and his players. Outside, though, it was Jack versus Greg Hartley. That was the season they went to war with one another and everyone was sucked down the sinkhole.

Jack's distrust of referees hadn't abated since that muddy afternoon on grand final day in 1963 when he'd told Noel Kelly that Darcy Lawler had backed St George. It had been a recurring theme during Jack's time as a coach. Keith Page. Dick Humphries. But now with Hartley—this is when it got serious. 'My other blues with refs have all been one night stands,' Jack said.

By 1981, Hartley's refereeing style bordered on vaudeville, according to his critics. Jack didn't do vaudeville. He was more Robert Mitchum. He abhorred theatrics in his own players. 'Let them know how tough you are,' he would tell them. 'Don't advertise it.' What chance of him copping this malarkey from a referee who berated a big heaving forward while digging an index finger into his chest? Once described in the press as a cross between a ballet dancer and a cop on point duty, Greg Hartley was the antithesis of Jack Gibson.

Hartley's feud with Parramatta, though, had ignited three seasons earlier. As far as anyone associated with the Eels was concerned, that try on the seventh tackle in the 1978 semi-final replay against Manly had cost them the match and possibly their first premiership. So poisonous had the situation become since then, Hartley had been banned from matches at Cumberland Oval because of fears for his safety.

When he fronted at Cumberland for the Eels' Craven Mild Cup match against Manly in mid-March, fans wore T-shirts emblazoned with the words 'I HATE HARTLEY'. The man himself entered the playing arena surrounded by a heavy police escort. The Eels won. The match passed without incident.

It was the final of the pre-season competition, against Easts, when the relationship with Hartley unravelled. Jack and Massey pored over video footage all weekend, picking the eyes out of his handling of the match, which had been won by the Roosters.

Then they fired a letter of complaint to the director of referees, Eric Cox, pointing out fifteen errors Hartley had apparently made. Two of the most contentious concerned errors in the tackle count. After looking at the video tape, Cox replied that as far as he was concerned, there were only two gaffes.

Three weeks later, against Canterbury, Jack was fuming again. 'This club hasn't got the players or the ability to contend with this man,' he told the press. 'And that goes for me too. That was an outstandingly bad refereeing performance. I will protest again if I'm allowed to.' Two days later, Fitzgerald said: 'I won't be standing in his way.'

Something ugly was brewing. You could smell it. Hartley appeared to be itching for a fight. On 9 April he launched an astonishing broadside in a column in *Rugby League Week* at Jack and Wests coach Roy Masters, who had been railing against Hartley with similar verve.

I challenge Jack Gibson and Roy Masters to forget about publicly blasting referees and start talking about the personalities of the game—the players! I don't know what I have done to Gibson or Masters—there has to be a motive behind their constant barrage. I don't tell Jack Gibson how to coach his side and I certainly haven't spoken to players in the manner alleged in some sections of the media.

Jack copped that one. He was the shrewdest manipulator of the press in the business. Hartley worked in the advertising department of *Rugby League Week*'s publishers. When Hartley fronted a meeting of the referees' association, its executive issued him with the same warning it had issued him midway through the previous season: 'Shut up and treat the players properly.'

Soon after, Jack was sitting in his study at Cowra Place, sifting through his mail, when he found a letter that seemed rather formal. It was a letter of demand from Hartley's solicitors seeking to prevent Jack from making further statements about their client. Then Jack picked up the daily newspapers. Hartley had circulated a copy of the letter of demand to them, too. Jack was furious: in three days, the same man would be officiating at Parramatta's match against Cronulla at Endeavour Field.

The weeks and months that followed were a tempest of angry faxes, legal letters and narky headlines between the warring parties. Jack Gibson and Denis Fitzgerald were in one corner; Greg Hartley, referees' boss Eric Cox and New South Wales Rugby League boss Kevin Humphreys were in the other. The more Hartley was appointed to Parramatta matches, the more fuel was poured onto the fire.

Newspapermen and lawyers seemed to be the only ones winning. In an interview with Channel Ten sportscaster Ray Warren, Hartley revealed the personal toll. His son was being harassed at school. 'And I am taking four anti-stress B complex tablets a day,' he reported.

Jack was not budging. 'I'm not apologising for anything. Not now. Not in the future. I stand by what I have said in the past. I intend to continue making fair and correct statements in future. I'm not apologising.' Jack made these comments in *The Sun*, beneath the headline: 'GIBSON: NO APOLOGY ON HARTLEY'.

The letters were so large they could've been read from outer space. War type, as they called it in the newspaper trade. Most stories about Jack and Hartley appeared under war type. This one was typical of Jack's defiance and timing. Parramatta's executive were due to face the New South Wales Rugby League that night and try to explain why the club should not be fined $15 000 for allegedly bringing the game into disrepute.

The simple fact of it was that this crusade went beyond Jack's distrust of referees and Parramatta's long-standing feud with Hartley stemming from the alleged sins of 1978. This was something more than a verbal brawl with a posturing whistleblower. This was about Jack taking on City Hall. The Establishment.

In the early 1980s, rugby league was staggering about like the drunkest man at the party. Crowds were in freefall, and those who did turn up watched matches in decaying grandstands at suburban grounds. Gambling had its nefarious fingerprints all over the code. Rugby league was the city's lifeblood. It meant so much, not least out there in the fibro houses in the western suburbs. Parramatta was its heartbeat. But the game was as crook as Rookwood, the biggest cemetery in town.

Fitzgerald blamed what he called 'The Cartel'. Humphreys, Cox, Manly boss Ken Arthurson and Peter Moore from Canterbury. 'These were the days when a wink was as good as a nod,' Fitzgerald says. 'There was a set against Parramatta, because Jack dared to speak out. He dared to be critical of referees and their appointments. We weren't part of the power group.' Fitzgerald was still being outvoted at fortnightly meetings … 40–2.

Humphreys had been particularly defiant and he eventually hauled Jack before a newly formed disciplinary committee headed by himself. Jack remembered Kevin Humphreys as the desperate voice on the other end of the phone, looking to snip him for $34 000 to cover gambling debts. Now he wanted to sanction him for an issue Jack thought the boss of the game should be handling.

So Jack marched into Phillip Street with his solicitor on one side and his barrister on the other. They were there for a heartbeat. Jack handed Humphreys a letter, and then walked out. The letter explained that Parramatta wasn't accepting the jurisdiction of this newly formed disciplinary committee. Four days later, Humphreys dropped the threat of legal action. 'Damned decent of 'em,' Jack said. Then Parramatta declared they wouldn't breathe another syllable about Greg Hartley or referees again.

Those outside the club smelled a con. There was a belief among rival coaches that this crusade of Gibson's was nothing more than a disingenuous attempt to put pressure on officials. There was certainly a hint of it. At the Roosters, Jack's instruction to Arthur Beetson for matches controlled by Hartley was to ignore him. At the Eels, he wanted Edge, Cronin, Hilditch and O'Reilly to approach the ref at the one time should the situation arise.

Yet outside of matches, the man's name was never spoken. Indeed, the players were usually kept abreast of developments in the ongoing saga of Gibson versus Hartley in the stories that appeared underneath the war type in the daily press. 'Jack took on the fight,' recalls Peter Sterling. 'He took it out of our hands.'

Judy Gibson knew it was no con. She knew better than anyone. Only rarely did Jack bring football into the house, even if the whole family had a passion for rugby league. It was woven into their lives, but it never dominated the conversation. Yet this whole episode involving Hartley was seeing Jack withdraw more and more until one morning husband and wife were in the kitchen at Cowra Place and he spurted it out. 'This is affecting my life,' he said.

At the height of the tempest, a prominent figure not associated with the game, who Judy won't name now, phoned her. 'He's hurting his image,' the caller said. 'I can fix this for him.' No thanks, said Judy. 'The only image he worries about is the one in the mirror.'

•

The drunk two rows back had been driving everyone mad all afternoon with his slurred running commentary. Then the drunk saw what nobody else had. 'That try was off the seventh tackle!' he bellowed. He was sitting two rows back from Jack Gibson, who was sitting in the Members' Stand at the SCG.

The try in question had come with two minutes remaining in the major semi-final against Eastern Suburbs. The Eels had identified early that year that if any side were to win the premiership it would have to beat the Roosters to do so. They had led 8–4 and were just minutes away from a grand final appearance when Easts big man Noel Cleal speared a ball out to centre Ron Giteau on the blindside and he snuck over in the right-hand corner to make it 8-all. That's when the drunk stood to his feet and vented his fury. *'Seventh tackle!'*

Surely not. Not again. Another Hartley final-tackle miscount in a finals match. Jack ordered Mick Souter to run down to the sideline to tell Alf Richards, and he passed the message to Steve Edge. 'Jack wants you to make an official complaint,' Richards said. Jack never sent out messages to his captain. About anything. 'But this wasn't a message,' recalls Edge. 'This was an instruction.' TV replays confirmed later that you should never trust a drunk. The try was on the sixth and last tackle. It was all good.

After the match, Hartley said the protest 'broke my concentration', while the Easts players considered it a shameless attempt to put pressure on the referee in extra time. Mick Cronin had his own pressures to deal with. He was presented with two penalty goals. He'd blown these before, of course. This time he moved in, poked at them with his toe … and landed both. Parra won 12–8.

The Eels were in the grand final; it was the perceived injustice of the Giteau try that had seen them lift themselves in those twenty minutes of added time. Roosters players will still tell you they considered it a shameless ploy from Gibson to gain an advantage. Shortly after the siren, the drunk from two rows back who had got it so wrong but so right approached Cronin. 'You're right, mate,' Jack said. 'You've done your job.'

Then he pulled Cronin aside. 'How'd Hartley take it?' Jack asked him. 'Not good, Jack,' Cronin grinned. That's when Cronin and Edge revealed what had been said out there in the middle. After Edge made his on-field protest, he said Hartley had uttered these words: 'I thought you were a sportsman, but obviously you're not.' As Cronin lined up one of his match-winning attempts at goal, he alleged that Hartley said to him: 'They were smart tactics—but you'll pay.' Pay for what? And when?

Jack's eyes widened. 'Are you prepared to go to the league about this?' he asked them. It was the last thing either of them wanted to do. They could see no good in complaining about the referee who might be in control of the biggest match of their lives. 'Jack, I might never get another chance at this,' Cronin said. 'These young blokes mightn't get another chance at this.' But then he remembered the coach had gone to war all season for him and his players. 'Okay, I'll go down.'

Denis Fitzgerald made Edge and Cronin sign statutory declarations outlining what Hartley had said before firing off an official complaint. When the warring parties arrived at Phillip Street, Hartley was immaculately dressed in a grey suit with a Toohey's Brewery tie. The meeting turned out to be a fizzer, though, because nobody could locate the right video from the match.

The following weekend, the battlers from Newtown snuffed out Easts' premiership chances, and when Hartley was appointed referee for the grand final Jack and Fitzgerald wrestled with the idea of marching up the steps of the Equity Court of New South Wales in a bid to prevent him taking the field. Fitzgerald provided copies of the statutory declarations to the press, but at some point the Eels realised it was time to move on. All three grades were in the grand final. They had a witch to hunt.

●

John Singleton had first seen him in the Forbes Club in the 1960s. In those days, Singleton was making so much money he'd walk into banks, sign blank cheques and walk out with the money he would soon hand to the croupier and never see again. That's when he noticed Jack. 'He looked like a minder, a standover man and a debt collector,' Singleton remembers. 'It shook me up. But I didn't know him until the night of the 1981 grand final.'

By the 1980s, Singleton was the colourful multi-millionaire advertising man who was pumping tens of thousands of dollars into the Newtown Jets. They were his passion. At the start of the season he had wagered $5000 at 50 to 1 on the Jets to win the grand final with bookmaker Terry Page, one of the most feared bagmen of them all. That was a payday of $250 000. When Jack learnt of the bet at the start of grand final week, he made a heavy assumption. 'Jack assumed I'd got to Hartley,' Singleton recalls, suggesting that Jack suspected a bribe had been handed to the referee. It had not, and it has never been suggested that Hartley would have been party to such an arrangement.

Warren Ryan, signed by Singleton to coach Newtown that year, had performed the same sort of miracles that Jack had performed there in 1973 when the club had won its first club championship. It wasn't all miraculous, though—they still had players to fear. Fullback Phil Sigsworth could be lethal. Tom Raudonikis was possibly the toughest halfback the game had seen.

John 'Chicka' Ferguson and Ray Blacklock had the speed and uncanny ability to conjure a try from anything out there on their respective wings. Phil Gould played in the second row but often assumed the role of playmaker.

Come half-time in the grand final, Parramatta led 7–6 but how they were in the lead was anyone's guess. Terry Page was sufficiently concerned to ask Singleton if he wanted to halve the $250 000 bet. No way, said Singo.

That was the time when Jack had walked down from the top tier of the Members' Stand and into the rooms below to deliver his frank half-time oratory. Forty minutes to go. A lifetime to think about the result. He couldn't have made it any clearer.

When Jack left, he left behind a room of broken and bruised bodies. They had all carried injuries into that September and now ligaments and sinews and muscles and bones screamed about the prospect of going back out there. The senior players said a few words but none needed to be spoken.

When Tom Raudonikis scooted over from a scrum two minutes into the second half, there was a deadly silence behind the posts. 'There was no ranting and raving,' remembers Ron Hilditch. 'Just composure.' They knew their time would come, but it wasn't until there were thirteen precious minutes left in the season before it happened. Sterling sniffed the hint of a gap down the right. He zipped to the blindside, passed the ball, but the leather didn't land in the hands of winger Graeme Atkins. It landed in the hands of a forward. His name was Steve Sharp.

Jack had dropped Sharp to the bench for the grand final. He wanted the assassin-like tackling of Stumpy Stevens, who had missed the semi-final against Easts with a chipped bone in his elbow. Sharp was furious and he let it all out in the press; there were claims he wanted to walk out on the club.

When Ray Price had hobbled from the field with a mangled right ankle, Jack had sent down the message to get Sharp out there. Now he had the ball in his hands, scooting down the right touchline. He passed back inside to Sterling, who then passed back to Atkins on the wing. He scored. Cronin had another pressure kick, this time in a grand final, the southerly wind howling from left to right.

He kicked it way out to left, but the wind bent it back and over ... Parramatta: 12. Newtown: 11.

There she was. The witch. They were close.

With five minutes to go, with Parramatta pressing the Newtown line, O'Reilly coughed a ball out the back of the tackle. Replacement Paul Taylor dived on it. It was a 50–50 call. It could've been a knock-on. Hartley gave the Eels another six tackles. The ball sang as it was passed along the back line. Sterling. Cronin. Muggleton. Then Ella, who scored. Cronin poked at the conversion from the same acute angle, the southerly wind howling from left to right. Parramatta: 17. Newtown: 11.

Come here, witch.

In that final minute, Denis Fitzgerald came to the sideline with a magnum of champagne of 1947 vintage—the year Parramatta entered the competition. The Bear had already started wrapping his arms around his teammates. Nobody seemed to be paying attention when Brett Kenny darted down the blind, dummied on the inside and then kept running and running and running to score.

Unbridled joy. Grown men sobbing. 'A special thanks to an absolute genius ... Jack Gibson,' Steve Edge said in the post-match speech. Jack was only just making his way to the playing arena. That's when the coach gave Edge his second instruction of the season. 'Not that way,' he said to Edge. 'You run the victory lap *that* way.' Later in the dressing-room, the jubilation had been replaced by a sense of relief. The Bear cried in the shower. 'I can't get out of my system we haven't got another game next week,' Jack told Peter Frilingos.

In the Members' Bar later, he bumped into John Singleton. It was the first time they had met. 'I'll buy you a beer,' Jack said. Greg Hartley had left by then. He officiated in a smattering of international games after that grand final day, but a hamstring injury forced him to take the following season off. Then he retired. 'But not because of Jack Gibson,' he says now.

A decade later, Hartley ran into Jack in a lift at Lang Park during a State of Origin match. 'Hello, Gregory,' Jack mumbled. They talked briefly that night, but more than they ever had in the past. 'You've had the wood on me for years because of your status in the game,' Hartley said to him. Jack rejected it. 'I'm just a coach, like all the others.'

Says Hartley now: 'I always respected Jack Gibson's ability to coach. I respected him more than any other coach. But he wasn't going to put me out of the game, mate. But I don't think any of those Parramatta players ever forgave me because of Jack's hold on them.'

As the Parramatta team bus slowly made its way up Church Street on that grand final night in 1981, it became apparent what they had done. These streets were clogged with humanity. Very happy humanity. The bus could only drive to within 50 metres of the front steps of the leagues club. As each player and official fell out of the bus, they were lifted across the sea of fans to the entrance.

It took an hour for them to find their way from the front steps, and once inside Ray Warren commanded proceedings. After each of the players said a few words, he called on Big Jack.

The room fell silent. Charles Bukowski, the American poet and novelist, wrote about the ordinary lives of poor people and he once said this: 'Genius might be the ability to say a profound thing in a simple way.'

Jack didn't know any other way. And he knew precisely what needed to be said now. To say what this meant. Because it meant everything. This one was for the lost grand finals. The lost grand final replays. The Bear. The Crow. All of them. The injuries. The last match at Cumberland. The League. Eric Cox. Humphreys. Hartley. They had defied all of that and history and now they had finally done it, so somebody hand the supercoach the bloody microphone now. He's got something to say.

'Ding dong. The witch is dead.'

The joint erupted. Chaos ruled. Meanwhile, next door at Cumberland Oval, the inmates weren't so much running the asylum as tearing it down. 2KY broadcaster Ron Casey had held a grand final party at the old ground during the day, but come nightfall, with the heady and intoxicating mix of KB Gold in their stomachs and a breakthrough grand final in their hearts, the Eels fans proceeded to tear her down.

Fence palings were ripped off and thrown into the air with careless abandon. Signs and seats met similar fates while shower-heads from the dressing-rooms were souvenired. Men climbed and staggered up to the old scoreboard and tried to rip off the clock, while elderly women sat in the grandstand and quietly reflected as the mayhem raged around them. Someone had gone on a shooting spree with a tomato sauce bottle.

Then they set the grandstand alight and as Cumberland was razed to the ground the embers rose up and danced into the night sky over Parramatta and beyond.

And it was beautiful.

20 'WE EAT THAT STUFF UP'

IT WAS JUST your average green-and-yellow government bus, one
of the old Leylands from the 1950s that was living beyond its
expiry date. Jack had a predilection for collecting unusual things:
antique golf clubs, old typewriters, old guns, a chastity belt
complete with key that he handed to Judy one day with a smirk.
But unlike the chastity belt, the bus served a purpose.

Cumberland Oval had been turned to ash and it would be
another five years before Parramatta Stadium was built. Until
then, the premiers would play their home matches at Belmore
Oval and train at Granville Park. Good old Granville Park:
a dust bowl on a dry day, too slippery to do anything when
it was wet, no hot water left for the first-graders once training
was over.

Early in the 1982 season, the Parramatta players arrived at
Granville and found the green-and-yellow government bus
parked at the side. 'Get on the bus,' Jack said to his first-graders.

'All I know,' says Peter Sterling, 'is that you wanted to be on that bus. That was the place to be.'

The bus is where Jack would assemble them on Tuesdays and he and Massey would whip out their big pad with all the stats from the weekend's match. Every tackle made, every tackle missed, every detail imaginable. From their video analysis on Monday, Jack and Massey would give each player a rating out of ten.

Sitting on the bus, each player would wait for Jack's assessment of their game. Nothing was hidden, and he delivered his critique with typical deadpan humour, but the players knew if they had rated a five or six for the last handful of games they would be off the bus and introducing themselves to John Monie—the reserve-grade coach.

It was in the early months of that season that the players arrived at Granville Park and noticed someone had changed the destination sign on the bus: 'MANLY WHARF'. Parramatta players had privately feared the prospect of meeting Manly in the grand final the previous season. Not now. Not with the witch now dead. 'We got better the longer that season went,' says Brett Kenny.

Because Jack wasn't prepared to accept complacency. Eric Grothe knew that. In the opening match of the season against Canterbury, he had failed to back up Mick Cronin and blown two scoring opportunities. The Eels lost by a point. 'Get back to where I found you,' Jack told him. That meant a plummet from premiership winger one week to third grade the next. 'He didn't muck around, did he?' Grothe said later.

In another era, superstar players might throw their toys out of the cot at such admonishment. Grothe was prepared to suck it up. Premiership success had only made the bond between the players stronger, and the bond between player and coach unbreakable.

Sterling knew he could talk to Jack about the deep, personal issues that troubled him—but knew Jack would know anyway. Sterling had had an argument with back-rower John Muggleton, who in time would become his brother-in-law. Jack pulled them aside at training. 'If you don't sort this out you are playing reserve grade,' he told them. If Sterling had spent too much time at the Swamp at the leagues club, Jack knew. 'Those dancing shoes can be put away this week,' he'd tell his little halfback at training.

When Jack said this to Sterling, there is some possibility he might've thought he was talking to Paul Taylor. Taylor was the fullback, although if he was a few kilograms lighter he could've been riding top-weight horses at Rosehill Racecourse down the road. Taylor had a home on the Central Coast, but he was seen as a drifter.

Sometimes, Tazza Taylor would sleep in his ute. Sometimes, his teammates could smell the grog on his breath from the night before at Saturday morning sessions. But Jack would turn a blind eye, probably because Taylor would come out on Sunday and punch and play well above his 64 kilograms. After a match against Wests in which Taylor stood in for the injured Sterling at halfback, Jack said: 'I wound him up for 80 minutes and let him do his thing.'

Jack believed in Tazza Taylor and Tazza Taylor knew it. Part of Jack's family were his German Shepherds, which dozed at his feet as he spent hours at the roll-top desk in his study. Jack had given one of his dogs to Taylor, knowing he needed the companionship. That year, a reporter asked Jack about his fullback. Where did he think his weaknesses were as a player? 'He's about as big as Clive Churchill was when he played,' Jack said. 'And he owns an ugly dog.'

Jack's reputation with his players was without peer, but he also cared what others thought of him outside the bus. He defended his public persona vigorously. Competing against the government-backed TAB was too difficult, so he had wound up his SP bookmaking operation by now, yet his reputation would never go away. Jack Darmody had spent a day with Jack for a two-part feature story for *The Mirror*, and mentioned his bookmaking activities in the first edition.

Somehow, Jack found out about it after the first edition was published—old journos still around reckon Peter Frilingos tipped him off. He was ghostwriting Jack's column, after all. Jack called the editors of the paper and any reference to SP bookmaking was removed for the final editions of the newspaper printed that evening.

It was in April that year when Jack walked straight up the steps of the Supreme Court to save his good name again. On 13 September 1980, Ron Casey had been hosting his usual Saturday morning breakfast spot on 2KY when a female caller came on-air. 'Jack Gibson is a criminal and an associate of criminals,' the woman said. A frantic technician played a delay jingle over her words. But the damage had been done.

Jack wasn't listening but Roy Masters was. 'That must've hurt you a lot,' he said to Jack. It hadn't so much wounded him as enraged him. It had been that September day when the news of his appointment at Parramatta was whirring around the city. Claims that he was a criminal were hardly something he wanted aired at that time. Neither did the club. Jack was never afraid to fire off a legal letter, and did so now.

About eighteen months later, he was in the witness box in the Supreme Court. 'It was hard to believe, hard to take and hard to accept,' he told the court. 'I am not a criminal and I am not an associate of one.' Other witnesses were called to make it clear that they had heard the woman's comments above the sound of the delay jingle. Denis Fitzgerald also testified that the remarks troubled him. Jack had only just signed with the club a day earlier.

It was whether the remarks had been heard, not whether they were correct, that formed 2KY's defence. At no stage did their lawyers try to raise Jack's murky past, with his connections to Thommo's and SP bookmaking. Truth is a defence in defamation proceedings, but it was an avenue not pursued by the defence team. 'This would appear to be a very serious defamation indeed, attracting very considerable damages,' Justice Cross told the court. One hour later, the jury returned and found in favour of Jack Gibson. Then came the good part: $50 000 in damages. It was like winning the lottery in those days.

'It is very relieving,' Jack said on the steps of the court, with his eldest daughter Susan standing alongside him. 'It certainly lessens any effect the thing might have had. This will vindicate my reputation.'

●

'Who's that sitting up there with Ron Massey?' asked the Eels fan. 'Oh, I think that's Jack Gibson,' said the other. That was the running joke around Parramatta in 1982. Jack Gibson was the figurehead, the statesman, but it was the big bloke in the bucket hat and dark glasses with the bad teeth right next to him that made it work.

Mass had the razor-sharp wit, the quick one-liner, and the players loved it. 'Jack's got to look as though he knows what he's doing so I have to be a bit of a con-man,' Massey joked in one interview. 'My most important job is to get a really good clipboard so I don't look like a tackle counter.' 'He'd eat a curried jockstrap,' Jack said, in reference to Massey's fearsome reputation for eating.

While life at Granville Park was always fun, Jack was wagering his usual war with referees again. Early in the season, it had been

Kevin Roberts. But it was after his side's one-point loss to Souths late in the season that his fury boiled over.

Martin Weekes had been placed in the middle as referee for that match, which the Eels had lost in a thriller after Jack had inexplicably replaced four players while his side held a healthy lead. When the reporters approached him afterwards, he detonated.

'What can I do? Who can I turn to? If I knew anything about Aussie Rules I would get out now. I may as well tell my players to stay at home rather than come and get treated like that.' He was then asked if he would ask Denis Fitzgerald to do something officially. 'Officially? What can be done officially?' He then took a long swig out of a carton of milk and hurled it into a corner of the dressing-room.

Jack had been firing off lengthy submissions to the New South Wales Rugby League throughout the season, with forensic video analysis of where the referee had got it wrong in his eyes. He fired off another letter to the league. The situation had not reached the same level of feuding as the Hartley wrangle. Instead, other coaches were dragged into the imbroglio.

The way Newtown coach Warren Ryan saw it, Jack was doing nothing more than using vitriolic criticism of referees as a means to influence them. It equated to standover tactics, as far as he was concerned. 'Gibson asserts pressure on referees through newspaper articles,' Ryan said at the time. 'Referees, being only human, realise their first grade position can be jeopardised by what Gibson says or writes about their performance. Even when he makes a report on a referee to the league he leaks it to the press.'

Ever since the 1963 grand final under Darcy Lawler, Jack hadn't trusted referees. But he knew the value of publicly criticising them. From Parramatta's perspective, the Hartley controversy had been seen as an impasse the previous season; it was becoming clear down the stretch of the current season that Manly were now the immovable object.

The Sea Eagles, featuring a brutal forward pack, had beaten the Eels at Brookvale Oval late in the season, and they were the bull in Parramatta's china shop. Parramatta had lost Bob O'Reilly forever, a knee injury finally forcing The Bear into the retirement he had promised for the past two seasons. Yet standing above everyone else in the Eels pack that season was Raymond Price. Mr Perpetual Motion. The Dally M Player of the Year who had become a football gladiator. Manly had a whiz-kid half in Phil Blake, yet the Eels had Sterling, Cronin and Grothe, and then there was Brett Kenny with those rubbery ankles again, letting him step off left and right feet with ease.

When the two sides met in the major semi-final, with a grand final position beckoning, Parramatta held their own for half an hour before they were crushed 20–0. There was talk afterwards that Parramatta had been complacent. There were rumblings about referee John Gocher caning them in the penalties and not stopping Manly's forwards from using cheap tactics to unsettle them. Price was sin-binned for ten minutes for throwing a punch and Jack didn't allow him to return. The simple fact was that the Sea Eagles had been too good. 'They've got a lot to learn in a week if they are going to play us in the grand final,' puffed Manly captain Alan Thompson. 'The normal Gibson discipline wasn't there. They seemed to get frustrated with all the pressure.'

At training the following week, Jack talked to his players for 50 minutes with hardly anyone else breathing a word. 'Don't let them bait you,' was his clear instruction. Then Parramatta went out into the muddy slop of the SCG that weekend and beat Easts 33–0.

Manly and Parramatta. Here they were. Finally. Some reckoned it loomed as the greatest grand final of the modern era. It was the classic confrontation between a club dubbed the Silvertails from the northern beaches against the side from the city's gritty arteries out there in the west. Parramatta considered themselves the outcasts of the league, treated poorly by officials and referees, while Manly's secretary was a close friend and confidant of Kevin Humphreys. Manly looked at the Eels as the whingers, constantly putting pressure on the referee, constantly claiming a bias that did not exist.

Naturally, Jack felt a need to add fuel to the fire. Days before the grand final he said he had 'zero confidence' in referee John Gocher. 'If Gibson thinks he's getting to me he's wrong,' Gocher fumed. 'It doesn't worry me. Greg Hartley had to cop it last season and it didn't affect him.'

Blake scored a try after three minutes of that grand final, after Eels winger Neil Hunt had failed to take a high kick from the Manly half. 'Forget it or I'll belt you,' Cronin said to him, according to Hunt after the match. Manly hammered the Eels line, but when they couldn't break it the Eels knew within themselves that they could win it. Jack's men won 21–8.

Amid the jubilation of victory, the newly bronzed Winfield Cup sat on the stage where the presentations were about to be made. It took the form of Arthur Summons and Norm Provan embracing one another after the 1963 grand final played in the mud. Jack must've noted the irony. That was the grand final he knew Wests couldn't win because of Darcy Lawler. Now he had coached sides to successive premierships, despite his mistrust of referees, which still lingered from that match nearly three decades earlier.

When Jack was asked to address the crowd, he looked Kevin Humphreys in the eye and shook his hand with purpose before taking to the mike. 'What do you say when you win?' Jack said. 'We eat that stuff up.'

When the moment presented itself later, Jack approached Cronin. Neither of them had discussed their conversation in the Members' Bar on grand final day in 1980, when Jack had asked him what he wanted out of football. Not a syllable about it. But it was never forgotten. Cronin had wanted a premiership. Now he had two.

Jack shook Cronin's hand. 'Got greedy, didn't you?'

21 THE BIG LEAGUE

WHEN HE WASN'T coaching young men he was being a father to them. To his three sons—Luke, Matt and John—he wasn't the supercoach. He was their old man. All three attended St Gregory's at Campbelltown just as he had, although by the time his sons became pupils it had developed into a thriving nursery for league talent. When the boys were playing rugby league, Jack would never coach. He'd stand on the hill from afar and watch.

As a young man in the 1950s and '60s playing footy and working beneath the swinging light bulbs at Thommo's, Jack presented like a character straight out of Damon Runyon's New York, with its hustlers and hard men. He had played that part during his life, yet he felt most comfortable in the blue haze of the bush. The bush appealed to his sense of adventure, which he never lost. He would take the boys camping, finding old houses and ripping up floorboards to see what might be hidden underneath. They would go shooting, Jack cooking their kill on an old Portagas stove before they fell asleep beneath the stars.

Rugby league was such an important part of his life, but he didn't always like the scene. He liked to escape it. Whenever he visited his old friend Peter Toohey at Mittagong in the Southern Highlands, he would rarely talk footy. On one visit, he handed Toohey an envelope. Two thousand dollars in cash was inside. He'd heard Peter had been doing it tough financially. 'I can't believe you've given this to me,' Peter said. 'You'd have given it to me,' Jack said.

The farm at Beechwood near Wauchope was his sanctuary. It was where he would take his players during the pre-season to train and swim and eat watermelon. They played trial matches against the local Wauchope side, and it was here in the early months of 1983 that back-rower Peter Wynn snapped his ankle.

It had crushed Wally Wynn, but Jack gave him some incentive. 'If you get fit, I'll pick you.' Yet walking, let alone playing, seemed an eternity away. Because you wanted to be on the bus again that season. Price. Sterling. Kenny. Cronin. Ella. Neil Hunt. Grothe. They all played State of Origin for New South Wales that year. When it came to the Sydney premiership, it appeared to be a race between Parramatta and Manly.

After the grand final win of the previous season, a deep rivalry between the clubs was forming not because of who they were but what they represented. Manly represented the wealth and luxury of Sydney's North Shore. And there was concern that their secretary, Ken Arthurson, was gaining too much influence at Phillip Street. Parramatta was the antithesis of all this. Their fans lived in houses made of the fibro manufactured by the major sponsor emblazoned on the players' backs: Jamess Hardie.

Manly were not the only threat. Not in Jack's eyes. He was still rumbling with the officials. He continued his attacks on John Gocher to the point where the referee threatened to sue. Then, in late April, a letter from Eric Cox hit the desk of Kevin Humphreys.

Dear Sir

I desire to lodge an official complaint against Mr Jack Gibson, coach of Parramatta DRLFC on Sunday 24 April 1983.

I was standing just outside the Referees Room in the passageway leading to the Referees Room after the 1st Grade match Parramatta v Canterbury Bankstown had concluded when Mr Jack Gibson walked past me and directed to me this remark:

'You would make a Pig vomit'

I then said to Mr Gibson 'I beg your pardon' and he immediately turned, glared at me and repeated the remark 'you would make a pig vomit'. He then spat on the floor about five (5) metres from me. At no stage did I speak any other words than 'I beg your pardon'.

I feel his remarks were insulting and not in the best interests of the game, nor the good conduct of Rugby League. Finally, as I have already stated, the remark I consider was not only insulting but obscene.

Yours sincerely
Eric Cox
Director of Referees
NSWRFL

Denis Fitzgerald was sending off some correspondence of his own. He lodged an official complaint to the special committee of the League saying referee John Gocher's handling of the match against Canterbury had been 'totally unsatisfactory'. Only eleven days earlier Fitzgerald had sent a similar letter in which Jack and Massey had given Gocher's refereeing of the match against Manly their typical forensic treatment. They found a litany of errors.

You would make a pig vomit. 'Doesn't sound like him,' says Steve Edge. Weeks later, though, Jack sent a letter directly to Eric Cox. 'I did not intentionally say anything that I felt would make you feel uncomfortable,' he wrote. 'If I did I withdraw such.'

Once again, the anger between Jack and officialdom was stirring. Against the backdrop of this animosity, there was talk that ABC investigative program *Four Corners* was putting the finishing touches to a heavy exposé of the game. The delay in its broadcast had fed rumours that it had been cancelled for legal reasons. Executive producer Jonathan Holmes told Peter Frilingos that the story was on track, although behind the scenes there was a very real chance of it being pulled.

Then, on the night of Saturday, 30 April 1983, 'The Big League' report was aired and rugby league changed forever. Reporter Chris Masters and senior producer Peter Manning had months earlier begun an investigation into corruption across a range of sports. But, they found, rugby league had more than enough controversy to focus on.

This was Masters' first story for *Four Corners*. He was the younger brother of Roy Masters, the former Wests coach now at St George who had risen up against Hartley, as Jack had done. When Chris Masters met Jack for the first time, he thought of him like a mobile version of the Blue Mountains. 'He is large and appealing and doesn't say much.' Jack repeated his often-drawled line about Kevin Humphreys: 'There's so much shit in his boots ...' So Masters and Manning went and found it.

Jack was interviewed at training wearing a blue-and-gold team tracksuit. His remarks were the first of the program. 'It's a violent game,' he explained. 'It's a body contact game. You don't care if he doesn't get up. You don't care if you broke his ribs. But that's the scene.'

The first part of the program focused on the administration of the NSWRL, especially the referees. Masters pointed out that no other team consistently complained about refereeing more than Parramatta. 'We have to be an eight-to-ten point better side to win that game,' Jack told him. 'With one or two referees?' asked Masters. 'Yes.' 'How can you say Parramatta has been discriminated against when you've won the last two grand finals?' You could scrape the frost off Jack's reply. 'Listen,' he said. 'We won those grand finals in *spite* of them.'

Then came the second, explosive part of the report. Masters revealed Kevin Humphreys' close relationship with SP bookmaker George Freeman. The fact that Humphreys had attended his wedding. Then Masters outlined, in atomic detail, how Humphreys had misappropriated $52 219 from the Balmain Leagues Club in 1976—and how Jack had lent him $34 000 to repay some of that debt.

Cut to Jack Gibson in the blue-and-gold tracksuit ...

Kevin was very agitated. He was a man in trouble. I spoke to him on the phone previously to that. He wanted money so I made arrangements. I borrowed some money myself. The only conditions were that he didn't have another bet. I told him that I wasn't giving it to him. I thought that giving him this money I was doing something for the game of rugby league. I was wrong in that statement. One of the conditions was that he never had another bet. He broke that promise.

He took an oath that he'd never punt again. That lasted barely 24 hours. He was playing two-up two nights later, and then the races that weekend.

By the end of the program, Masters' report had dragged in bigger fish. It alleged that New South Wales chief stipendiary magistrate Murray Farquhar had placed pressure on the magistrate hearing Humphreys' trial to acquit him. Premier Neville Wran was also implicated.

John Singleton had been watching all this at his home in Beecroft in Sydney's north-west and he phoned his friend Kevin Humphreys as the credits rolled on the *Four Corners* report. 'The good thing is they might've just gone too far,' he said, suggesting the report was libellous. 'I hope so, mate,' was Humphreys' glum reply.

Three days later, Humphreys resigned as chairman of the Australian Rugby League on the grounds of poor health, and soon after quit the New South Wales Rugby League citing the toxic publicity that had engulfed him and the game. Months later, a Royal Commission was held and Neville Wran was forced to stand down temporarily. Royal Commissioner Sir Laurence Street found that Farquhar had influenced the case but not at the request of the Premier. Farquhar was jailed.

On the direction of the Royal Commission, the case against Humphreys was reopened and once again Jack had to testify. The hearing was held in October. After seven days Humphreys was found guilty of fraud and stealing. He was fined $4000 and placed on a two-year good behaviour bond. When Jack fronted court in 1977, he was angry about being dragged into Humphreys' personal shitfight. This time he saw it as a chance to clear his name of any suggestion of wrongdoing or involvement in shady activities.

The entire episode was a holocaust for rugby league and those involved. Luckily, the sport had always been resilient and it swiftly rebuilt itself. The *Four Corners* report, in most eyes, had been for the greater good. 'That story changed everything,' Denis Fitzgerald recalls.

Jack felt comfortable in his decision to speak out. When it came to the rugby league material in the report, he had been the star witness. 'It was a big step for Jack,' Masters wrote a decade later. 'The Sydney underworld-mateship code of behaviour demands silence and self-protection. I suspect Jack felt Humphreys had lost the right to that protection.'

Because he'd promised not to bet again? Others were not so sure that that gave Jack such a right. Of all the contradictions embodied in Jack Gibson's personal life and career, this one resonated the loudest. He respected the code of mateship, yet he'd given Humphreys up. Cold. Stone cold.

The issue was his past. Jack had worked for Joe Taylor at Thommo's. He had been one of the city's biggest SP bookmakers. They were dark areas of his life and the unwritten law of the 'underworld', as Masters called it, was that one never spoke of them. Never publicly, at least. This was sacred ground. Humphreys had made it a grey area by breaking his pledge to Jack and now Jack had illuminated it all, with devastating consequences.

That's when the rumour mill cranked up. Those close to the situation say that Humphreys privately inferred that Jack hadn't actually loaned him the money—it was money Humphreys had lost through Jack's SP. 'Kevin never had a bet with Jack's joint in his life,' says one figure who was close to both men. 'Jack just lent him the money, which he got back.'

There was a belief that Jack's actions were vindictive payback for the battles waged over Hartley and Gocher in which Jack got no support from Humphreys. Then whispers started that Jack had been displeased that he was never approached to coach Australia when others had advocated it for so many years. 'If the opportunity came along I'd probably accept it,' he'd said at the end of the previous season. The call never came.

In June, Jack consented to an interview with 2GB sporting director Richard Fisk. The first question asked in a wide-ranging interview was about the claim that he had given up Humphreys.

> Fisk: What about the fact that you did come out and say that he was betting when he broke that part of the agreement, which, really, to a lot of people, was a telling factor?

> Gibson: Well it wasn't a telling factor—they wanted to know why I'd lent him the money. I told him I would for the game on the proviso that he wouldn't punt ... and I didn't want any favours as far as the league was concerned. The only one he lived up to was the last one because I never got any favours from him—because I never expected any. It wasn't so long ago he got his organisation behind him to fine me $15 000 for bringing the game into disrepute and that certainly didn't do my confidence in him or anyone else's any good. As far as the money was concerned, he let that secret out of the box—not me.

In the years that followed, Humphreys and Jack respectfully chatted on the rare occasions they saw each other at rugby league functions. Humphreys regularly tried to break his gambling addiction. Right up until his death at the age of 80, as he lay in a Drummoyne nursing home with his legs amputated from the diabetes that had ravaged his body, he was watching races and betting on them.

'The great irony is Kevin forgave Jack,' says John Singleton. 'He never blamed Jack. He only ever blamed himself. He would say, "It's not Jack's fault. It's my fault. It's my weakness." It was his weakness—and he paid for it.'

●

Jack inched around the dressing-room and every movement hurt. His back. His bloody back. It had flared up again. It wasn't helped by the kangaroo fur coat he was wearing. That thing weighed a tonne.

They had reached the grand final against Manly, but the bus had taken the longest and hardest possible route to get there. By their own admission later, the Eels players had underestimated the Sea Eagles in the major semi-final. Manly had players like Graeme Eadie, Phil Blake, Alan Thompson, Chris Close, John Ribot and Paul Vautin, and they were very good. The Eels lost 19–10.

In the preliminary final against Canterbury, they rediscovered their mojo. Peter Wynn had come on as a replacement and was at the end of a sweeping movement when he stumbled close to the line, got up, crawled forward, reached out … and scored. He'd come back from the broken ankle to put his side into the grand final. 'I think you're fit,' Jack told him after the game. Then he picked him in the starting side for the decider.

Now he was listening to Jack in the rooms at the SCG minutes before the grand final, their third in a row. The coach left them with a vintage one-liner: 'This is our last game of the year—so we might as well win it.'

Jack watched the first half from the first row of the second tier of the Members' Stand, leaning forward, chin on his hands, looking through darkened spectacles, a position that helped ease the inflammation at the base of his spine. Massey, Monie and Bob O'Reilly sat to his left, transfixed by the game.

It made for pleasant viewing. Parramatta led 12–0 at half-time and Jack felt they were in total control. What could he tell them?

His half-time addresses were legendary for what he didn't say. The players had heard some memorable ones over the past three seasons. They'd been playing so well at Belmore Oval one afternoon that Jack came in long enough to tell them this: 'You blokes know more about this game than I do. See you when it's over.'

Mick Cronin recalls him dumping on them only once, during a midweek match, but they'd had it coming. 'Jack had no pearls of wisdom,' Cronin says. Jack's pearls of wisdom were delivered during the week. He had a simple philosophy to coaching. Players didn't lose ability in 40 minutes of football. They had problems at home or money troubles, or they were injured. These couldn't be rectified during a ten-minute break in play.

But on this day, in this grand final, Jack made the most memorable speech of his coaching career. He said nothing. Not a word. There is a corner of the Gibson legend that tells you he wasn't even there. The players don't recall him being there. Massey can't recall him being there, although he reckons he would've been, somewhere. It was a grand final.

'Part of me wants to say he didn't come down,' says Peter Sterling. 'But the fact he didn't say anything to us was the greatest show of confidence we had ever had. When he didn't come in and say anything to us we knew what he was saying: "You're going fine. You know what to do."'

Then they went out and did it. Parramatta won 18–6. Three consecutive premierships. No rugby league side has done it since.

Jack barely features in the images in the minutes and hours after that victory. Australia's new Labor Prime Minister, Bob Hawke, is front and centre, posing with the likes of Sterling and Kenny and Edge and all of the others. Over the years, Jack and Hawke regularly enjoyed one another's company, even if Jack's political persuasions were different. He voted Liberal his entire life.

After the match, Jack was asked about his coaching future. 'I haven't even got a game plan for tonight,' he laughed. As the celebrations cranked up, Jack snuck out of the dressing-room and into the Members' Bar. Judy was there with Noel Kelly and his wife Chris. 'Let's go have dinner somewhere,' Jack said to them. As the two couples ate dinner at a restaurant at Double Bay, Noel had to ask. 'What are you doing here? Shouldn't you be with your players?' 'It's their night,' Jack said. 'Let them go.'

They didn't talk about the match, either. He preferred to talk about the old Clint Eastwood flick, *The Good, the Bad and the Ugly*. He eventually made it out to the leagues club later that night, and again Ray Warren handed him the microphone in front of a delirious auditorium. 'We'll be there in '84.'

Parra might have been—but Jack wasn't. Five days after the grand final, the newspapers rolled out the war type again. 'GIBBO QUITS PARRA.' 'I am now a spectator,' he told *The Sun*. 'I am sick of being the oldest coach in the game.'

His age had nothing to do with it, although Massey knew better than anyone that three years had wearied his friend. He had known Jack wasn't going to coach Parramatta again. He was equally certain he would coach nobody next year, despite renewed interest from Cronulla.

Jack's philosophy was that three seasons was long enough at a club. He reckoned the magic wore off after that. But there were other reasons. He wanted it known that he had no issue with

Parramatta. 'I'm not trying to paint Parramatta as the football version of the Love Boat, but it was a great outfit to be associated with because it wanted to work hard for success.' Finally, after all these seasons, Parramatta turned out to be the first club that worked with Jack Gibson—not against him.

What had finally got to him was the fight. The fight with Hartley. The fight with Humphreys. The fight with Cox and the rest of the Establishment. 'It's no secret that I have not been happy with the way the game has been administered from the top.'

Jack always walked out of a club leaving it in better shape than when he first arrived. It had been his calling card since 1967. But Parramatta had been the convergence of everything he had learnt and wanted from football. And this wasn't about winning premierships, but more to do with the people who had made it so.

He spoke to Steve Edge after his decision. 'In the three years I've been here, I've never once thought about dropping you,' Jack said. Edge almost exploded with pride. He had been at the club five minutes and Jack had made him captain ahead of the likes of Price and Cronin, and now he had made three victory speeches on grand final day as their captain.

Others also had first-hand experience of Jack's belief in them. Sterling and Kenny were players of promise before Jack arrived. Now they were international superstars. Players like Paul Mares and David Liddiard had come along that 1983 season. Neil Hunt and Steve Sharp appeared certain for permanent reserve-grade spots before Gibson took over. Now they had been key parts of another premiership.

As for those around him, Jack's coaching team had become the best in the business, the best that had ever been. Mick Souter was the best conditioner, Alf Richards the best trainer and medico on the run. And Massey's reputation was such that many regarded him as one of the game's most brilliant minds. After that grand final win, they presented him with the game ball.

John Monie was given the first-grade job. Jack had identified him when Monie was coaching Woy Woy, but there had been another moment that season that had convinced Jack that Monie was the right man to replace him for 1984 and beyond. Steve Sharp was playing reserve grade one week, but Jack wanted to bring him on for firsts at some stage. The rules meant Sharp had to complete the reserves match to come on in the top grade.

With five minutes remaining in reserves, Monie thought Neil Hunt sitting on the replacement bench could do the job. He hooked Sharp and replaced him with Hunt. Caught up in the pressure of the match, he had forgotten Jack and Massey's instructions. After the match, Monie walked into the sheds and was met with deathly silence. Jack scowled. 'What were you thinking, Monie?' 'I was just thinking about winning the game, Jack,' Monie said. 'What happened?' Jack fired back. Hunt had scored the match-winner. Jack paused. 'That's what I pay you for.'

Parramatta's success was also about the people it was for: those from The Hills and parts of greater western Sydney who had been considered of lesser importance than the snobs living east of Anzac Parade or on the North Shore. They were still Westies, but they were also successful ones. Jack had given them a club to be proud of. This was the house that Jack had built them.

Moving away from coaching once again gave Jack more time to spend with his family at Cowra Place. And while the Gibson household was usually a cheerful one, there was an underlying sadness.

Luke Gibson was a beautiful kid but a troubled one. Jack and Judy had spent hours taking him to doctors and psychiatrists in search of an answer. They were in this together, although of course both parents were aware that they had five other children. None of the professionals they sought out were prepared to diagnose Luke. They thought he might be suffering from schizophrenia but didn't want to label him.

Jack and George Piggins had remained close since they had parted ways at South Sydney. Jack still liked Piggin's head and Piggins still liked Jack's. They had bought shares in racehorses together, despite Jack's famous adage: 'Never invest in anything that eats.' That year, they bought a nursery on Gardeners Road in Kingsford and that's where Luke would work. Jack paid his wages.

One day, Luke told him he was giving up drugs. Jack dropped everything and took him to the farm near Wauchope for a week. But when they returned, Luke turned to alcohol. The old police sergeant at Cronulla who they had known for years would knock on the front door. 'Here's your boy,' he would say sympathetically.

This was crushing Jack, although he would rarely talk about it. That wasn't his style. He didn't want anyone to know his business. The great irony of it was he had shaped the lives of young men for years, but when it came to one of his own flesh and blood the supercoach was as helpless as any other father beset with the same circumstances.

'You can't go and get smashed all the time,' Jack told Luke. 'That's not the answer.' So Jack directed him to Alcoholics Anonymous meetings and Luke took it on with typical intensity. He attended sessions at Bundeena directly across the bay from the Gibson home at Cowra Place. He would ride the trains to Tempe and Hurstville and attend meetings there. Then he started to be banned from sessions. Luke had been sending the wrong message. 'You all come here and say, "I haven't had a drink",' he'd say. 'Well, I'm telling you that a couple of drinks won't do you any harm.'

On 4 December, Luke turned 21. But there was no party. No yardglass. Not even a small family celebration. 'What do you celebrate?' Judy recalls. 'We didn't know what we were supposed to be celebrating. There was no promise of him getting any pleasure out of his life. He hadn't got any pleasure out of his life. His life was never going to be free.'

22 COMMENTS FROM THE SUPERCOACH

The next person who asks me if I am having a rest may not like my reply. It seems to me that some of them think I have entered a nursing home after leaving Parramatta. Or that before I started coaching I was hiding in a cupboard. This year I won't have the responsibility of a football team, which means I have automatically eliminated about 50 phone calls a week along with the anxiety that never goes away. My heart is still with the Parramatta players and fans. I will continue to dispute blatant bad calls by officials or referees and I will still resent the players who, through lack of toughness or skill, resort to unnecessary roughness or violence.

THE TRUTH OF it was that Big Jack could never hide. In his first *Daily Mirror* column of the 1984 season he made it clear that he was also off the leash. He had already played a major role, albeit buried deep in the shadows, instituting important change at Phillip Street. When Kevin Humphreys departed the game in shame, rugby league needed a new boss. John Quayle wanted the job.

Jack and Quayle had remained firm friends. When Jack's daughter Tracey announced her engagement, Jack went to Quayle, who was the general manager at Easts Leagues, and told him to spare no expense for the wedding: 'I want it real good,' Jack said. 'I'll give you this to get started.' He whacked $5000 in cash into Quayle's hand.

Quayle was destined for a higher office than Easts Leagues. Anyone associated with the game could see that. After Humphreys had gone and the position of chief executive of the New South Wales Rugby League had been advertised, Quayle approached Kerry Packer. 'You are fucking kidding aren't you?' Packer said. 'They're all crook. Come work for me.'

Then Quayle approached Jack. 'I want the job at the New South Wales Rugby League,' he told him. Jack gave him that shrewd look. Quayle knew the look. He had seen it a hundred times. 'I think you'll be good. If you want to get the job, I'll get someone to organise it. There's no use me ringing anyone.'

Quayle was appointed general manager on a salary of $50 000 per annum. The league was incorporated within three months, answerable to a board comprising nine directors. One of them was Denis Fitzgerald. Rugby league's powerbase had changed forever.

'Take your time,' Jack told Quayle. 'There's a lot to do. You've got some bad people there. There's a few you have to be careful of.' Jack also told him that he should go to America, and organised for him to attend the Super Bowl and take a trip to the Dallas Cowboys.

When he returned, Quayle was single-minded about fixing the festering situation of the game's referees and the mistrust of them. Certain clubs had been putting pressure on Ray O'Donnell of the referees' appointments board to give them the referee they wanted. 'You do it,' Jack told Quayle. 'Nobody will have a go at you. They trust you.' Jack was hearing whispers, and they were gaining volume. 'It's comin' into the gambling,' he said to Quayle.

Jack was concerned about referees betting on matches. There was a whiff of it in English soccer. He knew that the outcome of a single rugby league match could hinge on a single penalty. So Quayle went to Ken Arthurson and NSWRL chairman Tom Bellew and said he wanted to make a change. Fitzgerald couldn't move quickly enough to endorse one.

Quayle became the man who decided who officiated which match and where, telling referees and clubs the night before the match. He'd switch them around at the eleventh hour and clubs would be furious.

The common line about Jack Gibson was that he brawled with the referees and officials for his own nefarious reasons. Now he could only be accused of meddling for one simple reason: the good of the game.

●

It was the kangaroo fur coat that drew the attention. He was making his way up the steps of the grandstand, through the heaving crowd at Lang Park minutes before kick-off, and the natives were becoming restless. Queensland was about to meet New South Wales in the opening match of the State of Origin series.

That kangaroo fur coat. Holy hell, he loved that coat. On this night in late May 1984, it made Jack look bigger than ever. Much bigger than Mike Gibson, who was walking a step behind and maybe even closer as the insults started to come from the crowd, which had already marinated itself in Fourex beer at the bars on Caxton Street. Jack and Mike had just done their piece-to-camera on the field and were now making their way back to the Channel Nine commentary box.

Now it was becoming ugly. Jack had to defuse the situation. In another life, he might've used those big hands of his. Now his mouth was a better option. 'Don't mess with me, brother,' Jack said to one of the Maroons fans. 'This bloke behind me is my bodyguard.' The crowd exploded with laughter. He had them eating out of the palm of his hand, as he did with most people.

David Hill was the head of sport at Channel Nine and when he heard Jack Gibson had left Parramatta and might be at a loose end he made an approach. Hill understood the mysticism of the coach. He had identified how American coaches were considered demigods, and how Jack had been the first one to attain such status in rugby league. 'He was the most charismatic person I could bring in,' Hill says. Jack agreed to join play-by-play callers Darrell Eastlake and Ian Maurice. As he said to Hill: 'I was comin' to the game anyway.'

When Jack took his seat in the commentary box, he was agog at the technical equipment and instrument panels before him. 'I feel like I'm going into space.' Commentating had never seemed like a natural progression for the supercoach. He never enjoyed speaking for the sake of it. Sometimes, at training, Ron Massey would have to finish his sentences. Sometimes, Jack would visit Kerry Packer, the owner of Channel Nine, and the two of them would often sit in silence. 'I think Jack thought Kerry was a goose—and I think Kerry thought Jack was a thug,' reckons John Singleton. But there was always respect.

He reckoned he struggled through that debut call at Lang Park but still managed to reel off some trademark Gibson-speak. When Eastlake criticised a New South Wales player for catching the ball while standing off-side, Jack remarked: 'Well, if you are in the position and the ball comes your way, you haven't got time to hold a committee meeting.'

When Jack arrived home from Brisbane the following night, he asked Judy for her assessment. 'I could understand you,' she smiled. 'But I don't know if anyone else could.'

By the weekend, the focus had shifted from Jack's commentary to an all-out verbal war with Australian and New South Wales coach Frank Stanton. Jack had revealed to reporter Ian Hanson in *The Mirror* that Stanton had savaged New South Wales halfback Peter Sterling in the dressing-room after the Blues' defeat. Stanton was apparently enraged that Sterling hadn't obeyed his instructions and apparently threatened to drop him from the side if he did it again. Apparently.

Jack launched an impassioned defence. Insulting the boy Sterling was akin to insulting one of his own sons. 'Sterling was singled out as the main offender for the defeat,' Jack said. 'The reason given was that he personally abandoned the coach's game plan. I wonder if most fans would agree. It's a little harder to perform behind a pack that was out-muscled on the night. I was of the opinion that Peter Sterling was the main contributor in keeping Frank Stanton's record intact on the 1982 Kangaroo tour.'

Stanton—a giant of the game in his own right—was never going to let that slide. 'Gibson is obviously good at criticising the actions of other coaches in positions he is afraid to take on because the conditions don't suit him and he couldn't get his own way,' he said. 'Maybe if he did take on a job of this nature and found out what it was like he would not be so quick to rush in and defend the players or criticise the coach.'

Here they were, two rugby league bulls locking horns, and it was a perfect storm for the newspapermen. Yet Stanton was right: if Jack Gibson was the so-called supercoach, why had he not taken charge of his state, let alone country? Apart from the feeling that Humphreys had always blocked it, the likely reason was the obvious one: his personality. 'I would want a major say in who I'm going to coach,' Jack said. 'I'm not going to say I could pick the team because when you pick a Kangaroo tour it's a certainty that the best players don't always go.'

For the second Origin match, played at the SCG, Jack again introduced a whole new vernacular to the commentary box. Players had 'done good' or 'done fine'. They'd 'crossed the stripe' for a try. The play was a sequence of playmakers makin' yards, wingers lookin' upstream instead of at the ball, skinny dee-fences, centres stayin' alive. While David Hill whacked Darrell Eastlake with a rolled-up program to amp-up his excitement levels, Jack would tap Eastlake or Ian Maurice's leg once he had finished speaking to signal he had finished. When Queensland won the match 14–2, thereby winning the series, Jack was asked for his thoughts about the final game. 'Maybe they can make it a benefit match.'

By the following afternoon, the result had become the secondary story on the back page of *The Mirror*. 'ARKO, GIBSON: BLAZING SCG ROW' screamed the headline. On the day of the match, Jack had predicted in his weekly column in the same newspaper that there would be an all-in brawl in Origin II. He accused judiciary chairman Jim Comans along with Arthurson and—surprisingly—Quayle of condoning punch-ups during play.

Minutes before kick-off, Jack bumped into Arthurson in the laneway alongside the Members' Stand. Harsh words were spoken and voices raised, much to the bewilderment of spectators and officials who witnessed it.

Both men confirmed the incident in *The Mirror*. Arthurson reckoned he was merely defending himself. Said Jack: 'He must have thought the laneway was a suitable place to discuss the matter otherwise he wouldn't have brought it up.' The simple fact was that Jack's prophecy came true: after the second tackle of the match, almost every player in the field was involved in an ugly brawl that lasted 45 seconds.

This anger in the press was not reflected in his commentary, which became legendary with every appearance. In July, Great Britain played a Test series against Australia and Gibson-speak came to the fore. After Eric Grothe scored from an off-load from Gene Miles, he said: 'Eric was just gonna shake his hand and all of a sudden he's got the ball and he ran that 20 metres with nothin' but green grass in front of him.' As time ran out for Great Britain, he drawled: 'They've got three plays to blow up the bridge.' He'd used that one as coach. When Mal Meninga hit the upright with a kick for goal after a string of missed attempts: 'He's getting closer.' Of trigger-happy New Zealand referee Tony Drake: 'He must have an egg-timer there because every four minutes he blows the whistle.'

His commentary seemed too good to be true, and in many respects it was. His philosophy about preparation hadn't changed now that he wasn't coaching. He was a student of the game of rugby league, and thought carefully about what he might want to say. And then he wrote it down in his long, sloping hand in a notebook. He would discuss it with his commentators before each match.

'A lot of our stuff was rehearsed, but nobody knew,' Eastlake recalled years later. 'He'd say to me, "If Garry Jack drops a high bomb, come straight to me." So I've gone, "Oh look at Garry Jack, he never drops the ball! He's the safest fullback!" Jack comes in and says, "It's a hell of a time to have a board meeting." '

●

Jack and Arthur were playing golf at The Lakes, which was hardly a surprise to anyone because they loved to play golf at The Lakes. Anywhere, really. Arthur was wearing a Queensland Rugby League tracksuit jacket, and whatever paddock he had been in over the last few years had been a good one. 'That's not a beer gut,' Jack quipped. 'That's his contract.' It had just been announced that Arthur Beetson was returning from Queensland to coach the Roosters in 1985. Weeks earlier, Jack had signed on to coach Cronulla.

Jack had made a promise upon leaving Parramatta that he would never coach a side against Steve Edge, Mick Cronin and Ray Price. Edge had retired at the end of 1984, but Cronin and Price were still going. None of them seemed to begrudge the supercoach forgoing his word: they wanted him coaching again.

So did Terry Fearnley, who had coached the Sharks for two seasons but had decided to have a break from the game. Financial problems meant that Cronulla had been staving off extinction for seasons, but Jack had decided to coach them anyway because he knew how good the football team would be, having been coached by his former front-row partner. Jack would be taking the same coaching machine with him—Massey, Mick Souter, Alf Richards—and he would not be building an empire.

'We are not going into the Cronulla club with a three- or five-year plan for success,' Jack told Peter Frilingos. 'We are looking for an immediate reaction from the Cronulla players next season.' It was a bold promise: the Sharks had never won the premiership since entering the competition in 1967.

As Jack and Arthur sat in their golf cart, hacking their away around The Lakes on a grey and miserable Sydney afternoon, the topic slowly drifted towards the subject of football and players and their teams. The talk turned to halves and playmakers. The normal footy chat.

There had been an issue gnawing at both of them since their respective appointments. Kurt and Dane Sorensen were tough, volatile Kiwi internationals who had played for the Sharks before playing with the Roosters for one season in 1984. They had agreed on a handshake to rejoin the Sharks, but Beetson had told the Roosters management he wanted to keep them at 'all costs'. They signed with Cronulla anyway.

Jack pulled the golf cart to a stop. 'Let's make a pact,' he said. 'Oh yeah, what's that, Jack?' Beetson asked. 'You don't take my players and I won't take yours.' Months later, Arthur took one of his players.

Olsen Filipaina, the son of a Samoan heavyweight boxer, was another Kiwi international who played at centre but mainly five-eighth. Filipaina didn't so much tackle as cut men in half. He had agreed to sign with Cronulla before phoning Jack one night. He'd signed with Easts, who had offered him extra cash. Filipaina had gone back on his word, but it was the friendship between Jack Gibson and Arthur Beetson that suffered—it was cleanly ripped in half.

'We agreed that wouldn't happen,' Jack said to Arthur. 'I never agreed to that. I never agreed to anything at all, Jack,' Arthur said. That wasn't the end of it. Asked about their mateship by *The Mirror*, Jack fumed: 'Straight out the window. It was Arthur's decision and as far as I'm concerned we're finished.'

Days later, Arthur responded.

Let's get it straight: there's no-one outside my family who means more to me than Jack Gibson. Jack is from the old school and I reckon he expected me to automatically drop off Olsen Filipaina because we've been like brothers for the past 10 years ... I still think Jack is a great bloke and I hope our friendship can survive this. We didn't buck when Jack won the race for Steve Rogers and we certainly didn't cry when Cronulla signed the Sorensen brothers before last season had finished. I'm not going to judge who is right or wrong in this bust-up. Just let me observe that by the words Jack Gibson used, the split is likely to remain permanent.

It never did. They got back together—over a round of golf, of course—only to fall out again a few years later when Arthur used material out of Jack's coaching manuals from his time at the Roosters without asking permission. It was an oversight by Beetson—and Jack had freely plucked information from many others over the years—but Jack again considered it an act of treachery. 'I've had fallouts with good mates over the years but my experience is that if the friendship is strong enough it'll survive and life goes on,' Beetson said of it years later.

So it was with Jack. He fell in and out with many people over the years, but he always managed to find his way back to his mates. That was the important thing. He was headstrong and he only liked men carved from similar stuff. He was stubborn but never so stubborn to hold a grudge long enough against those who he considered worth having in his life.

These were the wounds that could be healed. Others were never so easy.

The horse that deeply wounded Matthew Gibson wasn't Exile Prince, but Matt remembers that it was on the day a horse called Exile Prince won for the first time.

Matt had moved to Jack's farm near Wauchope. He wasn't doing much with his life, and it had been agreed that working with the quarter-horse stallions on the farm would be good for him. Matt thought it would be good for him.

In early December, a Sydney businessman Jack had known had sent Exile Prince to the farm for some work. The horse kept coming second to all the best thoroughbreds racing at the time and couldn't crack it for his maiden win.

Jack and Matt loaded him on to their old Bedford horse float and drove out of the farm, bound for Taree races, and one of the quarter-horse stallions followed all the way to the gate. When they returned later that night, with Exile Prince in the back having finally won his first race, they found the stallion still standing at the gate. As the truck approached, the horse started to buck and one of his hind legs got caught in the bullbar.

Matt jumped out of the passenger seat and started whacking it in the face, hoping the distraction would help the horse dislodge his leg. When a horse's leg is caught like that, it has the same instincts of a dingo: it would rather bite the leg off than have it caught. The stallion was snapping at his own leg, but it caught Matt just above one of his ankles and flung it back and forth in the air like a rag doll before finally letting go. When Matt tried to walk, he found himself standing on his own shin.

By the time Jack and Matt had flown by air ambulance to the Prince of Wales Hospital in Sydney, where Matt was to have microsurgery in a bid to save his leg, the story was all over the front page of the daily press. Whatever happened in the life of Jack Gibson always sold newspapers. He was a giant of the city.

But he was still a father and like anything that happened with his family he quietly blamed himself. It had been his farm, his horse, and this was his son who had suffered a terrible trauma.

One of the first people he phoned when he arrived in Sydney was George Piggins. He knew that Piggins would give him straight advice, if he needed to hear it. The pair were sitting in the waiting room when the doctor emerged. 'You've got a big decision to make,' the doctor told Jack. 'The leg's got gangrene. The boy will have to lose his leg.'

Jack asked Piggins what he would do. 'There's no choice to make,' Piggins said. 'It's gangrene. You are playing with his life.'

Matt had the lower part of his leg amputated, and while it ended his football career, it didn't become a hindrance for the rest of his life. 'He wasn't one to dwell, and neither was I,' Matt says. Then he says something you'd expect his father to say. 'Maybe I needed some slowing down.'

23   HAROLD HOLT

GAVIN MILLER HAD just woken up in Sutherland Hospital and he was looking at his thumb covered in plaster. Surgery had put it back together. Then he noticed Jack Gibson and Ron Massey standing at the end of his bed.

'What are you trying to do?' Jack grumbled. Miller was still groggy. 'He's one of the most respected players in the game. You don't need to do that.' It was 1980, and the previous afternoon Miller had thrown a swinging arm while playing for Cronulla against Parramatta. The swinging arm had hit Mick Cronin, yet Miller's thumb had come off second best.

Now it was early 1986 and Jack was about to speak to Gavin Miller again. His career had turned that day at Sutherland Hospital because of the advice from Big Jack. He never played dirty again. He had left Cronulla in 1983 because the club had asked him and others to take a 50 per cent pay cut, so dire was its financial state. He had played for Easts and then Hull KR in

England, but now Jack was trying to entice him back.

'Do you want to have a game?' Jack asked him. 'Sure. Where were you thinking?' asked Miller, who had played rounds of golf with him in the past. 'Bonnie Doon? The Lakes?' Jack chuckled. 'How about the Sharks?'

Jack needed his help because he could not effect this revolution in the Shire alone. When he'd signed on for the 1985 season, he'd been asked if he felt like he was putting something back into the local community, the one he had been a part of for most of his life. 'I'm not a benevolent society,' he snapped in reply.

Nor was Jack going to tolerate ego. Steve Rogers was at that moment the Prince of Centres, arguably the best of the post-war period. He had left the Sharks two years ago like Miller because of the pay dispute, but returned two years later having played for two years at centre, five-eighth and lock for St George. 'Where am I going to play?' he asked Jack. 'I'll scratch where it itches,' Jack replied. It wasn't a joke.

Rogers had his jaw broken in the opening match of the season and later took Canterbury hooker Mark Bugden to court over the matter. For the club, it never improved from that point on, despite some moments of hysteria at the start of the season that suggested they would be playing in the grand final. Despite some promising local juniors like Johnathon Docking, Andrew Ettingshausen, Mark McGaw and Barry Russell, they finished eighth.

The true believers in the Shire expected more. They were hoping Jack could do for them as he had done for Parramatta. *Win us something.* They had made grand finals, but they needed someone to kill the witch.

So Miller agreed to come back to Cronulla for 1986, even if it was a bad move considering how the club had screwed him and his teammates three years earlier. That was his better judgement speaking. His heart told him to come back because of Jack Gibson.

●

It had been Jack's idea for John Quayle to run the game. Now it was his idea for Quayle to protect the referees. 'You'll fix it when you fine them,' he said. 'Nobody wants to pay out of their back pocket.'

Quayle wanted to reef the stories appearing almost every day under the headline war type from the back pages of the tabloids and replace them with stories about the footy. Nobody had gunned for the whistleblowers over the years like Jack, but this time the coach agreed. The criticism of the refs was trashing the reputation of the game.

Then Jack went and spoiled it all by saying something stupid on the National Nine News like: 'There are a number of referees who can't handle it. They shouldn't be in first grade because they keep making the same mistakes.'

He had been aggrieved about an early season loss to Balmain. Referee Greg McCallum had allowed a crucial try to the Tigers off a forward pass from Garry Jack to winger Ross Conlon. But he also criticised his own player, Dean Carney, who had held the Tigers' Michael Perry as the Sharks scored.

The radio airwaves ran wild with the remarks the following morning. The obvious question: Would John Quayle fine Jack Gibson? And why should he? When Jack speaks, it usually makes sense. Where's the free speech in this game?

NSWRL chairman Tom Bellew sensed blood in the water as soon as he awoke. 'You've got your first coach,' he said to Quayle. 'Jack Gibson. He's all over the news criticising referees.' Quayle had only one thought: 'Why Jack? Why did you have to be first?'

Jack knew what was coming. 'I hear you're gonna fine me,' he said to Quayle. 'What for? That wasn't criticism.' 'You've breached the rule, Jack,' Quayle said.

Days later, Quayle stood before a specially convened committee in the NSWRL's boardroom in Phillip Street. He recommended Gibson be fined $1000 for criticising referees, then walked out of the room. Jack had been sitting outside the boardroom, and Quayle's assistant Nicky Braithwaite had noticed the anger percolating inside the supercoach.

'Have you watched the tape?' Jack snapped when he saw Quayle. 'Yes, it's in the boardroom,' Quayle said. 'They'll play it.' 'I want you in there.' When Quayle walked in behind Gibson, the committee chairman Dick Conte was puzzled. 'Do we need the chief executive here?' 'No, I need him here,' said Jack. 'Mr Gibson, there's been a complaint. Are you aware of the rule?' Conte continued. 'Yeah, I'm aware of the rule.' 'Would you like to add anything to it?' 'No, you've watched it.'

Then Jack turned to Quayle. 'Who put you up to this?' he asked. 'I brought in this rule with the endorsement of you,' Quayle replied. 'To get the referees out of the limelight. But this is a breach. You've criticised the referees publicly.' 'Who put you up to this?' Jack said again. 'I've recommended a fine. A thousand dollars.'

Jack got up and walked out. Later that night he called Quayle. 'Look at the unedited tape,' he said. Jack had seen it, and the VHS tape tucked away in his archives reveals it all. Apart from blaming his own side for a lack of discipline, Jack said this:

I think the standard of refereeing has improved every year in the last three years. It's come a long way. It's a terrible amount of pressure on the way they structure the rules.

When they structure the rules, they should take the pressure off the referee. He needs 20–20 vision to come out of there scot-free. He's going to make a certain amount of mistakes, but we just hope it's not in crucial periods.

Then reporter Tim Sheridan asked: 'They're only human, I suppose.' 'I'd like to think most of them are,' Jack grinned.

As soon as Quayle watched the unedited interview, he phoned Jack. 'I've watched the tape, Jack,' he said. 'I screwed it up.' When the interview was viewed in its entirety, it was clear that Jack had been complimentary towards the refs.

Jack hung up the phone. He didn't speak to Quayle for another two years.

●

South Brisbane had come last in 1977, but two years later Wayne Bennett had them one victory away from the grand final. Jack Astill was the chairman of Souths Juniors and was prepared to do whatever it took to ensure they got there. 'Wayne, what can I do for this team?' Astill asked in the week leading up to the preliminary final. 'How can I help you?'

Bennett had one wish: he'd love Jack Gibson to fly to Brisbane to speak to his players. Calls were made, and Jack agreed in a heartbeat to fly up. The plotline probably appealed to him: from wooden spooners to grand finalists.

The night before the match, Jack spoke to Bennett's players and then showed them a film, *The Value of Preparation*. 'You'll win tomorrow,' Jack said to Bennett after dinner. 'But I can't get back next week to help you, so you'll be in a bit of trouble.' It was a joke, of course. Souths won the final but lost the grand final.

Jack and Bennett were similar men, with a similar economy of words when they spoke and similar magnetism that drew players in, made them feel wanted, made them 'done good', as Jack would say. Bennett was a winning coach because of the belief he showed his young men. He knew that Jack was the original supercoach, but Jack knew that Bennett could become one, too.

Eight years later, Bennett was in the first season at Canberra as co-coach alongside Don Furner; his mouth was full of ulcers because of stress. He had no idea he was about to be offered the job of a lifetime. Brisbane businessmen Barry Maranta, Gary Balkin, Steve Williams and Paul 'Porky' Morgan had been given the licence to enter a team in the New South Wales Rugby League competition in 1988. Fundamental to its long-term success would be the founding coach. They needed the right man.

So all four of them caught a plane to Sydney and asked a man who might know. 'If you want your club to head in the direction that you hope it can, there is only one guy for the job,' Jack told them. Who's that? 'His name is Wayne Bennett.'

Williams spoke to Bennett days later. 'We've just been down to Sydney to see Jack Gibson,' he said. 'Jack says you're the coach we've got to get. We want you to coach the Broncos.' Bennett had agreed to coach Canberra for four years but had not signed a contract. The Broncos kept chasing and chasing until they got their man. The word of Jack Gibson had made them pursue him so single-mindedly. Wayne Bennett coached the Broncos for the next 21 years, and won six premierships.

While Jack was putting others on the course to greater heights, his Cronulla side kept spiralling downwards. They finished tenth in 1986, and the following year was barely any better. Jack's hands were tied: he couldn't buy a big-name player, because there was no cash to buy the big-name player. Newspaper reports suggested that the Sharks were about to be kicked out of the competition because of their flailing finances. Then the joke became serious. Dressed in a white suit and with a slicked-back mane of hair, Doctor Geoffrey Edelsten announced at an anniversary dinner at the Regent Hotel that he was making an audacious $2.5 million bid to buy the club. It was a gift for his wife Leanne, whose cleavage lit up the room and momentarily the hopes of a dying club.

As Cronulla struggled, Jack's star as a television personality continued on its upward trajectory. He had become an icon by now. While the rest of the Nine rugby league commentary team wore blue blazers on the orders of sports boss David Hill, Jack did not. His kangaroo fur coat had been lost in transit at Los Angeles airport and while the loss broke his heart he felt comfortable wearing a faded blue cardigan to matches and on air.

'What's with the cardigan, Jack?' Mike Gibson asked him on-air one night. 'Love in every stitch,' Jack smiled. 'Judy knitted it up for me. Love in every stitch.' Judy was watching at home at Cowra Place, shaking her head because she knew it was a lie. She hadn't knitted it at all.

The fans loved the cardigan and they loved the comments from the supercoach. On the Blues being convincingly beaten, he said: 'New South Wales were in the game right up to the national anthem.' On the performance of the New South Wales pack: 'If the meek are going to inherit the earth, our forwards are going to be land barons.' On the riotous Lang Park crowd: 'They'd boo Santa Claus this mob.' On Balmain prop Steve Roach: 'He's tough enough. He's just purchased one of those Tarzan chest wigs.' On Canberra prop Sam Backo: 'Legs like tree trunks? He'll have to watch out for white ants.' On Canberra winger John Ferguson: 'A freak. I would play him with measles.' On Cronulla centre Mark McGaw: 'He butchered that play.

He'd get in the Meat Packers Union for that.' On Cronulla winger Andrew Ettingshausen, the quickest player in the game at the time: 'He's so quick he could turn out the light and get into bed before it gets dark.'

That last one became iconic and it was typical of his commentary. The pun had been used in America for years, and was only mildly amusing. When Jack brought it to life in the context of State of Origin and on television, it was the line every smart-arse at school or the workplace would be saying the next day.

Billy Birmingham only enhanced the legend. He was the brilliant comedian who was earning a living off mimicking Nine's cricket commentators, Richie Benaud, Tony Greig, Bill Lawry and Ian Chappell. When he released *Wired World of Sports* in 1987, he featured a mock exchange between Jack and Darrell Eastlake as Wayne Pearce came off and Ron Gibbs—who never actually played for New South Wales—came on.

> Eastlake: Pearce off Jack, Gibbs on.
> Gibson: What did you say to me?
> Eastlake: Pearce off Jack, Gibbs on.
> Gibson: Don't tell me to piss off, fuck knuckle. [*Sound of Jack belting Darrell*]
> Eastlake: *Ho! Ho! Ho!* Big Jack's king hit me and I've gone crashing to the deck.

When Birmingham met Jack years later, he was worried about how Jack might react. Then they became friends and golfing partners.

Channel Nine's listeners never saw his one-liners coming, much like Jack never saw Ray Price's sledge. Left in the capable hands of John Monie after Jack's departure, Parramatta had reached the grand final in 1984 only to lose to Warren Ryan's Canterbury before beating them in the grand final in 1986. As Price and Mick Cronin hobbled through their victory lap of honour at the SCG that afternoon, having played their last match for the club, barely a bottom lip did not quiver.

The following year, Price released his autobiography *Perpetual Motion* and the most fascinating part of it concerned Big Jack.

> Jack was not the best coach I played under. But Jack Gibson and Ron Massey were the best coaching combination I played under. Gibson is called the 'mastercoach' but that is only half the truth. He would never have been as great without his right-hand man Massey.

Then Price said this of Terry Fearnley, who had coached Parramatta in the years before Jack:

> If Terry Fearnley had had a right-hand man, or an extra gun on his belt, he too would have gone down in history with a record similar to Gibson's. That is what Massey was to Gibbo, the gun on his belt, and in many ways his eyes and brains.

Price's Parramatta teammates past and present did not agree with him. Some dismissed it as a sensationalist way to pump the sales of his book, while others thought the comments looked worse in the two-page exclusive extract that appeared in *The Mirror* than they had in his book. Either way, Jack was seething.

For all his hardness, there was a belief that Price didn't mind the good old 'dry dive'—in other words, a player feigning injury to make himself appear like a warrior. Jack had identified it in the early days at Parramatta when he told Price to spend less time coming off the field on a stretcher. As Massey once joked: 'Two blokes lost their jobs after Jack started coaching Price: they were the Parramatta stretcher bearers who used to cart him off the field every week.'

When Peter Frilingos approached Jack for comment, he played it straight. 'Price's comments read as if Massey and I should have swapped jobs while we were at Parramatta. But it's nice of Ray to say I did contribute.' As for Massey, he was flummoxed. 'Sounds to me as though Ray Price packed into too may scrums.'

For all the adoration he had been afforded, criticism cut Jack. He never took it well. Proud men rarely do. 'I know I never did anything to hurt him,' he said solemnly to Mick Cronin amid the firestorm.

There was a belief then, and it has grown with the years, that Ray Price was on to something: that Massey was the brains behind Jack Gibson's success. 'That's unfair to both of them,' says Mick Cronin now. Jack and Mass never thought in those terms anyway. They knew what they were to each other. They would prefer to laugh about it. 'What does a coaching co-ordinator do?' Massey said once. 'As little as possible.' Massey was never Jack's right-hand man but his hand in glove.

While Jack was mostly feted as a giant of the game, there were some of rugby league's cognoscenti that hadn't fallen under his spell. His premierships at both Eastern Suburbs and Parramatta had been won with sides stocked with internationals or players packed with potential, they said. The premierships at the Roosters came after the leagues club had flipped open its chequebook, they reckoned. The seeds of his success at the Eels had been sown years previously by Fearnley, they declared.

By 1987, Warren Ryan had gently cruised past Jack as the most influential coach in the game. He had created the 'Dogs of War' at Canterbury and won titles upon the foundation of relentless defence. The type of defence Jack would've admired. Ryan—and others—privately thought he had a better football brain than Jack Gibson. A smarter tactician. And he was undoubtedly right. But Jack always figured the footy was only part of being a decent football coach. Five premierships suggested there might be something in that.

Jack also knew that it was about passion. Winning starts on Monday, as he often said. And after three seasons at Cronulla—a team struggling with injury in his third season at the helm—the start of the week seemed to be popping up too quickly. 'I don't know what will come up,' he said when he announced he was standing down as coach. 'I won't knock the present by planning for the future.'

Jack's record never escaped the fact that he could not do for Cronulla what he had done at Parramatta. The way Jack saw it, maybe they just didn't have a premiership in the woodwork of the joint. It took a Prime Minister presumed dead to explain it.

Harold Holt was the Prime Minister who went missing when he went swimming in heavy surf at Cheviot Beach near Portsea, Victoria, in December 1967. 'Waiting for Cronulla to win a premiership is like leaving the porch light on for Harold Holt,' Jack said upon his departure.

They never found Holt's body … just as Cronulla are yet to find their premiership.

24 LUKE

JOHN SADLER WAS a big Cook Islander who had biceps the size of watermelons, and the tight white T-shirt he wore every day clung to them for dear life. Within the walls of Parramatta Jail, he was the man. Nobody crossed John Sadler. He had been sentenced to twenty years for murder—retribution, he claimed, for a crime committed against his niece.

When he was released in 1992, the register had only two entries for those who visited Sadler during his time in jail: his niece, and Jack Gibson of Cowra Place, Cronulla.

Sadler had written to Jack and told him of his plight. Jack had been dropping into jails since the mid-1970s when Lionel Potter had first sent a letter asking for the Eastern Suburbs first-grade side to train at Parramatta Jail. Jack thrived on making men better men. He'd staked a reputation on it. Jack called a few blokes he knew. Coppers. Lawyers. He thought John Sadler needed someone to believe in him.

It was late 1987 when Jack convinced some of the biggest names in sport and the media to front Parramatta Jail one morning. 'We'll meet at the gates of maximum security,' he told them. 'Tell them you're with me.' Steve Mortimer. Peter Sterling. John Monie. Wayne Pearce. George Piggins. Ian Chappell. Gavin Miller. Even the little jockey Ron Quinton, who was approached by an Everest of muscle as soon as he crossed through to the other side of the prison. 'If you'd rode the last winner twelve months ago last Saturday I wouldn't be in here,' the prisoner told him.

One prisoner walked up to Peter Sterling. 'Sterlo, you know that yellow Mazda RX7 you had pinched from Baulkham Hills?' he asked the Eels halfback. Yes, Sterling remembered it. He owned it. He had been quite fond of it. 'That was me!' Sterling nervously laughed along with him. Craig Coleman, the Souths half, felt more comfortable than most. 'I've met ten blokes in here I went to school with,' he said.

Jack had felt comfortable here. He had been seeing Sadler for several years. Jack had convinced the players to come in for a game of touch against some of the inmates. Ray Hadley was calling the football for 2UE then. He'd first met Jack in 1981 when he would sit on the sideline at Parramatta games and call into a tape recorder, trying to get his foot in the door. Now Jack enjoyed calling in a favour.

As the teams took their place on the field for the match, Hadley's mind raced with the possibility of who could be behind these walls. He could smell the Asian food cooking somewhere in the place. The Asian inmates had their own wing, and were never allowed to mix with the other inmates because the Aboriginal inmates often bashed them. Those responsible for the brutal rape and murder of nurse Anita Cobby had been sentenced earlier that year, and the bastards were in here somewhere. Hadley put it to one side as he called the match over a PA system. He knew the players, of course, but not the prisoners.

John Sadler was giving him the names as the ball was flung along the back line. 'And now the ball goes out to Darky,' Hadley said. The inmate was furious. 'Nobody fucking calls me Darky,' he said, slamming the football down. Sadler calmed the situation. And Big Jack? 'He was laughing his head off,' recalls Hadley now. 'He liked taking blokes out of their comfort zone. And we were all out of our comfort zone.'

Jack liked to challenge people, no matter who they were. He saw benefits for all concerned. Peter Sterling knew why Jack was there. 'He didn't give up on people,' he says. 'He believed they deserved a second chance.'

He believed John Sadler deserved a second chance. When Sadler was released from Parramatta Jail, Jack found him a job on the door at Easts Leagues as a bouncer. Then Sadler assaulted a man soon after, and he was deported to Auckland. Nobody ever heard of him again, but there was talk he found his way back behind bars.

It reminded Jack that there were some men he couldn't reach.

●

Frank Sinatra. Whitney Houston. Peter Allen. The gala presentation for the opening of the Sanctuary Cove Resort on the Gold Coast promised to be a special night. A night of magic. Jack? He figured the golf would be enough. He and Judy had flown there in the private jet of their good friend and businessman Tony Power and booked into the newly built Jupiters Casino at Broadbeach.

Jack was out playing when the call came through to their hotel room, and Judy answered. It was Everett Bell, one of the neighbours who had known the family for years. 'Is Jack there?' he asked. Judy still remembers how he said it. The tone in his voice. 'What do you want him for?' she said, half-joking. 'I've got some terrible news,' he said. Judy wondered what could be so terrible. 'Luke's died.'

'Oh no,' Judy said. 'That's not right.' Then Everett Bell got firm. 'Now I'm here in your house, and you know I wouldn't make this call for any other reason unless this had happened.' That's when Judy lost control of her emotions. 'I'll put Father on.'

If that hadn't been the worst moment of her life, the next one was. She somehow tracked down Jack at the golf club and told him what had happened. Tony Power flew them to Sydney in his private jet. They had flown there to see Sinatra. Now they were flying home to see their son's body.

Luke Gibson died on 9 January 1988. He was 25.

The Gibsons had known for two years that his odd behaviour could be attributed to schizophrenia. They had been tuned into the ABC on television one evening, and presenter Trish Goddard had been talking about her sister and how she suffered from the affliction. It all lined up so easily. 'That's Luke,' Susan said.

When he was diagnosed with schizophrenia, there was a pervading sense of relief for the family. At least they knew. They would take it in turns to drive him to and from psychiatrists for a fortnightly injection of medication that would hopefully unlock the beautiful child they had known before the mental disease had taken him prisoner.

Luke wanted to get better. They'd consult an endless line of doctors. One on the North Shore prescribed a diet of no bread, no sugar, no caffeine, no alcohol. Luke stuck to it for a month and life swung his way. Then he turned around one day and said: 'I'll think I'll get myself an ice-cream.'

He'd kicked the drugs. The heroin at least. He hadn't touched it for four years. *Four years.* But his last hit had come from a bad batch, which was always the gamble you took when it came to the Hammer. When he was found in his bedroom at Cowra Place, the needle was right there on the carpet floor. That alone convinced his parents that it was lethal gear. 'If he had that shot he would've made sure he got rid of that needle so there was no discovery,' Jack said. 'The boy could hardly make it one yard from where the needle was to his bed.' One bad hit of heroin. Had there ever been a good one?

Jack was concerned about Judy, but she was more concerned about him. They both stoutly believed they had help from above during this time, and they had prayed at St Aloysius' Catholic Church in Cronulla for their son, just as Jack had prayed there on occasion as he came back home from working at nightclubs in the morning hours during the 1950s and '60s.

Out of respect for Jack, the football community flooded the church for Luke's funeral. John Quayle was there. They hadn't spoken for two years, but those wounds were only skin deep. 'I'm very sorry,' Quayle said, shaking his hand. 'Appreciate you comin',' said Jack.

Quayle still can't hold back the tears when he talks about the day. Jack had taken the kid who'd come down from Manilla to play for Easts in 1968 and thrown him in the back of a white Cadillac and introduced him to a new world. 'He'd been so good to me,' Quayle says. 'He'd been so good to all of us. He'd been a mentor to all of us and his own life had fallen apart.'

Days after the funeral, Jack phoned Gavin Miller. 'I'll pick you up in ten minutes,' Jack said. When Miller jumped in his car, Albert Tabone—who Jack had known through gambling and football connections for years—was sitting in the back of the car. He drove to South Coogee, where he picked up George Piggins. And then they drove to Kings Cross.

In another life, this is where he'd taken Judy, around the corner at the Carlisle Club at No. 2 Kellett Street, to play cards. This is where he came years later to settle his SP. That's when The Cross had a sense of style, or at least decency. Now it was an open sewer and Jack was looking for the filth who had sold his son the lethal gear.

The four of them walked along the strip, and then up the stairs and into a grotty nightclub. 'Holy god,' Piggins thought to himself. This wasn't his scene. It wasn't the scene for any of them.

'What corner does she work?' Jack asked to the bloke on the door. Jack had heard this was the prostitute who had sold his son the drugs. The four of them walked over to the bar, waiting for the girl to arrive, all eyes on them in that seedy place. Then, suddenly, Jack had had enough. 'Let's go.'

As they drove away in the car, Jack broke the silence. 'What am I doing here?' he said out loud, although to nobody in particular. 'That girl can't help me. She's dead anyhow. What am I doing here?'

Piggins knows why he was there. 'You had to be there. Because he had just lost his son ... and he was your friend.'

Jack did not shy away from the media interest. He and Judy posed for photos for *The Mirror*, the grief written all over their faces. Jack appeared on *The Today Show* on Channel Nine a fortnight after the funeral. The Gibsons had led a public life, and now this was a very public story. Jack consented to a story with *60 Minutes* reporter Mike Munro from Channel Nine. They walked the streets of Kings Cross, too, and still nothing. He narrowed it down to about 'three or four people' but never found the dealer. Mike Munro asked him what he would do should he ever find him. 'What would I do? I don't know what I'd do, Mike.'

Years later, Judy took a call at Cowra Place and it was a girl who had some information. 'I know the bloke who gave your son the drugs,' she said. Judy couldn't go there. She couldn't crank all that up again. 'If you've got any information, you take it to the police.'

And still, in those months after Luke's death, Jack never hid from it. He fronted *The Midday Show* with Ray Martin. 'In death, he left us plenty,' Jack said. 'He made us aware of a lot of different things. It's unified our family a lot more. He left a lot of things with us. Maybe it was a sacrifice.'

And while all the interviews and newspaper stories and books were cathartic and purified Jack in some way, it could not wash away the pain inside. Jack could not let go. It had long been the cruellest irony when it came to Luke: Jack had found the key to so many young men since he'd become a coach in 1967, but he hadn't been able to find the key to the one that mattered most. And now his eldest son was gone. 'We didn't know,' Judy said as he and Jack had dinner with John Quayle one night. 'We didn't know.' Jack sat there in silence.

Then, one day late that horrible year, life changed again. It flew in like a howling southerly off Port Hacking, straight through the sliding doors of the balcony, and it grabbed Judy and grabbed her tight. She couldn't do this any longer: 'I'm going to have to move on.'

She had felt like a piece of elastic. She wanted to move on, but Jack wasn't budging, pulling her back. She was leaving him behind in their grief and if they were to move on it had to be together. Everything had been together, from the moment when he'd arrived outside the picture theatre at Bondi Junction in 1954, with the flowers filling his Pontiac all the way up to the windows. He had always been in her life.

So she went and found Jack. 'Luke would want us to be moving on,' she said. Jack was stunned. 'Why are you saying that?' Judy smiled at the supercoach, who just so happened to be her husband and the father of her six children. 'Because today is a brighter day.'

25　WHEN ALL IS SAID AND DONE

RAY HADLEY QUITE liked his legs. He didn't fancy someone breaking them.

Hadley had made comments that offended a well-known colourful racing identity during a 2UE broadcast and it didn't take long for the word to come back to him that they wanted to do him some physical harm. So Hadley asked Mick Cronin, who he'd known since those Parramatta days, what he should do. 'Ring Jack, he'll know these characters,' Cronin told him.

'You've upset the wrong bloke,' Jack said down the phone line. 'This bloke is capable of making good on those threats.' 'What should I do?' asked Hadley. 'First thing you should do is shut your mouth,' Jack replied. 'I know someone who knows him so I'll have a talk to them to see if they can tell him you are not such a bad bloke and you'll drop off and everything will be fine.'

Then Jack told Hadley this: 'Just one thing: what time do you leave to go to work?' Hadley was reading sport on the breakfast show on 2UE at the time, and said he left in the dark at about 4.30 a.m. 'Carry a torch with you to the garage. You know. Just in case.' *Clunk!* Jack hung up.

Three days later, Jack phoned and asked Hadley to be the auctioneer at a black-tie function he had been organising to raise funds for schizophrenia research. 'I've got all that other stuff sorted, that's fine,' Jack said of the colourful racing identity who allegedly wanted to break Hadley's legs. 'I told him you are a good bloke. Most importantly I told him I need you to do the auction for me in October, so he said you are sweet.'

Then Jack told Hadley this: 'But after October you are on your own.' 'Jack,' Hadley said, 'this is a joke isn't it?' 'Wait until October.' *Clunk!* Jack hung up.

Hadley became Jack's go-to man whenever he needed an auctioneer at a charity function. He called in a lot of favours in those early years after Luke's death. He called on the likes of Kerry Packer, John Singleton, Rupert Murdoch and Bob Hawke to sign cheques for one dollar, so he could mount them and auction them off at a black-tie event at the Regent Hotel. 'He organised everything,' John Quayle says.

They raised $400 000 or more. The charities came out of the woodwork, but in the end Jack decided to give it to the Prince of Wales Hospital. Luke had spent some time in their psych ward. The money went towards schizophrenia research, and if they hadn't donated it to them, the research being done into the disease would've closed up. They asked Jack if he wanted to go onto the committee. 'No thanks,' Jack said. He'd never liked boards or committees as a coach, and he wasn't slipping onto one now. Judy became a director instead.

From the moment Luke died, the Gibsons went about their lives in the same pragmatic manner in which they had always conducted themselves. Judy had five other children to look after. Jack had sold the farm near Wauchope and bought a bigger one down past Nowra on the New South Wales South Coast. It became his sanctuary, where he would take mates or just himself, building a haven away from the city. The blue haze of the bush still appealed to him. Yet raising funds for charity became his crusade. It was his way of dealing with the pain of not being able to save his own son.

For years he had risen at 4 a.m., and with black coffee in one hand and Craven A in the other, he would pore over newspaper and magazine articles, trawl through periodicals and books from overseas, and note what he found in that beautiful long, sloping handwriting of his. These maxims and quotes were his search for The Knowledge—as he would call it—and it was relentless.

He had always had a solid relationship with respected rugby league writer Ian Heads, and they gathered all the material up and arranged it into published books. *Winning Starts on Monday* was the first. Then *Played Strong, Done Fine* just after Luke's death. The dedication on the first page reads: 'For Luke, a very special person whose presence in our lives made us look beyond ourselves—Jack and Judy Gibson.' Then came *When All is Said and Done*. All the money raised from these went straight into schizophrenia research.

His mates have no doubt this was Jack's cathartic way of dealing with his loss. 'They've got a demon in there,' Jack would say to John Quayle.

In his largely untouched study at Cowra Place today, you can find one of his diaries. Random scribblings of quotes from Hemingway to Henry Kissinger. On the inside cover, there is one quote, and you suspect Jack came up with this one himself:

'Invest in yourself.' He figured that was the best way to spend your money.

•

Jack knocked back the job John Quayle was offering three times before finally agreeing to it. The boss of the league wanted someone with some star power. When Jack was appointed New South Wales coach for the 1989 State of Origin series, NSWRL chairman Ken Arthurson laid out what was expected: 'We are delighted that Jack has accepted the position of coach of the Blues at a time when we are trying to restore rugby league supremacy to NSW.' No, no pressure at all.

Apart from the fact that Queensland had won the past two series, including a clean-sweep of the three matches in 1988, Jack had to deal with selectors in the form of Don Furner. When it came to choosing the side he would try his old trick from his St George days of arguing against the selection superstars so he could pick a player he wanted.

Jack never copped big Steven 'Blocker' Roach, the ball-playing Balmain prop who brawled with referees. He admired his passion, but not his lack of discipline. 'He's a player with a lot of talent but he'll never be a great player because of his ears. He doesn't listen.' Roach didn't play for New South Wales that year, despite being the best prop in the competition. Neither did his Tigers teammate, hooker Benny Elias. Jack felt the same about him, too.

Because Ron Massey had been appointed the chief executive of Cronulla, Mick Cronin was appointed Jack's co-ordinator for the series. 'More like translator,' Mick grins.

It was a bit like that. Jack couldn't remember the names of players at Parramatta, and found it even harder now that he had stepped away from the game. Origin was a different beast to anything he had coached before. In the past, he had a year and a pre-season to indoctrinate his players to his way of thinking. This was a week, for three matches, of brutal interstate football.

The game had also moved on. Jack's Spartan principles would stand the test of time, but Origin was the first sign that the game had passed him by. It couldn't be said at the time, of course. Greg Hartley had learnt that a decade earlier. If you took on the Gibson legend, you failed. You were the villain. Everyone loved Big Jack. Best to shut up.

Only years later did the criticism emerge. In his autobiography, former New South Wales forward Paul Sironen said:

> At the risk of sacrilege, I'm afraid to admit that when he coached the NSW side in 1989 ... it was all a bit of a mystery to me because the man spoke in riddles. As far as I was concerned there was no rhyme or reason to our plan and it was hard to know what was expected of us.

Said Roach in his autobiography, released in 1992:

> I think Jack temporarily lost it as a coach when he took over the NSW side in 1989 because he had been out of the club scene for a couple of seasons and had absolutely no experience of representative football—and it showed.

And he was right. Jack would tell the playmakers to take place-kicks, as if they were kicking for goal, when they had to find touch from a penalty. No Jack, they said. When Michael O'Connor asked if they would be using sliding or up-and-in defence, Jack looked at him as though he was a smart-arse. Jack told his halves to 'be a giraffe' when they had the ball. Translation: look over the heads of the defensive line and look for open space. It was a variation on the 'kick to the seagulls' edict he had given Peter Sterling in 1981.

A decade later, they sound like old words. These days, Canberra coaches like Tim Sheens were talking about 'red zones'—the 20-metre area from the tryline. They didn't talk about seagulls, but narrowed down areas of the field to the square metre. The game had progressed and now Jack's coaching sounded like a punch-line to a joke none of them had heard.

Yet nobody questioned Jack, because they didn't dare. Because it was Jack.

Arthur Beetson knew what Jack was talking about. He had taken over from Wayne Bennett as Queensland coach for that series. The night before the first game, the phone in his hotel room buzzed. 'What are you doing?' Jack asked. 'I'm coming over.'

So until the small hours of the morning, before squaring off against each other in Origin I at Lang Park, two old mates played cards—Clobyosh, of course—until the early hours. Wally Lewis popped his head in to speak to Beetson briefly, and shook his head at the sight.

Jack won the game of cards, but Beetson and Queensland won the series 3–zip.

The following year, Jack took the job but was shut out of the selection room altogether. Ben Elias was made hooker and captain. Steve Roach was picked in the side. Jack brought his German Shepherd, Taylor, to the medicals at the Sydney Football Stadium, and they all smiled for the cameras. Fact was, Jack was steaming about not having a say in selections.

New South Wales won the first game 8–0 at the SFS, and then wrapped up the series at Olympic Park in Melbourne when halfback Ricky Stuart intercepted and scored a length-of-the-field try. Stuart was beaming in the rooms after the match. 'You should've improved your position for the goal kicker,' Jack mumbled to him afterwards, because Stuart had planted the ball down out wide.

Before that match, a young bloke had come into the side called Brad Fittler. He was the lethal centre for Penrith who fired off a left-foot step like a shotgun. 'What's your name?' Jack asked, shaking his hand. Fittler told him. 'Righto Fred,' he said. Fittler had a new nickname; Freddie stuck like superglue.

●

Jack had first met Nick Politis in 1976, and they had stayed in contact since. Politis had been the first to emblazon his company name of 'City Ford' across the front of the famous foundation club jumper. 'Jack understood that,' says Politis. 'He was commercial.'

In 1990, with Politis now chairman of the club and his side struggling, and former glamour fullback Russell Fairfax sacked as coach, the millionaire car salesman with a deep passion for the Roosters convinced Jack to come on board as a director of coaching. The Roosters had been dubbed the 'transit lounge' because players dropped in, gobbled up big pay packets and then left.

Jack was having none of it. Upon his arrival, five players tested positive to marijuana and Jack stood them down immediately. Before that, he had been interviewed on ABC television by Warren Boland who had said smoking pot was akin to drinking beer and smoking cigarettes. An ugly slanging match ensued on live television. Jack knew how dope had precipitated Luke's slide into the abyss. 'All marijuana smokers are on the heroin trail,' he said.

Jack's first job was to find a coach, and while others pushed the likes of out-of-work coaches like Frank Stanton and Roy Masters, he cast a wide net. The legendary Bob Bax in Queensland told him one name: Mark Murray, the former Test halfback. Murray joined the coaching team. Together, Jack and Murray signed halfback Gary Freeman from the Tigers. Jack and lock Paul Vautin fell out, but Jack refused to pay him out the final year of his contract, so he stayed.

For the next four seasons, the Roosters failed to reach the finals, Jack sitting high in the stands, trying to find a solution. In another life, he had found the key to unlock the men in the red, white and blue. But now the game was not recognisable as the game he had known.

In late 1993, Jack and Murray were furious when Freeman reneged on a handshake agreement to join Penrith for the following season. Jack placed the blame squarely at the feet of Phil 'Gus' Gould, the Panthers coach who had won two premierships and Origins for New South Wales.

Jack did not like Gould for reasons known only to him. When asked about Gould's success in Origin, he said: 'You could coach that side over the phone.' *The Daily Telegraph*'s Ray Chesterton wrote a scathing critique in response, referring to Jack's colourful past.

'Did you put him up to it?' Jack asked Gould. 'No Jack. I swear I didn't,' Gould said. 'You might have to,' Jack replied, intimating that Gould might have to appear in the witness box in defamation proceedings. The matter was later settled out of court, and Jack cut out the apology published in *The Telegraph* and stuck it in one of his scrapbooks.

When the Roosters struggled down the stretch of the 1994 season, Politis had had enough. When Murray was sacked, it infuriated Jack. Then the whispers started that Gould would be coming in as his replacement. 'He didn't like Gus,' says Politis. 'He hated Gus. I was out in the cold with Jack for a while.'

The game's newest supercoach came in, and the original supercoach was out.

EPILOGUE

THE HANDS GAVE it away. They'd always done the talking, those massive hands, and now they were telling him what he did not want to know and they weren't listening to what he had to say. *Stop shaking.*

There was a whisper doing the rounds that Jack would live forever, and he was too proud to let anyone know he wouldn't. To let anyone know that the slide had started. He'd keep his hands in pockets, or arms folded, tucked away from sight. He'd throw an arm around a mate instead of shaking his hand. A man afraid of no one was suddenly afraid of what they all thought.

He had commanded the fairways of the golf course for years, and he could still knock it gun-barrel straight down the middle, and then lay-up on to the green. But then he would wrap those big hands around the two-iron doubling as his putter and he couldn't caress the ball towards the cup like he once did. He had the bloody yips, he'd say to Judy, when he knew it was something harder to fix.

Judy had noticed it around 2003 when he launched *The Last Word*—his fourth and final book. His long, sloping handwriting had always been immaculate, but as he signed autographs on the opening page his hand was barely controllable and the pen danced all over the page.

Stop shaking. But they would not. He preferred to drink beer out of a schooner glass, but then he went to drinking middies of beer in a schooner glass. Then beer from a stubbie. And then a can. Then his mates started discreetly cutting his steak into small pieces whenever they went to lunch.

And the worse the affliction grabbed hold of his mind and he lost control, the more he felt unheard. Everyone had wanted to listen for decades to every single word Jack Gibson had to say. Not now, or so it seemed to him. He turned to his old mate Peter Toohey one morning, shook his head and said it: 'Nobody's listening.'

Until then, everyone had been listening. After his bitter split from the Roosters, he was never going to retire; he just slowed down. You stop coaching, but you never stop being a coach, and his former players kept knocking on his door, seeking his sage advice.

Michael Wicks turned up there one day wearing a pair of Speedos, dripping wet. He had swum the length of Gunnamatta Bay to see Jack. The large knife in his hand was in case he found a shark. Jack had coached Wicks at Cronulla, but after that the player's life had unravelled. Drugs and alcohol: Jack knew what they could to do a young man. 'He cared for me,' Wicks said years later. Jack's belief saved him, and that saved others. Wicks became a drug and alcohol counsellor on the mid–North Coast.

Dan Stains, who had also played under Jack at Cronulla, asked him to give some advice to one of his players in the lower grades at Balmain. Luke O'Donnell was Jack's style of kid and player: respectful with a big engine that never stopped. 'Just concentrate on your defence,' the supercoach said. 'Make an impression on that first tackle.' Jack kept in contact with him right up to the moment O'Donnell received the phone call informing him that he'd been selected for Australia.

When the Super League war erupted in the mid-1990s, Jack kept his distance, but in the darkest hours, as the Australian Rugby League and Rupert Murdoch's News Limited picked the eyes out of the game, John Quayle would call for advice. Yet this time Jack had nothing for the son a preacherman from Manilla. 'Is it true that coach is getting that much money?' Jack would ask Quayle. 'Close,' Quayle would say. 'Doesn't sound right,' was the reply. He'd been the first one to fight for the rights of the coach; now he was ashamed of their greed.

He kept himself busy collecting antiques and buying fire-trucks and old guns and auctioning them off for charity. And playing golf and heading out bush with Arthur Beetson as his old captain scouted the land for rugby league talent recruiting for the Roosters. Wherever they went, everyone knew Jack.

He'd play in the Jack Newton Celebrity Golf Tournament, and on one occasion was paired with Wayne Grady, who had won the PGA Championship—one of world golf's major tournaments. 'Dumb as a post that bloke,' Jack said to Arthur Beetson back in the clubhouse. 'He didn't listen to a word I said.' Then Grady walked in. 'He drove me crazy,' Grady said. 'I should've shot eight-under par.'

On lazy Saturday afternoons, Jack would walk out of the house and his family didn't know if he was going to drink with his mates down at the surf club or drop in to see Kerry Packer. Around grand final time, Bob Hawke's secretary would call Quayle. 'Prime Minister would like to know if Jack Gibson will be there. Is he going to the football?'

When he turned 70 in 1999, Nick Politis invited him to a small gathering at Easts Leagues to celebrate. (They had reconciled, and later in life booked their colonoscopies at the same time.) When they swung open the door of the function room at Easts there was a room of a hundred or more people. His eldest daughter Susan explained how the King of the Castle had loved his dogs and lived on a diet of leftover baked dinner for breakfast, fried fish, bread and custard for dinner and the obligatory apple pie and ice-cream at 3 a.m.

Then she said this:

Dad has always given us everything we've ever needed and most things we want. He still plays a big part in our lives and the lives of his granddaughters. If someone were to ask me 'What did your dad teach you?', two things come to mind. First, take people for what they are. Don't be impressed by popular people for that alone. Dad could be equally attracted to and respect the neighbours' gardener as he could a Prime Minister. The other? The most important lessons you can teach your children are not through what you preach, but by what they see and experience at home.

A year earlier, Jack was attending a charity function at Wollongong Leagues Club. Andrew Speedy was 31 and ran a memorabilia business and happened to be seated at the same table. Ron Massey swapped seats so Speedy could sit right next to the five-time premiership-winning coach. At the end of the evening, he asked Jack for a piece of advice. One tip for life. Jack stared him down and the pupils in his eyes narrowed. He told him to do a good deed every day for the next month—call an old schoolteacher, for instance—and on the final day to call him. Speedy obeyed the order to the letter, and phoned Jack on the final day. 'I hope you're not thinking this is the 30th deed,' Jack quipped.

From that moment on, they formed the last unique relationship in the supercoach's life. Soon after they were making the 800-kilometre drive out west to Bourke in Jack's silver Toyota Prado Landcruiser, off to attend the Louth races, when they came across a giant kangaroo lying in the middle of the road. 'You better move that,' Jack said to him. Speedy was apprehensive. Was it alive? Was it dead? Just as he went to touch the enormous beast, Jack honked the horn and Speedy could've died from the fright of it. Jack just smiled when he got back in the car. 'Bet that scared you.'

Another trip, another stretch of road. Jack noticed an abattoir and decided to drop in. As they walked the floor, the workers resplendent in their footy jumpers—mostly the red and white of St George—noticed the supercoach and they looked and hushed and whispered. 'Productivity just increased,' Jack said.

Jack Gibson could see the potential in Andrew Speedy, and Andrew Speedy wanted to be the best bloke he could be around Jack Gibson. They would watch Friday night footy together on the couch, and Jack would predict what was going to happen three plays ahead. Or they would be riding in Jack's truck down to the farm at Nowra, his golf clubs in the back, an Anticol throat lozenge in his mouth and a Gracie Fields cassette playing. 'Ho, ho, ho!' Jack would say, smiling as they drove on down the road.

●

It was about 2005 when he knew it was time for a diagnosis. His regular doctor had for years been Peter Malouf, the club doctor at the Sharks. He obeyed what Malouf said. When Jack was suffering from a severe chest infection, Malouf ordered him to give away cigarettes; as hard as it was, Jack took his last drag of the Craven A, pinched between middle finger and thumb and sucked right down to the cork-tip filter, and flicked it away for good.

At first they thought it was Parkinson's disease but couldn't be sure. They traipsed around the city before a professor at Westmead Hospital brought him in for more tests, more research. While nobody could put their finger on it, he was in the dementia family.

Then he started to prowl, sneaking out of the house around 4 p.m. every day. He was diagnosed with 'sundowner syndrome', but all Judy knew was that she had to change the locks to prevent him from walking up the road to the service station and asking for money. One day, they were down at the farm in Nowra and Jack flogged the keys to the car and sped off down the back road to Gerringong. Judy and Susan were in a panic, and hoped that he might've been heading for Mick Cronin's pub there. Whenever he went to Nowra, he saw Cronin. When Judy pulled up, Jack had already arrived. 'Thank god you're here,' he said, handing her the keys. 'I couldn't have lasted another minute.'

That's when the Gibson family made the call. It broke their hearts like everyone else to see him placed in a nursing home at Taren Point. Andrew Speedy was there, feeling completely helpless, almost pleading with Jack: 'What do you want?' Jack came back with one word: 'Decorum.'

It was Jack's way of saying he knew what was going on, he knew this was the next step, he didn't want the world to know. This was a time to be respectful, for all concerned. And for the next two or so years, that's what happened. Such was the respect for Jack, few let it be known what was wrong. In the end, he was diagnosed with Dementia with Lewy Bodies, a severe form of the disease. Whatever it was, it didn't seem to matter, because it had robbed the supercoach of life.

That's why some would visit, others could not. A member of the family was there every day. Ronnie and Barb Taylor were there almost every week. And so was Massey. Norm Provan visited once. 'We had good memories over the years, didn't we, mate?' Provan said, tears welling in the eyes of the legendary former St George captain and those present. Jack cracked the faintest smile, looked up and drawled a remark that only he could.

'Would someone peel this bloke off me?'

They could all laugh. They had to. One night, one of his fellow patients was swearing at the top of his voice. Jack rarely swore himself, let alone in front of women, and he expected the same of other men. So he belted him. 'Old habits die hard,' Noel Kelly laughs when reminded of the story.

And the cruellest irony in all this was that the same thing was happening on the other side of the world—to Dick Nolan. Alzheimer's had torn down the 49ers coach, just as dementia had cut down Jack. His son, Mike, was now a coach himself and he knew something was wrong when Dick stopped gently needling him whenever his side lost. 'When that started to diminish, I knew something was up,' Mike Nolan said. 'That was his whole life.' Dick let go on 11 November 2007. He was 75.

When Jack's condition slid further and he was moved to Garrawarra Centre, sitting within the warm peach walls, in his big blue chair in his flannelette pyjamas, the visitors came less often. Men like Peter Sterling could not. 'I'm ashamed that I didn't but

I know why I didn't and it's because I didn't want to see him any different.' Men like Mick Cronin felt they had to. 'He would get up and wander off, but I had to go there. I felt I owed him that.'

Shortly after Jack let go on 9 May 2008, aged 79, surrounded by his family and just an hour before the Centenary Test, the Gibson family released a statement:

> Jack passed away comfortably today, at 6.32pm at the Garrawarra Centre, Waterfall, surrounded by his family. We greatly appreciate the wonderful care he had received at Garrawarra, and also the caring and kind support afforded to us, the family. We are dealing as well as we can and would ask that Jack's many friends in their sadness that he is no longer with us do not feel too sorry. Jack would not want that; it was his own strong belief and appreciation that he had a very fortunate life, and we knew he would have wanted that to be the spirit of this time.

The funeral was held five days later at St Aloysius', the same place where he would sneak in for Sunday morning mass on his way home from working at Thommo's, and it swelled with almost every soul who had been touched by him. John Quayle delivered the eulogy, and a large crowd watched outside on the big screen that had been wheeled in for the occasion.

Then the present-day Roosters players formed a guard of honour, and the hearse drove the supercoach to the Woronora Cemetery. Jack Gibson was buried in an Eastern Suburbs tracksuit, right next to Luke.

●

Big Jack has let go, but he has not gone.

His name is writ large all over the game, even if it is unrecognisable as the one he played and coached. Listen carefully. You will still hear the experts and coaches recall his turns of phrase, his deeply held philosophies, because as much as every corner of preparing a rugby league team has been explored and investigated, the way Jack did it in the first place remains the best way to do it now.

Yet it was never just about the game for Jack. It was about people. His name is writ large, too, in the effect he had on others. He is there in his former players who still turn up to meetings early because they are on Lombardi Time. To those who know, any success they have in this world is through discipline and preparation, and never luck.

He is there in Wayne Bennett, who won premierships with the Broncos and then the Dragons that Jack could not, and while the experts say it made Bennett a *better* coach than Jack there can be no comparison. Bennett knows who the original supercoach was.

He is there in Judy and her family, who have played on since Jack's death knowing he will always be with them, the oil painting of him on the wall at Cowra Place giving the supercoach a permanent view over Port Hacking. He is there in John Gibson's first-born son: Jack.

Big Jack has let go but these people have not. And they are all here now, still together, right here under the roof he provided. Here in the house that Jack built.

ACKNOWLEDGEMENTS

Jack Gibson would never consent to a biography while he was alive—and probably would've been less thrilled about the idea after his death. Ian Heads approached him twice about such a project. 'But Jack didn't want to go down that track,' he recalls. Ian suspects it had less to do with the dark corners of his past and more to do with the man himself. Jack Gibson was never afraid to speak his mind but he was a private man who was surprisingly shy.

He may never have wanted a biography written about him, but it didn't stop Big Jack from archiving parts of his life like he was preparing for one. He kept scrapbooks from the day he played third grade for St George in 1950 through to the late 1990s. He kept VHS tapes of grand finals, unedited television interviews and speeches from the Dally M Awards. He kept diaries and notebooks full of his long, sloping hand. The impression I got was that Jack wasn't driven by the publicity he received, but deeply proud of what he achieved in football and life.

This project was spawned out of a profile piece I wrote for *The Sydney Morning Herald* in April 2008, and thanks go to Ian Fuge and Fairfax for granting permission to reproduce part of that story in the Prologue. Thanks also to my present editors at *The Daily Telegraph*, Phil Rothfield, Ben English and Tim Morrissey, who gave me crucial time off so I could finish the book.

I've lost count of how many people I've interviewed, but it would be more than a hundred. Some spoke on the condition of anonymity,

ACKNOWLEDGEMENTS

others gave up hours of their time. Alas, there isn't enough space to thank them all but their advice, patience and candidness have been greatly appreciated.

There are some people, though, who I must mention. Without question, this book would never have happened without the approval then support of Ian Heads, whose advice was immeasurable. I'd also like to thank Ron and Barb Taylor, Bob Dodd, Peter Toohey, Ron Massey, Terry Fearnley, John and Diane Quayle, Arthur Beetson, George Piggins, Mick Souter, Geoff Carr, Nick Politis, John Singleton, Mike Gibson, Wayne Bennett, Chris Masters, Neil Cadigan, Mike Munro, John Brady, Gavin Miller, Peter Sterling, Mick Cronin and Noel Kelly. Cheers also to Garry Linnell for getting me started and Paul Kent, Eamonn Duff, Graem Sims, Stephen Gibbs, Ray Hadley, Rupert Guinness and Candace Sutton for keeping me going.

I'd also like to thank the team from Allen & Unwin for believing in this project when others decided they would not. Richard Walsh was the first port of call, and then Stuart Neal and Kathryn Knight have been absolute pros to deal with since. Thanks, too, to my agent Bruce Kennedy, who has been alongside me since day one.

Special mention needs to be made to two sources that were invaluable. *From Where the Sun Rises* became a bible for Jack's time at the Roosters. Equally important was *The Mighty Eels*, a video documentary, which contained many insightful interviews.

It was an honour to write the story of a true giant of Australian sport, but the most rewarding part has been getting to know the Gibson family. Their trust and support has been fundamental to making this book happen. I've spent hours at Cowra Place talking to Judy, and her willingness and warmth over the past three years is what got me to the finish line. Thank you, Miss Pacific.

The abiding theme of Jack's life was that he backed people. My beautiful family has always done that for their unpredictable son and brother. So too did Greg Hunter and James Carey, former sports editors who passed away during the writing of this book.

Huntsman and Jiggler: a raised glass to them.

NOTES

p. 10	**Joe 'The Boss' Taylor was ...**	David Hickie, *The Prince and the Premier*, pg. 150
p. 21	**When he was gambling ...**	ibid. pg. 152
p. 44	**I recognised some familiar faces ...**	Tom Prior, *The Sinner's Club*, pg. 107
p. 110	**Why didn't you make ...**	*Second Effort*
	Confidence is contagious ...	ibid.
p. 111	**Fatigue makes cowards of ...**	ibid.
	He saw his chance to run ...	ibid.
	You're absolutely right ...	ibid.
	My name is Vince ...	ibid.
p. 121	**I don't know how else ...**	ibid.
p. 247	**It's a violent game ...**	'The Big League', *60 Minutes*
	We have to be an ...	ibid.
	Kevin was very agitated ...	ibid.

NOTES

p. 277   **Pearce off Jack . . .**   Billy Birmingham,
    Wired World of Sports

p. 278   **Jack was not the best . . .**   Ray Price, *Perpetual
    Motion*, pg. 105

    If Terry Fearnley had . . .   Ray Price, *Perpetual
    Motion*, pg. 105

p. 287   **In death, he left us . . .**   *The Midday Show*

p. 291   **For Luke, a very special . . .**   Jack Gibson, *Played
    Strong, Done Fine*, pg. ii

p. 293   **At the risk of sacrilege . . .**   Paul Sironen, *Sirro!:
    Tales from Tiger Town*

    I think Jack temporarily . . .   Steve Roach,
    Doing my Block

Excerpts on p. 293 taken from Jack Gibson's scrapbooks

BIBLIOGRAPHY

Arthurson, Ken, *Arko: My Game*, Ironbark Press, Sydney, 1997

Bennett, Wayne, *The Man in the Mirror*, ABC Books, Sydney, 2008

Beetson, Arthur, *Big Artie*, ABC Books, Sydney, 2004

'The Big League', *Four Corners*, television program, Australian
    Broadcasting Corporation, Sydney, 1983. First broadcast 30 April
    1983. Reporter Chris Masters, Producer Peter Manning

Birmingham, John, *Leviathan*, Random House, Milsons Point, 2000

Gibson, Jack, *The Last Word*, ABC Books, Sydney, 2003

Gibson, Jack, *Played Strong, Done Fine*, Ironbark Press, Randwick, 1991

Gibson, Jack, *Winning Starts on Monday*, Lester-Townsend Publishing,
    Paddington, 1989

Gibson, Jack, *When All Is Said And Done*, Ironbark Press, Chippendale,
    1994

The Good, the Bad and the Ugly, film, United Artists, Beverly Hills, 1966

Heads, Ian, Geoff Armstrong & David Middleton, *From Where the Sun
    Rises*, Playright Publishing, Caringbah, 2007

Heads, Ian, *True Blue*, Ironbark Press, Randwick, 1992

Hickie, David, *The Prince And The Premier*, Angus and Robertson
    Publishers, North Ryde, 1985

The Longest Yard, film, Paramount Pictures, Beverly Hills, 1974

'A Losing Game', *60 Minutes*, television program, Channel Nine,
    Willoughby, 1988. Reporter Mike Munro, Producer Ben Hawke

BIBLIOGRAPHY

Masters, Chris, *Inside Story*, Angus and Robertson Publishers,
 Pymble, 1992

Masters, Roy, *Bad Boys*, Random House, Milsons Point, 2006

McGregor, Adrian, *King Wally*, University of Queensland Press,
 St Lucia, 1989

Maranis, David, *When Pride Still Mattered*, Simon and Schuster,
 New York, 1999

Mayhem on a Sunday Afternoon, television program, American
 Broadcasting Company & David L Wolper Productions, USA,
 1965. First broadcast 15 November 1965

The Midday Show, television program, Channel Nine, Willoughby,
 1989. Broadcast 4 August 1989. Reporter Ray Martin

The Mighty Eels volume 3: 1978–86, video documentary, Richard
 Bradley Productions for Parramatta Leagues Club Limited, 2005

National Nine News, television program, Channel Nine, Willoughby,
 1986. Broadcast 6 March 1986. Reporter Tim Sheridan

Peard, John, *Fine Thanks Mate*, ABC Books, Sydney, 2007

Piggins, George, *Never Say Die*, Macmillian, Sydney, 2002

Price, Ray, *Perpetual Motion*, Eden Paperbacks, North Ryde, 1987

Prior, Tom, *The Sinner's Club*, Penguin, Ringwood, 1993

Roach, Steve with Ray Chesterton, *Doing My Block*, Ironbark Press,
 Randwick, 1992

Second Effort, film, Dartnell Corp, Chicago, 1968

Sironen, Paul, *Sirro!: Tales from Tiger Town*, ABC Books, Sydney, 1997

Williamson, David, *The Club*, Currency Press, Sydney, 1978

Wired World of Sports, sound recording, Birmingham, Billy
 [The Twelfth Man], Little Digger Productions, Sydney, 1987